Managing Teachers
as Professionals
in Schools

Managing Teachers
as Professionals
in Schools

EDITED BY
Hugh Busher &
Rene Saran

**KOGAN
PAGE**

London • Philadelphia

in association with the British Educational
Management and Administration Society (BEMAS)

First published in 1995

Kogan Page Limited
120 Pentonville Road
London N1 9JN

British Library Cataloguing in Publication Data

A CIP record for this book is available from the British Library.

ISBN 0 7494 1774 9

Typeset by Kogan Page
Printed and bound in Great Britain by Biddles Ltd, Guildford and Kings Lynn

Contents

Acknowledgements

The editors gratefully acknowledge the support they have received from the British Educational Management and Administration Society (BEMAS) in the original development of this book. The idea for it first emerged from the Society's Annual Conference in 1992, held at the University of Bristol, on the theme 'An Education Profession for Tomorrow'. Several of the present chapters develop and bring up to date papers given at the conference. They stand alongside other chapters written especially for this book.

We wish to acknowledge the dedicated and determined work of Lesley Boyd, research assistant to Hugh Busher at Loughborough University, who carried much of the load of the data gathering for research on which two chapters are based. Neither would have been achieved without her conscientious and enthusiastic efforts. We are also grateful to the schools and to their teaching and support staff who willingly and cheerfully agreed to being questioned as part of this research.

Finally, we gratefully acknowledge the work of two people who acted as part-time secretaries: Amy Thomas who transcribed many of the interviews collected during the research based at Loughborough; and Alison Moore who typed up the myriad minor amendments to chapters which arose from the dialogues between editors and authors, and who prepared the final text for the publishers.

Series Editor's Foreword

The government's educational reforms have created an unprecedented rate of change in schools. They have also raised fundamental questions about the purpose of education and the nature of school management and leadership. Similar changes are occurring worldwide.

In this context, there is an urgent need for all of us with an interest in education to step back and reflect on recent educational reforms, to reaffirm old truths and successful practice where appropriate, to sift out and implement the best of the new ideas, modifying or abandoning those which are a distraction from the central purpose of schools: to ensure that an education of high quality is a guaranteed opportunity for *all* our children and young people.

This series aims to satisfy the growing need for short, readable books designed for busy people and with a focus on single issues at the forefront of school management and leadership. Written by reflective practitioners who are either working in schools or directly with those who do, the series celebrates the ideals, skills and experience of professionals in education who want to see further improvements in our schools.

For many years there has been an unresolved debate in education about whether or not teaching is a 'profession'. At times of industrial action, the view of many outside education, certainly the right wing press, is that teachers are not behaving like professionals. However, the genuine desire by most groups directly involved with education to see the establishment of a General Teaching Council to define, monitor and develop standards for teachers, suggests that there is an inherent sense of professionalism within these constituent groups.

In several respects, the working context of established professional groups like doctors and lawyers has been changing rapidly and now has many similarities with education. For example, the philosophy of the marketplace and the predominance of economic imperatives has radically transformed most areas of professional and public service. Certainly the best of the qualities traditionally associated with the professions are found within teaching. Their formal recognition, redefinition for the future and extension to become normal and accepted practice would provide an enormous boost to embattled and often demoralised teachers.

This book is, therefore, a timely and important addition to the Management and Leadership in Education series. It addresses four main themes. Firstly, several writers explore the unstable environment in which schools now find themselves. Recent changes in government policy for education have threatened to deskill teachers and undermine their professionalism. However, paradoxically, they have also created new opportunities for an extended professional role.

Secondly, the relationships between teachers as individuals and the school as an organisation are discussed within the context of the research on effective organisations. This stresses the importance of ongoing staff development rather than more narrowly defined training, the involvement of all personnel in whole school planning and the empowerment of individuals to bring their full range of talents to bear on school improvement.

Thirdly, the essential differences between leadership and management are explored. Both are important as the visions and values of leaders cannot be implemented without good management but, on the other hand, management must not become a stifling bureaucracy with no sense of purpose.

Finally, the authors discuss the meaning of professionalism in the late twentieth century, particularly as it relates to education and public service. Their view is that those in positions of leadership should enable all the key stakeholders – teachers, support staff, governors and parents – to articulate and implement a vision for moving schools forward. Key elements for implementing this vision will be effective team work and wide involvement with planning and decision making. Central to the task will be the professionalism of teachers in their role as 'leading learners'. This book explores a vital theme for effective teaching and learning and for school improvement into the twenty-first century. It is commended to a wide readership.

Howard Green
Eggbuckland
October 1995

Notes on Contributors

John Beresford began his primary teaching career in ILEA and moved to Cambridgeshire where he was elected branch secretary for the NUT and teacher representative on Cambridgeshire's education committee. He has written a number of articles for teacher journals and lectured on LMS issues to teacher groups. In 1994 he was awarded an MPhil at the University of Cambridge Institute of Education (UCIE) for research into local management of primary schools. He is currently working as research officer attached to the UCIE's School Improvement Project (Improving the Quality of Education for All – IQEA).

Hugh Busher is a lecturer in the Department of Education, Loughborough University. Previously he taught in comprehensive schools for many years before spending a brief period at the University of Leeds. He now focuses much of his work on management and policy making in schools as organisations, and is responsible for the Loughborough University Headteacher Leadership and Management development programme which is being run in partnership with Leicestershire LEA. He is a member of two BEMAS committees and co-ordinates a BERA group on research into the management of autonomous schools and colleges. He writes on teachers' professional development and the process and politics of managing change in schools. Most recently he has published jointly with Rene Saran *Teachers' Conditions of Employment* (1992).

Hilary Constable is Professor and Head of Research in the School of Education, University of Sunderland. She has a long-standing and continuing interest in the relationship between organisational development and teachers' professional development, especially in relation to educational change. She has written elsewhere on teachers' experience of school development planning.

Christopher Day is Professor of Education, Chair of the School of Education and Head of Advanced Studies, University of Nottingham. Prior to this he worked as a teacher, lecturer and local education authority adviser. His particular concerns centre upon the continuing professional development of teachers, teachers' thinking, leadership and school cultures. Recent publications include *Managing Primary Schools in the 1990s* (1990); *Leadership and Curriculum in the Primary School* (1993); *Insights into Teachers' Thinking and Action* (co-edited with M Pope and P Denicolo, 1990); *Research on Teacher Thinking: Towards Understanding Professional Development* (co-edited with J Calderhead and P Denicolo, 1993); and a series entitled 'Developing Teachers and Teaching' (1995). He is editor of *Teachers and Teaching: Theory and Practice*, a newly published international journal, and co-editor of *The British Journal of In-service Education* and *Educational Action Research*. He is currently Chair of the Continuing Professional Development Committee of the University Council for the Education of Teachers.

Bertie Everard, an Oxford chemist, on leaving ICI in 1982 as company Education and Training Manager became a Visiting Fellow of the University of London's Institute of Education, designing and delivering management training for heads. He is the co-author of the standard textbook *Effective School Management* and Vice Chair of the National Association for Values in Education and Training. He is currently chief verifier (Sport and Recreation) for the RSA Examinations Board.

Keith Foreman was, for 25 years, Warden of Comberton Village College in Cambridgeshire and Principal of Burleigh Community College in Loughborough, prior to becoming a Consultant in Educational Management in 1994. He is currently a senior tutor with the Leicester University Management Development Unit based in Northampton, managing its Head Teacher Leadership and Management Programme and teaching on the MBA School-based and Distance Learning Programmes. He also runs courses for governors and senior managers at the University of Cambridge Institute of Education. From 1989 to 1992 he was a member of the DES School Management Task Force.

Eric Hoyle has been Professor of Education at the University of Bristol since 1971. He has previously been Head of English in two secondary schools and Senior Lecturer in Education at both the James Graham College, Leeds, and the University of Manchester. He has published extensively in the fields of organisation theory, educational management and teaching as a profession. His books include *The Role of the Teacher, The Politics of School Management* and, with Peter John, *Professional Knowledge and Professional Practice* (1995).

Jenny Ozga is Professor of Education Policy in the Department of Education at Keele University (UK). Before that she was Dean of Education at Bristol, University of the West of England. She worked at the Open University for many years, and also taught in the Department of Administration at Strathclyde University after a period as Senior Administrative Officer in the Education Department of the National Union of Teachers. Her main research interests are in education policy, teachers' work, and gender and management.

Rene Saran is Honorary Visiting Fellow in Policy Studies at the University of London's Institute of Education. She worked for many years in industry, commerce and as an adult education and polytechnic lecturer. She is a BEMAS Council member, chairing its Research Committee. Jointly with Hugh Busher she was author of *Teachers' Conditions of Employment* (1992). Earlier publications, some in collaboration with other scholars, include *Policy-making in Secondary Education* (1973); *The Politics Behind Burnham* (1985); *Public Sector Bargaining in the 1980s* (1988); *Research in Education Management and Policy* (1990) and *Effective Governors for Effective Schools* (1995).

Michael Strain is senior lecturer and research co-ordinator in the School of Education at the University of Ulster, where he teaches education management. He has previously taught classics in secondary schools and served as an LEA education officer. He has published essays and articles on local government, education policy and organisation in the UK and Ireland, and on some political, moral and economic implications of recent education reforms. Since his two granddaughters recently started school, he has begun to reflect more critically upon the nature of learning and the role of the teacher.

Acronyms

AMMA	Assistant Masters and Mistresses Association
APT&C	Administrative, Professional, Technical and Clerical Staff
ATL	Association of Teachers and Lecturers
BERA	British Educational Research Association
BEMAS	British Educational Management and Administration Society
CCT	Compulsory Competitive Tendering
CSE	Certificate of Secondary Education
DES	Department of Education and Science
DfE	Department for Education
GCE	General Certificate of Education
GCSE	General Certificate of Secondary Education
GEST	Grants for Education Support and Training
GM(S)	Grant Maintained (School)
HMI	Her Majesty's Inspectors (of Schools)
HRM	Human Resource Management
ILEA	Inner London Education Authority
INSET	In-Service Education and Training (of Teachers)
IT	Information Technology
K	Underpinning Knowledge Requirements
KWS	Keynesian Welfare State
LEA	Local Education Authority
LFM	Local Financial Management
LMS	Local Management of Schools
MCI	Management Charter Initiative
NAHT	National Association of Headteachers

NAS/UWT	National Association of Schoolmasters/Union of Women Teachers
NC	National Curriculum
NCC	National Curriculum Council
NCVQ	National Council for Vocational Qualifications
NFER	National Foundation for Educational Research
NUT	National Union of Teachers
NVQ	National Vocational Qualification
OE	Outdoor Education
OFSTED	Office for Standards in Education
PAT	Professional Association of Teachers
PCs	Performance Criteria
RSs	Range Statements
SATs	Standard Assessment Tasks/Tests
SCAA	Schools' Curriculum and Assessment Authority
SEAC	Schools' Examinations and Assessment Council
SHA	Secondary Heads' Association
SRLB	Sports and Recreation Lead Body
SSA	Standard Spending Assessment
STRB	School Teachers' Review Body
SVQ	Scottish Vocational Qualifications
TQM	Total Quality Management
UCIE	University of Cambridge Institute of Education
UNISON	Union of Public Service Workers

Chapter 1

Introduction:
Schools for the Future
Hugh Busher and Rene Saran

Teachers in schools of the future

A vision of schools moving into the twenty-first century is that they are rapidly becoming centres of learning, not just for students but for all involved with the institution, including staff (both teaching and support staff), parents and members of the local community. This new role is not easily assumed by some teachers as they see learners primarily as students who are the recipients of knowledge which they transmit. It will be in addition to the other specified roles of staff, such as teacher, senior manager or site supervisor. This visionary view of schools points to an entirely new setting for the work of teachers, support staff and school governors. It has implications both for the management of teachers in schools and for understanding teacher professionality and staff development.

This vision is not far fetched. A review of school effectiveness research shows one of the 11 characteristics for such an institution to be 'a learning organisation' with 'school-based staff development' (Mortimore, 1995, p 11, citing Sammons *et al*, 1994).

A study by Wasley (1994) offers valuable insights into the lives and work of teachers who were changing their classroom practice to better meet the needs of their adolescent students by creating opportunities for independent individual and group learning. The epilogue to her book, *Stirring the Chalkdust: Tales of Teachers Changing Classroom Practice,* refers to images of teachers in the midst of change:

Teaching is not easily transformed, nor is the transformation process something that one completes; ... teaching is complex enough, compelling enough to provide teachers with a career of growth, change, and ever deeper understandings about how students are best supported. Teachers do not arrive. They do not learn everything there is to know about teaching. Although for some this is humbling, and for others discouraging, it also promises a career rich enough in complexity and potential inquiry to hold a professional's interest for more years than a typical working lifespan allows ... Teaching is ... only for those who can – learn, hone, reflect and then investigate again.   (Wasley, 1994, pp 202–3)

The contributors to this book have addressed various aspects of teacher professionality against a background of a rapidly changing social, political and educational context. This represents a critical community of researchers, practitioners and consultants engaged in learning through draft writing, considering comments and producing final chapters that embrace the impact of political, trade union and curriculum issues on the management of staff in schools. We perceive this breadth as necessary for an understanding of schools as organisations. In order to develop a fully rounded analysis of the functions and processes of management in schools it is necessary to relate them to the central teaching and learning purposes of schools. It is difficult to understand either of these comprehensively without being aware of the pressures on schools from the socio-political environment.

Over time shifts of meaning and emphasis have occurred about the essence of professionalism. Professionals have been seen as people with certain traits who were self-governing and had autonomy and specific qualifications. Often they formed groups to protect their professional identity and preserve their livelihood but, in the main, they continued to work as self-employed individuals. Although teachers were not self-employed, except perhaps when working as a private tutor, those in secondary schools laid claim to academic expertise, and many throughout the last century claimed or demanded a qualification which they said was the equivalent of the training of other professionals, such as solicitors or churchmen. If working in organisations precluded people from being acknowledged as professionals then, today, many accountants, architects and doctors would be in danger of losing their professional status, which is clearly not the case.

Another hallmark of professionality is often said to be the special relationship between service provider and client. Mutual obligations are negotiated, involving moral obligations by the professional to deliver a service in a way which gives priority to the interests of the client, and which almost acquire the status of a social contract. The client has to pay an agreed fee for this service, which used to be negotiated directly with the professional when that person worked on their own account. Nowadays the fee is likely to be regulated by central government or professional bodies or negotiated by the client with the firm for which the professional works. In the event of negligence by the professional the client can, in theory, claim damages, although this might involve considerable legal costs.

Teachers, too, in a sense negotiate a contract with their clients, both with each of their students individually and with their students' parents, agreeing to deliver a particular sort of curriculum, managed in certain ways to meet their students' needs. Teachers and students strike bargains, though not legal contractual ones, about how each will behave and what each will do. For delivering their side of the bargain teachers are paid indirectly by their clients through the agency of the school governors out of the fees which pupils bring to a school, whether directly or indirectly through LEA age-weighted pupil formulae. Teachers who fail to deliver what their students expect of them may well find themselves in trouble, either suffering the consequences of student misbehaviour or of parent and student complaints to headteachers or school governors. Ultimately, proven professional incompetence could lead to dismissal.

The diversity of circumstances in which professionals work may account for the fact that contributors to this book reflect a range of perspectives about teacher professionalism. Some place more emphasis on the teacher as an individual while others explore the nature of professionalism resulting from the interaction between individuals and the school as an organisation. However there appears to be some sort of consensus that the developing shape of teacher professionalism in the twenty-first century will involve teachers working together more closely in teams in schools than they have done in the past, developing a more collegial culture than the fragmented or autocratic ones to which many have been subjected previously.

This emerging culture is being fostered by increased opportunities for professional development, which involves acts of reflection and critical enquiry by participants (at whatever level in an institution) about their own practices. It marks professional development off from more superficial processes of training driven only by short-term institutional needs. Even when staff undertake development together, reflection and enquiry can only be ultimately meaningful when something is transformed in the minds of the individual participants.

Shared common features of public services

Education is only one of the public services, albeit one of the highest spending ones. It shares certain characteristics with other public services, as do professionals working in both the public and private sectors. It was suggested by the School Teachers' Review Body (STRB) in 1995 that 'there is evidence that workloads are increasing generally for professional groups and that teachers are part of the broad trend'. For teachers the main factor was the pressures resulting from the introduction of the National Curriculum and the related Standard Assessment Tests (STRB, 1995, para 153, p 43), to which the consequences of the increased administrative work generated by the introduction of local management of schools (LMS) should be added.

A 1994 survey showed the average number of hours teachers worked per week was 49 for classroom teachers and 55 and 61 respectively for primary and secondary headteachers (STRB, 1995, para 146, p 41). These average hours do not reflect the special intensity of teachers' work. When comparing teachers' workloads with that of other professionals it has to be borne in mind that teachers usually work with large groups of students for most of each working day, whereas doctors and solicitors, for example, usually deal with only one or two clients at a time. There is something special about having to cope with 30 clients simultaneously, both individually and collectively. It requires teachers to make huge numbers of decisions every day in response to a multitude of student demands, without losing sight of the aims, structure and purpose of a lesson.

Recent changes in the National Curriculum, brought about by the Dearing recommendations of 1994, should reduce the complexity of teachers' work and lessen the number of decisions they have to make. The increased numbers of support staff being used in schools in some capacities, such as classroom assistants (STRB, 1995, p 40), as a result of budgetary decisions being taken by headteachers and school governors may also reduce teachers' workloads to some extent. The latter, however, is also changing the nature of teachers' work, requiring them more often now than formerly to supervise and manage adults working alongside them, as well as the students in the classroom.

The need for continuing professional development is also a common strand amongst professionals inside and beyond the public services. Nurses are allowed at least five study days a year. Under the Teachers' Pay and Conditions Act (1987) teachers were given five days a year in school for school-focused training to supplement whatever other professional development they undertook in their own time. Doctors are required to undertake 30 hours per year further study. Architects and people employed in marketing expect to spend 35 hours a year on professional renewal or development.

The provision of education, like social services and health, is labour intensive – 70 per cent of school budgets are spent on teaching staff, a figure rising to 80 per cent when support staff are included. Where public services are 'free' or heavily subsidised at the point of delivery, as is education, the cost of staff will always add substantially to public expenditure, giving people in society an added incentive to be concerned about the efficiency of such services both as taxpayers and as users. Since the early 1980s central government in the UK has introduced a range of measures to curb public expenditure, including the extensive privatisation of public utilities, and to promote competition by public services to achieve cost savings and encourage fund raising.

An imposed market ideology is a further factor influencing the whole of the public sector since the early 1980s in the UK. It claims to serve efficiency and promote individual choice, ensuring that resources are distributed more precisely to meet expressed individual needs. However, this view overlooks doubts about the ability of everybody in society to make rational choices or to take advantage of particular choices even when they have made them. It would seem to run counter to the notions of equity which underpinned the establishment of the welfare state in the late 1940s, following the recommendations of the Beveridge Report during the Second World War.

Another feature shared by many public services is the paradoxes inherent in central government policy. On the one hand public services are subject to strong central control through legislation and financial constraints. On the other, power has been decentralised and/or delegated to local or institutional units (Busher and Saran, 1993), so that schools control resource allocation as do trust hospitals or funded GP practices within cash limited budgets. National levels of funding for institutions are tightly controlled by government departments or funding councils prescribing the formula or the amounts of money per service which local authorities may spend.

The granting of limited discretionary powers to local units to vary national agreements has not always been welcomed by trade unions because it threatens to unleash a flood of local bargaining. This may lead to people in different parts of the country being paid different rates for the same work, the situation facing teachers in different parts of the country in the early years of the twentieth century before national wage bargaining was established through the Burnham Committee. In 1995, nurses expressed widespread opposition to the implementation of local pay bargaining. Similarly, few schools have made use of governors' discretionary powers over teachers' pay.

In schools opposition to the use of pay flexibilities is based on disquiet over their divisive potential, not only between institutions but also within institutions. Teachers, trade unionists and governors have voiced grave concerns that performance-related pay for teachers would undermine the team work which seems to be essential for a school to be effective. Central government has made this situation worse by insisting that any performance-related pay awarded in schools should be for individual teachers' performances rather than for particularly successful teams, such as a department, for example. The greater effectiveness of team work in industry – rather than individual competition between workers – is a widely recognised feature of recent management literature.

On the other hand the flexibility which financial delegation has given senior staff in institutions to use resources in ways which more closely match identified school needs is beginning to be appreciated by headteachers. The Office for Standards in Education (OFSTED) has commented that the proportion of resources which schools spend on teaching staff should not necessarily be seen as a fixed cost for all time. A different allocation between different types of teaching and support staff could be considered (OFSTED, 1993, Part 5, Technical Papers, pp 52–3). For example, since LMS was introduced, the numbers of less expensive support staff and part-time teachers have risen at the same time as the numbers of the more experienced and more expensive full-time teachers have declined. The figures are quite striking. Between 1989 and 1994 the number of full-time teachers employed declined by 3 per cent while the number of part-time teachers rose by 26 per cent. Between 1991 and 1994 numbers of staff other than teachers in schools rose by 31 per cent (STRB, 1995, Table 2, p 11).

These changes have aroused considerable disquiet in schools. If the reason for changing a school's staffing structure is merely to cut costs, squeezing out professional staff who are more expensive than less qualified auxiliaries, then it may endanger the quality of service a school delivers. If, on the other hand, a change in staffing structure means, for example, that teachers spend less time on administrative work and more time working with pupils, this could lead to an improvement in the quality of service offered.

The changing nature of teachers' work

The main debates in this book revolve around notions of what is involved professionally in being a teacher. In the maintained sector of education, as well as teaching large classes of students, all teachers have to be concerned with aspects of developing whole school policies, with school development planning and with the management of the delegated budget, even if it is only within their departments.

The increasing use of adults other than teachers in classrooms is expanding the range of management responsibilities which teachers are having to accept. The statutory contract of employment imposed in 1987 made explicit teachers' duty to manage people such as classroom assistants, technicians, and special needs support staff as part of managing the learning process for students.

Teachers are beginning to work increasingly in teams, a process that was fostered in the 1980s by the introduction of the Technical and Vocational Education Initiative. In some cases, teachers of not particularly high formal status in a school may well take responsibility for aspects of curriculum development; while in some science departments in secondary schools these teams include support staff such as laboratory technicians as well as teaching staff. All are expected to attend department meetings and contribute to the discussions on an equal basis.

Major themes of this book

There are four main themes which emerge from and through various chapters of this book. They are not mutually exclusive, but their different focuses bring to the fore different aspects of the debate about professionalism and the management of teachers as professionals in schools.

The first of these themes concerns the unstable environment in which schools operate, which has profoundly altered the working world of teachers since the early 1980s; another is the relationships between professional teachers as individuals and the school as an organisation. The third theme we discuss focuses on the styles of leadership and management which might be appropriate to schools as institutions supporting communities of learners, including teachers and parents as well as students. The fourth theme probes what might be meant by professionality in the late twentieth century.

The unstable environment

In exploring this theme it is useful to examine separately the impact of the external environment of a school on its processes from that of the internal environment and to note the interaction between them.

Since the mid-1980s there have been a great many changes imposed by central government on the ways in which schools work. The extent of these and the impact which they have had on schools and the way in which teachers are required to work are discussed at length in Chapters 2, 3 and 6, as well as being referred to by other contributors. These changes arise from seven major Acts of Parliament since 1980 and their myriad satellite statutory instruments and circulars. Some commentors suggest that chaos theory offers the only possible framework of analysis to cope with such an avalanche.

The National Curriculum which was imposed in 1988 extensively remodelled the content of the curriculum for all students from the age of 5 years to 16 years. It had a major impact on teachers' professional tasks. Both Ozga (Chapter 2) and Foreman (Chapter 6) take the view that by 1995 teachers no longer determined the curriculum content (though they still largely influenced the pedagogy), but delivered a curriculum designed by others. At one extreme this loss of professional autonomy can be seen as deskilling teachers, turning them into mere technicians working to externally set specifications. But even Ozga, who comes nearest to this view, leaves open the question of deskilling. The extent to which that actually occurs may depend on the way in which senior staff run a school and whether or not they choose managerialism.

The charge of deskilling or disempowerment can be seen most strongly in the way in which the National Curriculum was introduced and subsequently managed. As Foreman points out, it was introduced with little consultation and no trialling. No sooner was the first wave of shiny covered curriculum statements lodged on teachers' shelves impelling teachers to try to implement them, than a review of their requirements was instigated and schemes of work changed. This threw many teachers into a state of confusion and despair. Many were very annoyed at having spent so much time beginning to make one set of changes to the curriculum only to find that they immediately had to make another. Many wondered at the impact of this waste of resources on students' schooling.

The system of national testing which was set up for each of the Key Stages of the National Curriculum, the Standard Assessment Tests (SATs), caused teachers as many problems as the curriculum itself. The original versions of these imposed unmanageable workloads on teachers and deprived students of weeks of teaching while the tests were set, taken and marked. Furthermore, for the many teachers who tested their students' performances regularly in any case, the SATs gave them neither new information about their students nor any information worth passing on to parents. During the summer of 1993 teachers, following the required balloting by teachers' unions of their members, boycotted the tests. Many governing bodies and headteachers were in sympathy with their teachers and resisted central government suggestions that it was the duty of school governors to insist on teachers administering the tests. In 1995 teachers' workloads for these tests were reduced when central government agreed to fund external markers for the tests in return for the teachers agreeing to administer them.

Beyond central government requirements there were changes to the organisational framework of teaching at local level. The reconstitution of school governing bodies in 1986 gave parents and the local community a much stronger position of influence in the running of the schools which their children attended, at the expense of the teachers' employers – local education authorities. The 1988 Education Reform Act turned this position into one of actual power as school governing bodies became budget holders for their schools and the de facto employers of staff. Consequently, teachers had to learn to work more closely with lay people in the management of schools, explaining more clearly what was involved in the processes of teaching and learning and managing a school. By 1995 this had already led to conflicts between teachers and governors in some schools (Esp and Saran, 1995).

These externally imposed changes catapulted schools into feverish activity, developing new strategies, structures and procedures to cope with them. One of these was the advent of school development planning, discussed by Constable in Chapter 9. These changes made heavy demands on teachers' time, ingenuity and skills, as Constable and Foreman point out, resulting in the development by teachers of new skills and possibly new types of professionalism. For example, headteachers had to learn to consult staff opinion before and during the development of whole school policies on a wide variety of topics from equal opportunities to occasional school closures, no mean feat in an averagely sized secondary school where there are, perhaps, 50 teaching staff and many support staff.

To cope with this situation many headteachers came to see themselves as managers of the boundaries of their school organisations. As best they could they protected their teachers from the full impact of externally imposed changes in order to sustain staff morale and, as far as possible, keep staff in a calmer atmosphere than that which existed in the frenetically changing external environment. As Strain explains in Chapter 3 this was an attempt to leave space for teachers to work professionally with their students in the classroom, the job for which they had been educated.

This suggests that what happens inside institutions is not entirely determined by external pressures. The coupling between the internal and external environments of schools can be quite loose, to adapt Weik's notion (1976), despite the valiant attempts of the central government of the UK in the 1980s to tighten it up to a high degree of rigidity. It tried to do this through its attack on the powers of local authorities, trade unions and professional autonomy in many spheres of economic and social activity. What matters is how people in schools respond to changes in the external environment. In some cases subversion and passive resistance have been quite successful. Grammar schools successfully survived into the 1980s and 1990s, despite pressure by earlier central governments in the 1960s and 1970s in favour of comprehensive schools. New funding arrangements in the late 1980s, such as grant maintained status, have since guaranteed their survival.

Individual professionals in institutional settings

Schools are institutions which are concerned with learning. To facilitate this students need the support of their teachers. Teachers need space, autonomy to cultivate that special professional relationship between teacher and student which fosters this learning. Whilst teachers in most maintained schools usually have to teach large groups of between 25 and 30 students they also have to create time for one-to-one interaction with individual students to inspire them and to tailor the teaching to each learner's individual needs. In Chapter 3, Strain sees the teacher–learner relationship as a moral one, in which the former serves the needs of the latter altruistically.

In order to work effectively teachers, too, have to be learners, as Constable points out in her chapter. They constantly have to be reviewing their understandings of the needs of their students, the pedagogy of how their students learn and their grasp of the contents of the curriculum which they have to teach. Their need for changing knowledge does not stop at the classroom door, since most teachers work in school organisations. They also need to be constantly up-dating their knowledge of how their school works as an institution. Their statutory contract as well as the demands made on them by senior management of the school require them to be so involved, whether considering, for example, whole school policies on student behaviour or on homework and marking schemes. They also need to negotiate for an adequate allocation of resources from their school to support those aspects of the curriculum with which they are concerned.

This leads Day in Chapter 7 to argue that teacher professional development should not be confined to narrow training just to meet immediate institutional needs. He prefers that staff development be used to encourage reflection about values and pedagogy which will help individual teachers improve their professional practice.

Leadership and management

To be effective as learning institutions schools need both leadership and management. It is important to distinguish between the two. Leadership is associated with vision; clear school aims; the development of a school ethos or culture which inspires professional staff; the winning of trust; the fostering of learning communities and of critical inquiry and reflection. Management embraces the efficient use of resources, both financial and human; the pedagogical and curriculum tasks of a school; the effective use of communications to ensure that suitable consultative structures are in place; effective processes of decision-making including those of delegation; the promotion of warm, open and honest interpersonal relationships and the implementation and development of school policies, staff development programmes and monitoring and evaluation procedures.

Esp and Saran (1995) found that headteachers and chairs of governors whom they interviewed gave themselves and each other numerous leadership and management roles: 'The most striking contrast is the perceived leadership roles for chair and head respectively. The chair is concerned with leading a group of people who together make up the governing body; the head has to give pedagogical leadership to professional staff' (Esp and Saran, 1995, p 29).

Perhaps institutional leadership and management are in a state of tension, but they also derive mutual support from each other. Professional leadership must be backed by professional management and vice versa. There would be little point in inspiring staff and writing the most exciting mission statements and policies unless the organisational structures and the will to manage policy implementation were also in place. For example, staff need to have their work sensibly timetabled and adequate resources made available to them if they are to perform as competent professionals in the classroom. Without the maintenance of clear codes of conduct for students and teachers, and support for those who are experiencing difficulties, good teaching cannot thrive.

On the other hand should effective management turn into managerialism, the fears which Ozga expresses in her chapter, that teachers would be deskilled, would loom large. By managerialism we mean school leaders maintaining the bureaucracy of an organisation for its own sake and for the sake of maintaining their power and control over a school rather than for helping a school's members to fulfil its purposes. Sets of bureaucratic rules and meaningless consultation would demoralise staff, would spread perceptions of conflict between senior management and the rest of the staff and would exclude staff from any real influence over decisions.

In such circumstances teachers would become like technicians, delivering a product designed by others rather than by themselves. Old-fashioned professional skills, which Hoyle rather applauds in Chapter 4, of curriculum development and design and of pedagogy and working with students would no longer be needed. Nor would there be any challenge to develop new skills except clerical/technical ones. Staff would be disempowered or deskilled.

The spectre of managerialism has much in common with the rational economic model of management which Beresford, in Chapter 5, explains has been promoted by the New Right. He argues that it is inimical in many of its aspects to effective educational and learning processes. He believes it should be replaced by a different model of management, the human relations model. He argues that this accords more closely with the notions of collegial relationships between professional colleagues in a school, which teachers' unions would like to foster, and with the idea of schools being institutions for collaborative learning.

The above debate leads us to the conclusion that management should be an instrument, not master but servant, for the running of schools. Headteachers and other senior staff and governors should never lose sight of the purposes of their schools as centres of learning. All management structures and decisions should support the school as a learning institution in which professional teachers and other staff can serve effectively the interests of the students of whatever age.

What might be meant by 'professionality' ?

A central cause of tensions in schools is the lack of an agreed view on teacher professionality. A decade of rapid change and the emphasis on school effectiveness and improvement have engendered a wide-ranging debate about what should be expected of teachers. Ozga, in her chapter, fears the deskilling of teachers. In her eyes total quality management (TQM) and human resources management (HRM) may just be a cloak for a new managerialism which enhances the power of senior staff and school governors and tightens bureaucratic processes of control, while leaving precious little space for teachers to exercise their professionality. She prefers to see teachers developing their range of professional skills. We would expect this to occur through increased team work and involvement in school decision-making at all levels in schools.

Beresford prefers a view of teacher professionality which emphasises participation in school decision-making, while arguing that teachers and their unions have to be realistic in accepting schools as hierarchical organisations, of necessity in larger institutions. Although teachers may aspire to senior positions within the school organisation, and some will achieve this, at any one time the majority of teachers are likely to be working in classrooms, mainly managing students and their learning, rather than working as more senior managers with wider responsibilities for a whole school or a department whilst continuing to have some responsibility for teaching.

What seems to be emerging in this debate is a view of a collegial system of running schools which gives scope to the development of teachers, and perhaps other staff as extended professionals, to use a term first used by Hoyle (1975). Such a system involves the participation of staff in the development of whole school policies, and the formation and implementation of school development plans by teams of teachers. These activities require the development of a range of new skills by teachers to allow them to work effectively in teams with their colleagues and to understand and make judgements about the wider processes of the school as an organisation. However, some of the existing skills which teachers have of working alongside students can be adapted, and are in any case still needed for teachers to retain their autonomy of decision-making when working with learners, a point emphasised by Strain in his chapter.

Collegially managed schools in which high quality educational leadership inspires staff will keep educational and pedagogical issues as the focus of their central purpose and the focus of staff decision-making. In such schools, all in the school community will need to be empowered as learners, since teachers will be unable to adapt their strategies to meet the changing needs of their students and of the external enviroment unless they are willing and able to reflect in a structured way on their existing practices in order to improve them in the future. Constable emphasises the importance of this aspect of professionality in her chapter, but points out that some teachers might find it threatening since it appears to question the authority of knowledge on which their power as leaders and managers of student learning is largely based. This gives expression to the possibilities for professional staff development well into the twenty-first century.

A brief resume of the book

The book is divided into two parts, the first (Chapters 2–6) looking broadly at how teaching as a profession in the 1990s has evolved historically and how conceptions of it have been affected by changing ideological and social frameworks. Some of the changes have been brought about by alterations in the legal frameworks of education, local government and trade union activity and the responses of teachers' unions to these. In Part Two (Chapters 7–11) the authors focus mainly on the work of teachers in schools. They argue that values are central to competent professional practice, implying that senior staff need to use the opportunities which can be provided through continuing professional development to raise the awareness of staff of the ethical under-pinnings of action. They also discuss the influence which school leaders and governors have on the development of a school's culture or ethos. They suggest this should be of a nature which encourages all staff, whether teaching or support staff, to work together to facilitate learning and school improvement.

In Part One, Ozga's chapter begins by providing an historical analysis of the changes in the ways teachers have performed their work. Through this she develops the concept of teaching as a labour market to complement the notion of teaching as a profession. Pressures in the labour market, she argues, are due to Britain's general economic decline in the 1980s. This has threatened the security of teachers' jobs and affected definitions of what is involved in being a teacher. For example, the introduction of the National Curriculum, which was discussed earlier, has changed part of the role of the teacher from one of curriculum design and implementation to one of delivering a curriculum designed by others.

The introduction of new styles of management she believes also needs to be examined critically. Processes such as TQM or HRM purport to empower people, placing emphasis on individuals working collaboratively in teams. In reality, however, they may represent a new form of institutional tyranny – the tyranny of the rule book and the school mission statement. These can give apparently rational grounds for reinforcing the control of senior management in place of the traditional person-centred autocracy formerly wielded by some headteachers.

Strain takes the argument forward by looking at the administrative frame-work which developed during and after the mid-1980s in England and Wales, and how this was affected by the ideology of the New Right and its views of the job of teaching. Against this background he then develops his own view of teacher professionality, discussing in what profound way the values which people hold personally relate to the values they hold professionally. This leads him to argue that it would be morally wrong and a denial of a teacher's professional role for teachers merely to comply with external controls or conform to management requirements, although he admits that the pressures inherent in the socio-political climate of the 1990s make it difficult to preserve this view. Yet, he argues, teacher autonomy exists for the benefit of the learner.

Since schools exist as institutions to foster learning, it is incumbent upon senior staff to use their hierarchically given authority to support teacher autonomy and innovation, not to stifle it.

The discussion of the chapters so far begs the question what new type of teacher professionality might be emerging in the socio-political climate of late twentieth-century Britain. Hoyle discusses this in his chapter, using a checklist to itemise the differences between what he perceives as the old and new styles of professionality. Like Strain he is concerned about the impact of the ideology of the political New Right with its emphasis on efficiency and on the distribution of resources by the mechanisms of the free market, to ensure that an institution or school meets its clients' or students' needs. In this rational instrumental world, headteachers are supposed to provide control and deliver services efficiently regardless of whether the service is effective or equitable. It risks providing students with easily achieveable targets and courses, which may or may not be in their best interests, rather than encouraging them to aspire to excellence. It was the last quality which Peters and Waterman (1982) linked to the most successful companies in the USA, not the former.

It is difficult to understand management processes without understanding the perspectives of organised labour. Beresford provides an account of teacher union views on themes like teacher professionalism and the school curriculum. He points out that teacher unions do not want to confront school hierarchies but to work with school leaders to foster genuine professional management which will sustain teacher autonomy. To do this, he suggests, a human resources model of management is likely to be more successful, and preferred by the teachers' unions, than a rational economic one. The latter, he argues, represents ideologies of social control and market place relationships between people. He notes that it is the dominant model nationally in the mid-1990s in the UK.

The concern with teacher autonomy leads naturally to an examination of that aspect of their work in which, until the mid-1980s, teachers had greatest autonomy, the management of the curriculum. An aspect of the curriculum reforms imposed by central government in 1988 was a renewed emphasis on the importance of subject specialist teaching at all levels of schooling, including primary schools. In his chapter Foreman discusses the impact of these curriculum reforms, particularly on the work of primary teachers, suggesting that they challenged school leaders and class teachers to think very carefully about what and how they taught. He suggests that it shifted the main concern of teachers from the content of the curriculum to the pedagogy, in particular leading them to focus on how they might differentiate the curriculum adequately to make it accessible to students of all abilities.

Part Two pursues the logic of this line of discussion. In such turbulent times teachers clearly need help and support not only in adapting to changing circumstances but in sustaining existing levels of performance. Day discusses how institutional leaders can create a school culture which supports teachers' reflection on practice at classroom and school level. He argues that this reflection is an essential part of their developmental process to meet and to implement change. In effect it encourages them to become learners, too, like their students and leads to the development of schools as critical learning communities.

At the heart of the argument about teachers, their professionality and appropriate styles of management for schools is the issue of values. Rutter *et al* (1979) and the National Commission on Education (1993) suggested that appropriate values are at the centre of school improvement. Of concern here is what values senior staff and school governors need to hold and implement coherently to facilitate particular approaches to teaching and learning. The main thrust of Everard's chapter is this. He argues that the way to promote 'right thinking' as well as 'right action' is to take staff through a training process in which values are linked to particular statements of competency. In learning to act 'correctly' in certain circumstances, staff will also acquire the values implicit in such actions. He suggests that such management learning could be linked to tests of competence such as National Vocational Qualifications.

Although the development of particular styles of leadership and certain values are important in creating schools which are communities of collaborative learners, these are of little use unless coupled with effective management, as we argued earlier. In her chapter Constable illustrates one means by which management can be effective and collaborative, discussing how a science faculty in a secondary school used school development planning to alter its pedagogy and develop staff skills. Through having to develop new teaching materials and introduce these to and evaluate these with their colleagues, teachers underwent an important learning process. As Constable points out, some of them found this painful because their images of learners were associated with the inferior status of students, not with the peer status of professional development.

Many different kinds of staff work in schools, though popularly and mistakenly it is usually only teachers who are denoted by the word 'staff'. Staff other than teachers also have a considerable effect on how teachers are able to work with students. They carry out a wide range of tasks as classroom assistants, clerical workers and premises supervisors. Some are unqualified manual workers, others have recognised technical or professional qualifications. Financial delegation under LMS has made clear the importance of these support staff whom Saran and Busher consider in their chapter. They discuss how the management of such staff should and can be an integral part of the management of all staff in a school. They point out that the relationship between teaching and support staff is a key element in the culture of a school and in facilitating student learning.

Having explored who are the staff of a school and the nature of their work, Busher and Saran discuss, in the final chapter, how staff might be managed professionally, ie effectively, to best promote the purposes of a school within the legislative, administrative and socio-political frameworks which emerged in England and Wales by the mid-1990s. Notions of different types of consultative procedures by headteachers (Busher and Saran, 1992, 1994) are developed and related to notions of collegiality and empowerment. It leads the authors to consider how collaborative management can be implemented so that schools can become communities of learners.

References

Busher, H and Saran, R (1992) 'Changing professional roles of teachers in the UK', paper to British Educational Management and Administrative Society (BEMAS) Annual Conference, 12–13 September, University of Bristol.

Busher, H and Saran, R (1993) 'Paradoxes of power under LMS' in Smith, M and Busher, H (eds) *Managing Schools in an Uncertain Environment: Resources, Marketing and Power* Sheffield Papers in Education, for BEMAS, Centre for Education Management and Administration, Sheffield Hallam University.

Busher, H and Saran, R (1994) 'The politics of school management' in Public Finance Foundation *How to Manage a School, Conference Proceedings*, Chartered Institute of Public Finance and Accountancy, London.

Dearing, R (1993) *The National Curriculum: The Final Report*, SCAA, London.

Esp, D and Saran, R (1995) *Effective Governors for Effective Schools*, Pitman Publishing, London.

Hoyle, E (1975) 'Leadership and decision-making' in Hughes, M (ed) *Administering Education: International Challenge*, Athlone Press, London.

Mortimore, P (1995) *Effective Schools: Current Impact and Future Potential*, Institute of Education, University of London, London.

National Commission on Education (1993) *Learning to Succeed*, Heinemann, London.

Office for Standards in Education (OFSTED) (1993) *Handbook Part 5, Technical Papers*, HMSO, London.

Peters, T and Waterman, R (1982) *In Search of Excellence: Lessons from America's Best Run Companies*, Harper & Row, New York.

Rutter, M, Maughan, B, Mortimore, P and Ouston, J (1979) *Fifteen Thousand Hours: Secondary Schools and Their Effects on Children*, Open Books, London.

Sammons, P, Hillman, J and Mortimore, P (1994) *Key Characteristics of Effective Schools*, OFSTED, HMSO, London.

School Teachers Review Body (1995) *Fourth Report Cm 2765*, HMSO, London.

Wasley, P A (1994) *Stirring the Chalkdust: Tales of Teachers Changing Classroom Practice*, Teachers' College Press, New York.

Weik, K (1976) 'Educational organisations as loosely coupled systems', *Administrative Science Quarterly* 21, 1, pp 1–19.

Part One

Teachers as Professionals in the 1990s

Chapter 2

Deskilling a Profession: Professionalism, Deprofessionalisation and the New Managerialism
Jenny Ozga

Introduction

This chapter seeks to review critically the concept of teacher professionalism, with the intention of providing a clear – if somewhat bleak – appraisal of the extent of teacher deprofessionalisation in the 1990s. The chapter's essential arguments concern the need to understand professionalism in its historical and political context, to appreciate its function as a form of occupational control and to consider its capacity for the concealment of differentiation in and stratification of the teaching workforce. Furthermore, it is suggested that these arguments are essential to a sound understanding of the scope of current and recent policy developments and in particular their potential for the separation of management and workforce in education. The review of teacher profession-alism which follows presents – albeit in summary form – the arguments which have been developed extensively elsewhere (Ozga and Lawn, 1981; Lawn and Ozga, 1986; Ozga and Lawn, 1988; Ozga, 1990). These arguments themselves draw on critical sociological work on the professions – especially that of Larson (1977) and Johnson (1972); and on labour process theory and historical sociology (for example Grace, 1987). The review is organised in relation to three themes; first an exposition of the sociological analysis of professionalism as a form of occupational control, second through a historical account of teacher–state relations which allows for the application of that sociological perspective, and finally through an analysis of the current restructuring of the teaching labour force.

The chapter adopts a standpoint external to the experience of teachers, and leaves to one side issues concerning teachers' everyday uses of concepts like professionalism, and their complex strategies for dealing with their ambiguous and contradictory status. This is not because I do not consider these issues to be significant, but because I want to deal with teachers here as an occupational group, managed by the state, through various strategies, including profession-alisation. My concern is thus to explore policy intentions towards the teaching workforce, and to consider the role of management in effecting those inten-tions. In addition, my purpose in reviewing the historical management of the teaching workforce is to illuminate the permanent tension in teacher–state relations, and to consider whether we may identify significant differences from past practices, differences that perhaps reflect the emergence of a post-Fordist core and flexible forms of education labour.

Professionalism in its social, political and economic contexts

It is pointless, as Hoyle and John (1995) well illustrate, to try to establish whether or not teachers are professionals in some abstract, absolute sense. Professionalism is best understood in context, and particularly in policy context. Critical analyses of professionalism do not stress the qualities inherent in an occupation but explore the value of the service offered by the members of that occupation to those in power. The growth of the modern state and the development of modern capitalism in the nineteenth century produced condi-tions favourable to the growth of new categories of professional workers. State mediation (Johnson, 1972) created a category of 'state professionals' incorpo-rated into the organised framework of agencies that were financially dependent on the state. As public service bureaucracy steadily increased with the growth of state responsibility for education, health and welfare, employment and so on, professionalisation – as an affirmation of expertise – grew in strength.

Bureaucratisation and the fostering of education as a route to social mobility opened up the possibility of professionalism to a wide variety of occupations. The main points that emerge from such a critical, historically located analysis of professionalism may be summarised as follows:

22

1. The characteristics of professionalism are not immutable and professionalism has been transformed in conjunction with the growth and development of capitalism and the related emergence of the modern state.
2. Therefore the modern professional may be most accurately characterised as a bureaucratised, state professional, and it is this model which is being refashioned in response to changes in the state.
3. Some residual elements of historical models of professionalism remain and inform the conduct of the modern professional: altruism or community interest, for example. These may be used by the state to manipulate the employee or by the employee as a defence against such manipulation.

The significance of these points is not so much that they challenge some ideal, essential professional status, but that they link professionalism to changing state activity. What we are experiencing now is just the most recent manifestation of shifting relationships between the state and professionals. The current transformation of the bureaucratised Keynesian Welfare State (KWS) into the small, strong state in the service of the market inevitably brings with it a reduction of professional power and status. Let us look now at that shifting historical relationship.

The history of teacher–state relations

This historical account takes as its starting point the premise that teacher–state relations are problematic, and that the management of the teaching workforce requires a strategic response from the state. Historical investigation allows us to chart the variations in that response, and the role of professionalism within it.

From central control to indirect rule and back again

The establishment of a state system of education in England and Wales required that, along with growing responsibility for the provision of schools, the state assumed growing responsibility for the provision of teachers, for their training and regulation. Before 1862, teachers – who could be certified, uncertified or apprentice teachers – were engaged and paid by the managers of the schools in which they taught. With the introduction in 1862 of the Revised Code, school managers received a single block grant, the amount of which depended partly on the results of examinations carried out by HMI – hence 'payment by results'.

The Revised Code was intended to be cheap and efficient, but its overarching aim of 'educating our masters' lay behind the narrowness of the curriculum and its rote-learning methods. Teacher initiatives had raised the quality of working-class education, and the code provided more 'appropriate' education, as Grace explains:

> Despite existing mechanism of surveillance and screening, the system had perversely developed its own dynamic which had resulted in forms of curriculum development, forms of teacher initiative and forms of cultivation of intelligence which had never been intended for working-class schooling. The costs of the enterprise had risen dramatically and new subjects had been introduced into the curriculum. Elementary teachers had become more confident and assertive. As standards within the provided system rose, the dreadful prospect that working-class education might soon surpass in quality that provided by many middle-class private schools suggested, as one writer put it, that there would be an 'inversion in the orders of society'. In short, the system in practice had turned out to be altogether too good for the working class. (Grace, 1985, p 7)

The responsibility for this distortion of the schooling system lay with the teachers, who had become an overpaid and over-confident vested interest in education. Lowe, President of the Board of Education, argued that, without the code 'a state of things will arise [such] that the control of the educational system will pass out of the hands of the privy council and of the House of Commons into the hands of the persons working that educational system' (Tropp, 1957, p 87).

Control over the system was reasserted through the application of the principles of a market economy to elementary schools:

> The code would define the product required, the inspector would assess the extent to which it had been achieved, the teacher would be paid in relation to his or her measured efficiency in production ... The dominant principle was now to be that of efficient pedagogic work production with an emphasis on 'basics'. (Grace, 1985, p 8)

Reaction to the code
The operation of the code provoked resistance from teachers, and was probably the single most significant factor in the development of an organised, unionised teaching force. By equating schools with factories and teachers with workers, the state revealed to teachers the advantages of organisation and of direct action for the improvement of working conditions. By treating elementary teachers as state servants, the state encouraged them to identify with those whose children they taught, rather than strive unsuccessfully for social promotion.

In the aftermath of the First World War, and especially in the post-1920 period when the bipartite division of educational provision based on social class came under strain, technical justification of such division based on the assessment, through testing, of intellectual ability, was invoked. The role of education as a means of maintaining class division grew in importance, as did the need for the state to ensure the co-operation of its teachers. This co-operation could not be relied upon in a period when the NUT had steadily increased its membership and engaged in two long local disputes, while campaigning throughout England and Wales for better working conditions and improved pay. H A L Fisher, the President of the Board of Education, warned that 'an embittered teacher is a social danger' (Grace, 1987, p 203) and sought ways of reducing that danger.

Licensed professionalism and indirect rule
The strategic response adopted by Fisher centred on teacher professionalisation, within limits. Teachers, including elementary teachers, were to be encouraged to think of themselves as professionals, through the fostering of their responsibilities in certain areas – pedagogic expertise, for example, and identification with the service:

> The National Union of Teachers had played a most valuable part in watching over the material interests of the profession ... but as the state takes a more and more direct interest in the material conditions of the profession, and as these material conditions become more and more improved, then I hope that the activities of the National Union of Teachers, which is such a powerful instrument for influencing opinion in this country, may be more and more concentrated upon what I may call the spiritual and intellectual aspects of the teachers' work.
>
> (Fisher, 1919, quoted in Lawn, 1987a, p 69)

Fisher's policy foundered because of the disparity between professional rhetoric and the worsening economic climate which led to the implementation of severe cuts in the level of central support for education in 1922. These cuts, and a review of teachers' salaries, superannuation and pension rights aroused fierce opposition from teachers. Teachers continued to drift towards the Labour Party (Lawn 1987a), and the NUT was involved in a protracted salary campaign which involved most of its local associations in extended disputes or strikes. Thus the teaching force presented an immediate and pressing problem to Baldwin's government.

Baldwin's President of the Board of Education was Eustace Percy, appointed in 1924. According to Lawn (1987b), Percy's correspondence with backbenchers reveals considerable concern about teachers in the Labour Party and the activities of the Teachers' Labour League. Some MPs demanded that teachers take an oath of allegiance, and a Subversive Teachings Bill was suggested, but Percy had a clear perception of the dangers of overt central control in a period when the Conservative Party could no longer assume electoral victory: 'What could be worse... than to encourage a conception that teachers are servants of a government in the same way as Civil Servants, and therefore must teach in their schools precisely what any Labour Government may tell them to teach'. (Percy in Lawn, 1987b, p 230).

It was this appreciation of the dangers of a highly centralised system which produced a certain relaxation in curriculum controls over elementary teachers. In 1926 the Board of Education changed the basis of curriculum control from prescription to suggestion, establishing the 'modern principle of curriculum autonomy' (Grace, 1985, p 10) which endured until 1988. White's convincing analysis of the motivation of the Conservatives in deregulating the curriculum concludes:

> If Parliament still controlled the content of education, the Socialists would change the Regulations... they would be able to introduce curricula more in line with Socialist ideas. To forestall this it was no longer in the interests of the anti-Socialists, including Conservatives, to keep curriculum policy in the hands of the state. ... If they would devise a workable system of non-statutory controls, the Conservatives had everything to gain and nothing to lose from taking curricula out of the politicians' hands.
>
> (White, 1975, p 28)

What we see here is a strategic response by the state to a number of related problems – the danger of an overcentralised system falling into the 'wrong' hands, the drift of some teachers leftwards and economic difficulties. It is also important to note that licensed professionalism was underpinned by *curricular* autonomy.

The strategy of indirect rule continued until 1944, when the political and social content of expanding demand permitted teachers to defend their 'licensed autonomy' (Dale, 1981) and resist more direct rule. They were in a strong market position in the period following 1944, when there was a shortage of qualified teachers, public demand for increased educational opportunity (allied to demands for a more just and egalitarian society), acceptance of a human capital approach to investment in education and the growth of pedagogic expertise, whether associated with intelligence testing or based on child-centred methods. A further important factor was that which had initially provoked the centre into promulgating licensed autonomy – the strength of organised teachers.

Throughout the 1950s and 1960s all these factors combined to strengthen teachers' claims to autonomy and to force the state to maintain the rhetoric of indirect rule, partnership and professionalism. It was only with the threat of economic crisis, in the late 1970s, that the centre began to move away from indirect rule.

Back to central control

The end of the 1970s and the 1980s saw a period of economic contraction and concern about educational standards linked to questions of competitiveness and national performance which echoed the historical conditions of the 1870s. We have witnessed a similar reaction: greater control over educational content and greater control over the activities of teachers. The idea of relaxed controls over the curriculum has, once again, given way to the need to prescribe centrally.

Criticisms of teachers also echo the old arguments, castigating teachers for their professional self-interest, their monopolisation of provision, their constant expansion of the curriculum and demands for greater resources. The rhetoric of professionalism left teachers vulnerable to such criticisms. Indirect rule had fostered distance between teachers and parents. That division permitted the co-option of parents into a new 'partnership' for the 'reform' of the education system. The capacity of teachers to resist such initiatives was weakened by the failure of education policy designed to eradicate inequality; it was becoming apparent to teachers that education could not, after all, compensate for society. Furthermore, teachers were having to cope with a simultaneous decline in both resources and pupil numbers. All these factors combined to create favourable circumstances for the reassertion of control over teachers in England.

The teaching labour force: marketisation and management

This final part of my review is intended to provide a brief discussion of the teaching labour force in the context of marketised provision. This discussion places teachers within the context of changing occupation structures. It attempts to avoid conventional thinking about teaching as having special status as a vocation or profession, as this prevents us from making use of some of the insights available from the study of work and occupations.

The emphasis on market-led policy and consumer choice in education has resulted in considerable exposure of the teaching labour force to pressures more commonly experienced in other, traditionally less secure, occupations. This adds force to the argument for studying this occupational group and its organisational context alongside others, and for the use of major themes in the sociology of work – themes like occupational structure, labour market position, occupational segmentation, labour process analysis – in relation to teachers and their managers. Moreover, as Knight *et al* (1993) have pointed out, teacher restructuring needs to be seen in the context of global change in work organisations, in management–workforce relations and in the identification of core and peripheral workforces.

A great deal is to be gained from placing teachers within the scope of theoretical and intellectual enquiry which is concerned with other occupational groups, particularly as public sector workers find themselves exposed to the stress and competition of the market-place. Ideas concerning the labour process and its management provide particularly rich connections to the historical and contemporary control of the teaching labour force, while maintaining a commitment to recording the messiness and complexity of such processes in relation to teachers' work. Connell has set out some of the ways in which we might explore these processes:

> Teachers' work can be understood as a particular *labour process* and as governed by a particular *division of labour*. In comparison with other workers, the object of teachers' labour is difficult to specify, so the definition of task can extend almost without limit, and the work could be intensified indefinitely. But it is governed by strong constraints – such as the nature of the classroom and other settings, class sizes, the timetable – which embody particular social relations and policies. The work of secondary teaching is most often performed by a technique of collective instruction on predetermined content. There are a good many refinements and variations of this technique... The timetable embodies a division of labour based on one set of principles, viz. content, difficulty and pupils' age. Teachers' work is also divided in ways reflecting experience, sex, administrative involvement, and the histories of particular schools... The division of labour changes historically, as in the emergence of new specialisms like computing.   (Connell, 1985, p 86)

The interest lies in exploring the extent to which these divisions, and the division between teachers and managers reinforced by current policy trends, are functional and rational in their consequences, or if they are better understood as deriving from the imperative to control the teaching labour force (Johnson, 1972; Edwards, 1979). A labour process perspective, within the broader field of the sociology of work, reveals more clearly than conventional approaches the fragmented nature of teaching as an occupation, with its segmented structures (particularly those of class, race, gender, sector and subject), its complex and contradictory functions and its ambivalent relationship with its employer, and thus allows further exploration of the nature of control.

In developing this analysis, the ideas associated with new management practices are significant because, as Hatcher (1994) has argued with reference to changing employment conditions, organisational cultures and staff management tasks, the importance of management in the marketised system is enhanced.

Before moving on to explore the nature of the new management, it may be helpful to review some of the recent policy activity that places education (and other public sector services) in the market-place.

The marketisation of education

It is not possible to address all the issues raised by marketisation of education. The emphasis here is on its consequences for employment practice. The particularly hostile context in which the restructuring of the education work-force has proceeded is significant. It is unnecessary to repeat widely discussed points about the major restructuring of state responsibilities in the face of the apparent failure of the KWS. Education was, and remains, heavily implicated in that apparent failure, and has been subjected to particularly harsh criticism on the grounds of malign inefficiency and producer capture (Dale and Ozga, 1993). Education and education workers were castigated for what was claimed to be their improper concern with attempts to redress naturally occurring inequalities and accused of squandering scarce resources on inappropriate ends, thereby contributing to economic decline, as well as to moral decay and cultural confusion.

These points are made because they remind us of the peculiar hostility with which teachers in England were scapegoated, and of the collision between market precepts and the informing cultural concepts of education workers. Principles of equality of opportunity and measures of success which do not connect directly to improved economic performance – for example enhanced confidence and self-esteem, improved co-operation – are very securely lodged within the work cultures of primary schools in particular (Pollard *et al*, 1994). There is then, good reason to anticipate some difficulty in identifying with the market by those expected to deliver it. Thus it is that management comes to assume such significance.

In considering the implementation of market-driven education policy, due weight should be given to the connection – the interdependence – of enhanced regulation (to ensure that the market works in a particular way) and deregulation/devolution. Marketisation in education is not accompanied by the elimination of mechanisms of control but by their reformation and relocation. The professional/bureaucratic mechanisms of the KWS are eliminated, but the efficient operation of the market is secured through a combination of legislative controls (juridification) and internal, institutional mechanisms, notably performance indicators and inspection, which ostensibly provide consumers with a basis for selection but more importantly provide powerful managerial imperatives. In addition, as Hartley (1994) has argued convincingly, the consequences of financial devolution for headteachers are to make them complicit in delivering predetermined policy:

> The surface impression is that devolved school management is all about local control and the quest for quality. At root, however, it is a new mode of regulation, a new discourse, whereby government retains strategic control of teaching, curriculum and assessment whilst it devolves to headteachers... the tactics for implementing that strategy.
>
> (Hartley, 1994, p 139)

Marketisation in education is most clearly visible in the provisions of the 1988 Education Reform Act, and in the Act of 1993 which enshrined 'Choice and Diversity' in law. The 1988 Act introduced formula funding, local management of schools (LMS), and the facility to opt out of local authority planning frameworks to become grant maintained schools (GMS), ie directly funded by central government. The 1993 Act extended choice and diversity through the financial encouragement of specialist schools and through the acceleration of opt out. Accompanying these changes in structures are changes in mode and method. The National Curriculum requirements and the publication of examination results as league tables contribute to marketisation. The logic of the market links funding to success, and consequently encourages schools to seek potentially successful pupils, while other pupils, with a low market value or expensive needs, are not targeted. Thus the steered education market is characterised by differentiation and stratification, though the rhetoric is that of choice, diversity, responsiveness and flexibility. This rhetoric is also abundant in the description of the emergent forms of the teaching labour force (School Teachers' Review Body (STRB), 1993, 1994), and similarly conceals stratification and segmentation, as well as the market's tendency to reinforce inequality.

Occupational restructuring

Occupational restructuring in teaching has taken place through two principal mechanisms: first the direct regulation of pay and promotion through the STRB (a quango appointed by the Secretary of State), and second through deregulation and devolution of financial control, which allows for greater variation in employment terms and conditions. The policy background – of reduced employment protection and an effective public sector pay freeze – is important for teachers, as it is for other public sector workers. Teachers' negotiating rights have been abolished and a contract specifying hours of work and duties has been imposed by the Teachers' Pay and Conditions Act of 1987, bringing to an end a protracted and bitter dispute which was as much about the control of the occupation as about pay and conditions (Seifert, 1987; Ozga, 1988). The abolition of the Burnham Committee and its associated three-cornered negotiations involving the Department of Education and Science, the local education authorities and the teacher unions and associations set the agenda for a move away from national pay bargaining towards the setting of a minimum rate and the encouragement of much greater local flexibility.

In 1987 a new pay structure was introduced, establishing a single scale for classroom teachers with five levels of incentive allowance for distribution by school managers. In 1993 this new structure was amended. Classroom teachers were placed on an 18-point spine and additional spine points replaced the five incentive allowances. Heads and deputies were already on a separate 51-point spine, paid within a certain range, depending on school size. The 1990 pay award was generous to managers and deputies, and the incentive allowance scheme worked in favour of senior teachers from its inception. In 1991 the STRB was established and policy since has confirmed the recognition of managerial responsibility by financial reward and strengthened headteacher and governor autonomy in allocating these awards. The third and fourth reports of the STRB continue the pursuit of flexibility, of reward for good performance measured against indicators and the encouragement of management discretion and control. Progress has not been unproblematic, however, and there have been differences of view between the STRB and the Secretary of State. The STRB remains concerned about the need to encourage excellence in classroom teaching (STRB, 1994, para 53).

If we move to the issue of deregulation/devolution and the consequences for occupational restructuring, a very significant factor in determining the developing character of the education workforce is the freedom of governing bodies to appoint as they wish, with regard only to the demands on the budget. This is a considerable freedom in LMS schools, while GMS schools need not adhere at all to national scales, but may devise their own. As a consequence new divisions are emerging, and the situation is further complicated by the use of ancillaries and auxiliaries (Lawn and Mac an Ghaill, 1994). Further incentives to flexibility may be discerned in the current and recent changes to initial teacher training, which permit greater variation in access to the profession, including school-based training run by schools, and considerably shortened BEd degrees for teachers in the early years of primary school.

Teachers are further stratified according to their access to in-service training. The virtual disappearance of financial support for individual in-service training (with the exception of limited National Curriculum updating) means that many teachers have to fund their own professional development. On the other hand there continues to be funding available for training teachers as managers, particularly at senior level, for example through the Headlamp scheme established by the Teacher Training Agency in 1995. This effectively discourages and disenfranchises many lower-paid teachers. Given the large proportion of teachers who are women and taken together with women's double burden of work and family/housework, these factors combine to decrease promotion opportunities for many teachers and create a pool of undertrained, unrecognised workers.

These initiatives – in devolution of financial management, in pay, in training – combine to promote flexibility which may be exploited by the employer. The consequences for the occupation of the employer's use of this flexibility are likely to be complex. It is reasonable to anticipate growing workforce segmentation. It is also apparent that segmentation and specialisation will not, in all cases, link automatically to deskilling – quite the reverse in some areas of secondary teaching and in management. In primary teaching we may see the emergence of status divisions and the downgrading of the generalist. The existence of different categories of teaching staff provides flexibility to the manager and is potentially a source of increased power to governors and managers. At the very least the solidarity of the primary teaching community is weakened, a community which could be characterised, before these reforms, as exhibiting all the characteristics of unalienated, integrated labour (Bowles and Gintis, 1976).

The significance of management

I have looked at professionalism as a form of occupational control and considered its historical use in the management of the teaching labour force. The essential elements of my argument may be summarised as follows: the teaching workforce is managed *either* through promulgation of a professional ideology, which regulates behaviour in particular ways (eg militant unionism is replaced by responsible cooperation) and which creates a climate of consultation and curricular autonomy; *or* through direct regulation, which permits curriculum control but which fosters militancy and reveals inequity. Neither management strategy is stable, historically each has led to instability, either through teachers extending the terms of their licence beyond permissible limits (Dale, 1981) or through inefficiency and loss of quality in a heavily regulated system (Arnold, 1862; Grace, 1985).

These ideas are important because they suggest the use of professionalism as a form of occupational control of teachers when there is a context that permits broad agreement about education provision – put briefly, a coincidence of economic prosperity, acceptance of human capital theory and of entitlement as a basis of provision. Professional ideology brought with it associated structures, for example relatively undifferentiated levels of reward, flat hierarchies, equality of status and the headteacher as academic leader rather than manager. As we have seen, the present context is very different, and it is to the role of management in the emerging occupational structures that I now turn.

Once again I would like to set discussion of the management of the teaching workforce within a broader context of changes in management in the 1980s and 1990s. A more detailed discussion of these points is to be found in Nicholls *et al* (1993) and Nicholls and Ozga (1994).

There is a need to understand management in education against the backdrop of the continuing process of restructuring of British business and industry, with its restoration of management's *right to manage*. That restoration was accompanied by the threat of unemployment and the decline of trade union power.

New discourses of management were required to legitimate this new order and its practices. These discourses were closely aligned with marketisation and its associated structures and processes: 'Our new enterprise culture demands a different language, one that asserts management's right to manipulate, and ability to generate and develop resources' (Legge, 1989, p 40).

Management discourses such as human resource management (HRM) and total quality management (TQM) have strong parallels with professionalism as a form of control. HRM harnesses the occupational culture to the delivery of efficiency and quality. Marketability ensures commitment which produces increased economic effectiveness and development. The tensions between individualism and teamwork, always prevalent in professional work, are effectively resolved by a strong corporate culture, which creates a cohesive workforce but avoids workforce solidarity. Professional workers are thus subject to management controls and processes that permeate their work: 'Strong culture/cohesion is achieved through a shared set of managerially sanctioned values (eg quality, service, innovation). Co-operation through the management of the culture reinforces the intention that management will be exercised responsibly' (Legge, 1989, p 37).

The echoes of professionalism as a form of control are, I hope, apparent. What is different is the shift in the locus of control – from a directive state, manipulating professional rhetoric in a relatively undifferentiated workforce, to the head-as-manager, working within a framework of regulations, and using management of the culture to internalise controls and ensure compliance. It is in this context that I suggest we explore the meanings of empowerment and collegiality, as these terms, along with the proliferation of management teams, may conceal the increase in monitoring and surveillance of teachers' work. Market success requires smooth production and the eradication of 'problems'. Deviations from policy are less likely to be tolerated by the senior management team. Class teachers must answer to postholders; indeed the growth of super-visory functions implicit in collegiality, which may 'extend' professionalism for some, but deskill others (particularly women and part-timers), connects to the bigger agenda of emergent post-Fordist production processes. The impor-tance of these new management discourses and processes in internalising control mechanisms should not be overlooked. The principles of 'steering at a distance' (Kickert, 1991) discussed by Ball (1993), where coercion is replaced by incentives, quality assurance and control and repressive tolerance have much in common with the new managerial discourse. As Ball argues:

> Management is a disciplinary practice. But *importantly,* as a discourse, man-agement is productive rather than simply coercive. It increases the power of individuals – managers and managed in some respects – while at the same time making them more docile. It offers flexibility and autonomy to some, although within the constraints and rigours of a market system and in relation to fixed indicators of performance. Management is both a body of precepts, assump-tions and theory, to be learned by managers, and a set of practices to be implemented, encompassing both managers and managed.
>
> (Ball, 1993, p 112; emphasis in original)

This is an extremely critical perspective of the new managerialism, and one that is opposed to the burgeoning literature on restructuring and self-management which accepts much of the HRM and TQM discourse, incorrectly perceiving it as an escape from the bureaucratic regulation and paternalistic hierarchy of modernity (Hargreaves, 1994). The education literature ignores the debates on industrial relations and power that surround these issues in the literature on management and organisation theory. These debates continue and are supported by detailed case study work that attempts to disclose what is really going on in the new industrial relations of post-Fordist, post-modern business and industry (Scott, 1994). Similarly, informed work is needed in education.

Conclusion

This chapter has looked at professionalism as a form of occupational control of teachers, and at its changing use from the establishment of a mass system of education in England to the present, marketised provision. The attack on producer capture that accompanied marketisation signalled the abandonment of professionalism as a means of control in its historical form. It has been replaced by managerialism, which is school based and which offers enhanced status and financial reward to those responsible for ensuring delivery of the service against a set of externally determined criteria and in pursuit of externally generated aims and targets. Senior teachers are thus co-opted in a redefinition of professionalism that is essentially managerialist, and may disseminate this definition through processes that extend surveillance, manufacture consent and render dissent illegitimate.

These processes operate within a policy framework that legitimates inequality of provision and outcome and supports increasing differentiation among the teaching workforce, in pursuit of flexibility, diversity and responsiveness.

Professionalism as a form of occupational control was always vulnerable to exploitation by teachers, as I have argued above. Its links to public service, and to autonomous judgement, and its inclusive character were features which strengthened teacher resistance to central direction, despite its use as a form of occupational control by the state. As a form of control it was always dangerous and contradictory. Managerialism is a different matter, in that it works with the fissiparous character of the occupation and against public sector collective identities. If senior managers in education choose to work within this discourse then they must recognise the consequences for other teachers, and particularly for the flexible, deskilled, part-time labour force. However there are invidious consequences for all teachers, managers and managed, in the acceptance of externally constructed agendas that contribute to loss of control over the meaning and purpose of work, which is the essence of deskilling.

References

Arnold, M (1862) 'The twice-revised code', *Frazer's Magazine*, London.

Ball, S (1993) 'Changing management and the management of change', paper to American Educational Research Association (AERA), Annual Conference, Atlanta.

Bowles, S and Gintis, H (1976) *Schooling in Capitalist America,* Routledge & Kegan Paul, London.

Connell, R (1985) *Teachers' Work*, George Allen & Unwin, London.

Dale, R (1981) 'Control, accountability and William Tynedale' in Dale, R *et al* (eds) *Education and the State Volume III*, Falmer Press, Lewes.

Dale, R and Ozga, J (1993) 'Two hemispheres: both New Right?' in Lingard, B, Knight, J and Porter, P (eds) *Schooling Reform in Hard Times*, Falmer Press, London.

Edwards, R (1979) *Contested Terrain: The Transformation of the Work Place in the Twentieth Century*, Heinemann, London.

Grace, G (1985) 'Judging teachers: the social and political contexts of teacher evaluation', *British Journal of the Sociology of Education* 6, 1, pp 3–17.

Grace, G (1987) 'Teachers and the state in Britain: a changing relation' in Lawn, M and Grace, G (eds) *Teachers: The Culture and Politics of Work*, Falmer Press, Lewes.

Hargreaves, A (1994) *Changing Teachers, Changing Times: Teachers' Work and Culture in the Post-modern Age*, Cassell, London.

Hartley, D (1994) 'Devolved school management: the "new deal" in Scottish education', *Journal of Education Policy* 9, 2, pp 129–41.

Hatcher, R (1994) 'Market relationships and the management of teachers', *British Journal of the Sociology of Education*, 15, 1, pp 41–61.

Hoyle, E and John, P (1995) *Professional Knowledge and Professional Practice*, Cassell, London.

Johnson, T (1972) *Professions and Power*, Macmillan, London.

Kickert, W (1991) 'Steering at a distance: a new paradigm of public governance in Dutch higher education', paper for the European Consortium for Political Research, University of Essex, March 1991.

Knight, J, Bartlett, L and McWilliam, E (1993) *Unfinished Business: Reshaping the Teacher Education Industry for the 1990s*, University of Central Queensland Press, Queensland.

Larson, M S (1977) *The Rise of the Professions: A Sociological Analysis*, University of California Press, Berkeley.

Lawn, M (1987a) *Servants of the State: The Contested Control of Teaching 1910–1930*, Falmer Press, Lewes.

Lawn, M (1987b) 'The spur and the bridle: changing the mode of curriculum control', *Journal of Curriculum Studies* 19, 3, pp 227–36.

Lawn, M and Mac an Ghaill, M (1994) 'Primary schoolwork', paper to Centre for Educational Development, Appraisal and Research (CEDAR) Conference, Warwick University.

Lawn, M and Ozga, J (1986) 'Unequal partners: teachers under indirect rule', *British Journal of the Sociology of Education*, 7, 2, pp 225-38.

Legge, K (1989) 'Human resource management: a critical analysis' in Storey, J (ed) *New Perspectives on HRM*, Routledge, London.

Nicholls, P, Muschamp, Y and Ozga, J (1993) 'Exploring the market: a report on progress in a comparative study of the impact of market forces on small service providers', paper to British Educational Research Association Annual Conference, Liverpool.

Nicholls, P and Ozga, J (1994) 'Manufacturing consent: markets and manageralism in primary schools', paper to Australian Association for Research in Education (AARE) Annual Conference, Newcastle, NSW.

Ozga, J T (ed) (1988) *Schoolwork: Approaches to the Labour Process of Teaching*, Open University Press, Milton Keynes.

Ozga, J T (1990) 'A social danger: the contested history of teacher–state relations' in Jamieson, L and Corr, H (eds) *State, Private Life and Political Change*, Macmillan, London.

Ozga, J T and Lawn, M (1981) *Teachers, Professionalism and Class*, Falmer Press, Lewes.

Ozga, J T and Lawn, M (1988) 'Schoolwork: interpreting the labour process of teaching', *British Journal of the Sociology of Education* 9, 3, pp 323–37.

Pollard, A, Croll, P, Broadfoot, P with Osborne, M (1994) *Changing English Primary Schools?*, Cassell, London.

Scott, A (1994) *Willing Slaves? British Workers under Human Resource Management*, Cambridge University Press.

Seifert, R (1987) *Teacher Militancy*, Falmer Press, Lewes.

School Teachers' Review Body (STRB) (1993) *Second Annual Report, Cm 2151*, HMSO, London.

STRB (1994) *Third Annual Report, Cm 2466*, HMSO, London.

Tropp, A (1957) *The School Teachers*, Heinemann, London.

White, J (1975) 'The end of the compulsory curriculum' in *Curriculum: The Doris Lee Lectures, Studies in Education, Vol 2*, Institute of Education, University of London.

Chapter 3

Teaching as a Profession: The Changing Legal and Social Context
Michael Strain

The legacy

The latest revision of the National Curriculum is intended to last for at least five years (*Independent*, 1994a). The new Secretary of State, Gillian Shephard, has called a truce (*Times Educational Supplement (TES)*, 1995a), one might say, in what has been a most protracted and wasteful conflict. The prospect for teachers is now one of opportunity to consolidate practice and stabilise conditions and working relationships. This tenuous hope follows ten years of conflict, and many of those involved now seem unsure of exactly what the war was about, though English teachers have probably, of all groups, remained most tenaciously sure of their professional reasons for opposing tests (*Independent*, 1995a). For some politicians and administrators the engagement was a campaign to obtain better value for money; for others a struggle for increased efficiency or higher standards; for still others the attempt was to obtain more influence for parents and employers in the running of schools and what was taught. For teachers generally, what seemed to be at stake was their public standing and their *raison d'être* as a profession. At any rate it seems appropriate now to review the consequences of what has been instituted legally since 1987 to determine teachers' conditions of employment (Tomlinson, 1993, p 51) and the implications of this new framework for the future, especially as it has come to affect the role of teachers, both in schools and in the wider society. This chapter briefly reviews recent legal changes determining teachers' working conditions and explores significant cultural and social developments which seem to threaten inherited beliefs concerning the nature of teacher professionalism. It is hoped the discussion might inform and guide teachers in their participation in new management structures and associated organisational tasks and, through their responsibility for the curriculum, in fulfilling their obligations to pupils as learners.

Management is now a legally stipulated element within what 'shall be deemed to be included in the professional duties which a school teacher may be required to perform' (Department of Education and Science (DES), 1987, 35.11). The language itself is significant; teachers are now to 'be available for work' and their activity is frequently described in terms such as 'planning', 'delivery' and 'performance'. There is also much about providing advice and ensuring co-operation, collaboration and co-ordination. Teachers' work is now subject to appraisal and governing bodies act as the employer in respect of appointments and dismissals. Will governors, with their extensive new powers, demand submission and loyalty to their own policies and perceived requirements for their particular school? If so, in what sense can teaching be understood as a profession, whose members share and embody a set of autonomous values and a commitment to the needs of learners, independently of the particular institutional setting in which they work? Can a teacher of a child with special educational needs participate in the statementing process with at least some freedom to act differently from the adopted priorities and policies of the school governors? A growing number of chief executives in NHS trusts are not afraid to politicise their role in such a way and require medical decisions to be circumscribed by and subject to the overall operational policies of the organisation. In a widely publicised recent incident, one such executive declared that a hospital doctor's first loyalty was to the employer (*Independent*, 1994b).

Teachers and the new ideology of schooling

The practical consequences of the changes brought about in teachers' conditions of working by the reforms introduced since the mid-1980s hardly reveal their full significance unless they are understood as not just technical changes but also imbued also with profound values resulting from attempts by the New Right (Jonathan, 1990, pp 17–18; Arnot and Barton (eds), 1992) to mould the popular or, to use an old-fashioned term, public (Feinberg, 1991, p 24) perception of teachers' proper function. Teachers may have won the battle to fend off the more mechanistic, performance-related versions of appraisal (Tomlinson, 1993, pp 95–106) and pay (*TES*, 1995c) sought initially by the government, but the longer and more profound struggle for a role comparable in dignity and independence with what they were traditionally accorded may already be lost in the face of an emerging, government-sponsored ideology of schooling. There are already indications that teachers will generally be judged by parents and members of the local community against the criteria implicit in the government's ideology. If this turns out to be the case, the power of this ideology to shape the reality of what teachers actually do and how they do it will become irresistible. The professionalism of teachers will be diluted and transformed despite the efforts of the academic and professional establishment to go on asserting, or redefining, teachers' traditional values and forms of responsibility. Eagleton's characterisation (1991) of how ideology works is succinct and instructive here:

> A dominant power may legitimate itself by *promoting beliefs* and values congenial to it; *naturalising and universalising* such beliefs to render them self-evident and apparently inevitable; *denigrating* ideas which might challenge it: *excluding* rival forms of thought.
>
> (Eagleton, 1991, pp 4–5, emphasis in original)

The following paragraph offers a brief sketch of the emerging educational ideology being promoted by the present government; its commitment to the sovereignty of individual choice and the superior regulatory conditions induced by competitive 'market' relations could quickly universalise certain general assumptions and beliefs about schooling. On the beneficiary side, a superficial perception of consumer empowerment, seemingly afforded to parents by open enrolment and pupil-led funding, could readily naturalise these beliefs in the public mind. If so, parents' concept of a teaching profession would be radically redefined with, it will be argued later, destructive moral and social consequences.

Professions in the market-place

Professions, according to what many would wish to become received wisdom, are fundamentally self-interested associations, a form of conspiracy against the public. In a modern democracy, built upon the twin pillars of representation and accountability, professionals cannot be relied upon to be accountable and to serve the interests of individual clients unless they are subjected to the same disciplines as commerce and industry, namely market forces. Instead of hiding behind claims to professional autonomy, called in aid of even vaguer protestations regarding professional dedication and commitment, professions should test the validity of such claims openly by putting a price on their services and allowing personal profit, consequent upon client satisfaction and 'professional' responsiveness to market demand, to proclaim the authenticity of otherwise unverifiable assertions. This inherently empiricist, Protestant and Anglo-Saxon belief in the efficacy of works and their product, wealth, will, by such mechanisms as if by an Invisible Hand (Jonathan, 1990) reveal pragmatically (no need for theories or abstract rules) the good doctor, lawyer, teacher and cleric. Full churches, like full concert halls, and over-subscribed schools, are by definition worth supporting. So let the funding follow the pupil, the grant be dependent on the prior support of the private sector, and the hospitals built according to the business interests of insurance companies, reflecting in their capital expenditure decisions the health care choices of the fit, able and economically most active members of society, as if society were a sort of club for self-help enthusiasts. In this way public morality becomes merely a common-sense formulation and practical expression of social efficiency: by their works shall ye know them; wealth (Tomlinson, 1993, p 144) to the wealth creators, strength to the strong.

The circular logic of this argument (whatever works successfully defines what is good) might be less unacceptable if our inherited political institutions more adequately fulfilled the democratic and developmental needs of late modern societies; in other words, if they enabled such ideological propositions to be articulated, challenged and mediated by a critical public debate before becoming a principle of social policy. Instead, everywhere in western societies, an unprecedented gulf between the reactive policies and ineffectiveness of purportedly 'representative' governments and the aspirations of their electorates gives cause for concern:

> But the malaise has much deeper roots. It reflects a crisis in the relationship between the political and non-political parts of society which has led many to question the very rôle of politics and political institutions in providing leadership for society. (Leadbetter and Mulgan, 1994)

The question of the professionality of teachers and of the kinds of operational freedom and scope for independent action they should be granted concerns the grounds on which public agreement is based. These require public debate over what values shall inform and define appropriate relationships and bonds of obligation between teachers and taught and so they must periodically be re-examined by reference to the ideology and prevailing values contested and endorsed within the polity. Education and the way it is organised and practised must always involve consideration of political choices. Contemporary British politics, over at least the last ten years, has narrowed the admissible criteria of such choice to those appropriate to exchange relationships in a 'market'.

Questions concerning a school's educational purposes have been neglected in face of a new political agenda in which efficiency and effectiveness have become the cardinal criteria of policy. Is the price right? Is the product what parents and employers demand? Is its cost justified by the quality and standard revealed by measurable outcomes?

Product or process?

The logic of this neo-classical economic framework, in which the rationality of choice is explained by the observable outcomes of behaviour, has come to redefine the nature of education itself. A good school will be revealed by its exam results (by their fruits...); such results should be achievable at competitive prices (or their proxy, the Office for Standards in Education 'value for money' checklist). Freedom of choice given to parents under open enrolment will ensure a process of adjustment within the education market-place, so that less competitive and successful providers conform more closely to the standards set by more popular schools. Indicators of 'performance' will provide an information base for purchasers so that these 'market' processes of consumer-led choice (Jonathan, 1990; Strain, 1995) and product specification[1] may be reliably and effectively sustained. Use of these 'mechanisms' facilitates belief that instances of underachievement in education are either the consumer's fault or can be corrected by improving the operation of the market, by improving the flow of information to consumers and the conditions of open competition among suppliers. Suppressed, if not altogether removed from consideration in this new ideology, are questions relating to the kinds of learning processes which schools should be seeking to establish and maintain.

From this ideological base, new 'professional' practices operationalise the new morality, an outcome-based verification of worth, entailing subjection of process to product as means to an approved end. Professional practice itself comes to promote and 'naturalise' (in Eagleton's terms), politically desirable popular beliefs and marginalise others. Education comes to be understood as a commodity or a range of products instead of a holistic process (Ranson, 1994). Process variables, the conditions of individual learning, come to be accepted as given, with a fatalistic resignation (the poor we have always with us), or marginalised within the spectrum of professional and public concern. Significantly, the psychology of children's learning has almost disappeared[2] from the curriculum of initial teacher education. This at a time when scientific interest in and capacity to analyse empirically the relationship between mind and brain (Fischbach, 1992), consciousness and understanding, sign and meaning in human cognition, has reached the threshold of redefining the very nature of the human condition and experience of reality. Yet few teachers any longer regard a knowledge of learning theory and its application to the curriculum and organisation of pupil activity as a central requirement of their work in the classroom.

From an ethic of service to conditions of employment
Early in 1995 HM Chief Inspector of Schools, Chris Woodhead, was reported (*TES,* 1995b) to be opposed to the encouragement of active learning and 'discovery' methods in schools. In the same week the Secretary of State resisted proposals from the Schools' Curriculum and Assessment Authority, from a number of examining boards and from Sir Ron Dearing, her chief adviser on assessment, to increase the proportion of course work in pupil assessment (*Independent,* 1995b). The paradox of a government policy which requires 'learning by doing' as the foundation of its arrangements for teacher training (Department for Education (DfE), 1992) but resists its extension in the learning programmes of children scarcely merits serious attention; the story of the National Curriculum by Graham and Tytler (1993) has already exposed the culture from which such statements derive their ephemeral political significance. But the implicit diminution of the role of the learner in learning makes it less surprising that teachers have come to see learning theory as remote from their professional concerns; the curriculum is now increasingly defined and regarded as something 'provided' and 'delivered', assessed by reference to universal objectives, leaving the individual learner a recipient, at best a client, whose individual contribution is encouraged as a motivational device rather than an intrinsically desirable end, a good in itself. This is not, of course, how teachers typically regard or fulfil their responsibility to learners, but it is an inescapable part of the logic of the role and responsibilities now thrust upon them. Similar conflicts and paradoxes are evident in the legal and other formal changes to the conditions of teachers' work introduced during the last 10 or 15 years.

The new legal framework

The new 'props' were mostly set in place between 1986 and 1989. The constitution and role of governing bodies were widened by the inclusion of teacher, parent and community representatives (Education (No 2) Act, 1986) and by giving them overall responsibility for the conduct of the school. More extensive and specific management responsibilities were delegated to them by the 1988 Act (Education Reform Act, 1988). Teachers, on the other hand, have been significantly, though by no means wholly (*TES* 1995a), marginalised. The abolition of the Burnham Committee and the introduction of the Teachers'

Pay and Conditions of Service Act, 1987, left teachers without national negotiating rights, enjoyed more or less continuously since 1919. Instead, initially an Interim Advisory Committee advised the Secretary of State on pay and conditions (Barber, 1992, pp 111–15), replaced in 1991 by the School Teachers' Review Body.

The local authorities, which formerly negotiated with teachers on pay through the Burnham Committee and on conditions through the Council for Local Education Authorities (CLEA), have also been excluded from negotiating processes following the 1987 Act. In subsequent Education Acts of 1992 and 1993 LEAs have been even more radically marginalised. Their residual powers and duties have turned them into a public 'holding company', with default powers (Strain, 1993) in respect of activities which most schools cannot easily undertake on their own and of pupils whose essential needs might not be provided satisfactorily by the new 'market'-based arrangements for admissions and school organisation.

The new conditions of employment (Tomlinson, 1993, pp 49-61) define professional duties as specific activities which teachers must carry out over a prescribed number of hours. These activities are wide ranging and, in addition, cover the provision of guidance, information and records, including assessment reports. School discipline, staff meetings, assemblies, co-operation and participation in school management, administration, school and public examinations are all now included amongst the duties a teacher 'may be required to perform'. These changes reveal an underlying redistribution of power in the education system. If the outcomes of education are examined along three dimensions of process, product and pattern of distribution, and the influential actors identified as learners, providers and managers, it becomes possible to see the direction of shifts in the relative positions of power for each group of actors, in respect of particular dimensions of change (Fig 3.1):

Learners	Less	More	?
Providers	Less	Less	?
Managers	More	More	?
influence over	Distribution	Product	Process

Figure 3.1: *Relative shifts in the power of actors to influence educational outcomes: 1980–95*

Managers, including governing bodies, senior teaching staff and central bureaucrats have increased their control over the form and composition of what is to count as a learning outcome (product). Learners, if they are adults, and parents on behalf of their children, can also now exercise more 'voice' regarding their level of satisfaction in relation to these outcomes. Managers enjoy a greatly increased capability to affect the distribution of educational goods within their sphere of responsibility. A governing body and a school's management team can alter learning opportunities for different groups of pupils by their timetabling and staffing decisions, choice of syllabuses and overall use of the narrow margins of actual discretion, or 'virement', within the school budget. Equally, central government affects learning opportunities for different categories of pupil and different localities by its policy priorities (eg nursery school provision; child care tax allowances for lone carers), global resource decisions and the distribution of finance through local government and funding agency grants.

Providers (a category which includes teachers directly responsible for and engaged with learners in learning, ancillary staff in schools and local authority advisory and support staff), have in many schools (Webb, 1994) experienced a loss of scope for the exercise of discretionary influence over day-to-day procedures and organisational activities in support of their work and its distributive consequences (ie its capacity to benefit some pupils more than others). It might be argued that teachers significantly affect distribution of opportunity when they construct school timetables. So they do, but they act in that capacity as managers rather than as teachers. The relation between the two functions is an issue in need of much more elucidation (Eraut, 1993) than has generally been attempted so far, in the rush to replace traditional subject-based in-service education and training with courses in education management, in the wake of the implementation of local management of schools reforms.

Many schools now manifest features of what has been termed by Hargreaves (1994) 'contrived collegiality', namely:

- a form of working together imposed by administrative or managerial authority rather than created spontaneously by teachers themselves;
- adoption of functions and conduct oriented to prespecified implementation outcomes;
- activities which take place within a relative fixed frame of time and space, determined by administrative or managerial decisions.
- preference for ways of working which lead to predictable outcomes.

It is apparent that changes in teachers' conditions of service and other changes in the way schools are run, considered in the wider context of shifts in the balance of influence and control, point to a significant change in the relative importance attached to the exercise of authority and control by the centre. This has been achieved at the expense of local interests whose opportunities for participation in and for formatively shaping the components of the learning process have been formalised and restricted. Definition of the desirable outcomes of education processes, of education as a product, has been removed from the direct influence of teachers and parents, who are ostensibly responsible for the educational progress and destination of the individual child. Teachers may choose what to buy, but have less influence over the uses to which those purchases are professionally applied. Parents may choose where their child attends school, but have less opportunity to participate in decisions affecting the quality and purposes of the learning processes in which their children are engaged.

To sum up: recent shifts in the distribution of power have made it easier for authorities to control educational outcomes. They have kept closed possible avenues by which beneficiaries might have learned to participate more influentially in educational decision-making, and made it more difficult for those professionally committed to learners' interests to affect the quality and purpose of what is provided for their benefit. What remains unclaimed, if not uncontested (*TES*, 1995b) territory is the process of learning itself; in subsequent sections some of the possibilities generated by profound changes in the intellectual, cultural and social conditions in which teachers now prepare children, for lives whose real needs are increasingly difficult to foresee, will be explored. It might be possible to formulate new grounds on which teachers stake a moral claim to be accorded a different and less self-interested kind of autonomy.

Changing conditions

A new meaning for professionality

Professionality is inextricably bound up with widely shared values, understandings and attitudes regarding the social order and the rules by which others, in certain relationships, may instigate a claim on us. When the claim nowadays is made for a social activity to be regarded as 'professional' it is not only a claim for status and a higher level of reward, but an assertion about the expectations which others might properly hold in relation to all those admitted to the 'profession'. Thus, to claim the standing of a professional has come to mean adherence to an ethic, a moral principle, which derives from a freely undertaken commitment to serve others as individual human beings, worthy of respect, care and attention.

The commitment should be made without regard for the other person's power to purchase, demand or in any way coerce the professional to provide the attention sought. It is this independence (Gellner, 1983, p 64) from the normal interplay of inducement and obligation, through the medium of real (monetary) and authoritative (non-monetary) differentials, which confers a particular status on professions. Attribution of independence and impartiality also frees the endowed professional from some of the normal forms of accountability. Enjoying a standing, a role, and a form of protection from the everyday claims which persons may make upon others, the professional enjoys some of the autonomy of the confessional, the jury bench and the home, privileged or 'private' domains in which, subject to some default provisions (such as those of the criminal law, in respect of cruelty, abuse, corruption etc), persons are not required to account for their actions. Our actions in those 'domains' are, we say, our own business. Whereas submission to the kind of accountability which asks, 'was that resource spent prudently?' is functionally necessary in market relationships, freedom from such obligations is a necessary condition for the success of relationships which are defined by and fulfilled in acts of giving, caring and serving.

Such freedom may be understood as an endowment (Strain, 1995), conferred on agents by their willingness to participate meaningfully and constructively in social life and implying an obligation to render an account. In return for the privilege, we undertake to make visible, public expression of our answer to the claims of the 'other'. Shared rules and routines by which 'self' is revealed to 'other' facilitate free and creative gift exchanges, between generations (as with provision of child care), or within groups, such as reciprocally formed networks (Thompson, 1993, pp 54–60), or individuals engaged in conversation or musical performance. Such exchanges, by transfer of gifts, form a significant and much underexamined part of social and economic life (Boulding, 1973). Not all exchanges in social life are transacted under market conditions. The market introduces a framework of social discipline which will accord a high degree of freedom at the operational level for unimpeded individual action. But when the rules are broken (eg in the case of faulty goods, broken contracts, unfair exploitation of knowledge and opportunity in share dealings), the good order and social benefits of the totality are paramount. Whereas in personal relations we are morally obliged to render an account to each other, in market conditions we may by force of law be held to account by a superior authority. External authority, imposed for a socially agreed purpose, requires individuals to answer for their accomplishment of a task or mission authorised within the collectivity. It is an essential element of the apparatus necessary for securing order within market exchanges.

For teachers, however, in their relations with learners, it will be crucial for them that, in their readiness to be accountable for their new financial responsibilities, they should hold on securely to some zones of freedom from a narrow functional, legal accountability, especially in respect of their response to the claims of learners to the educational 'gifts' we make available. Learners are, for teachers, the 'other' to whom accounts are rendered as part of the learning process itself. The form of accountability appropriate to teaching must be defined in terms of the teacher's personal response to the learner's 'How shall I know ...?', 'Where shall I find ...'? Friendship entered into for one's own purposes is not true friendship, in the sense of a mutual relationship constituted by the actions of each to promote the good of the other. Similarly, learning for purposes chosen by others, and by rules and specifications formulated by authorities far removed from the learner's lifeworld, can at most have only an instrumental (Bauman, 1993, p 184) place and should be subordinate to the moral, 'gift-giving' enterprise on which education is founded.

The hallmarks of professionalism

Downie (1990) has analysed the idea of a profession and identified the characteristics which give the role and practices associated with professionalism a special social importance. These are:

1. skills or expertise proceeding from a broad knowledge base;
2. a special relationship with beneficiaries consisting of an attitude (a desire to help plus a sense of integrity) and a bond (constituted by the role relationship with beneficiaries);
3. recognised authority to speak out on matters of public policy and justice, beyond any duties to specific clients;
4. independence (in at least some respects) of the state and of commercial interests;
5. possessing education as distinct from training.

Downie's first and last criteria seem to be disregarded in recent changes to regulations governing teacher education (DfE, 1992; DES, 1983; Tomlinson,

1993, pp 14–19), which emphasise practice at the expense of theoretical training and require a specialised rather than a broad knowledge base for intending teachers. And yet, with regard to skill and expertise, a broad knowledge base is an increasingly common occupational characteristic, as knowledge production and diffusion replace physical production in advanced economies. The fourth criterion is entailed in the third, since 'speaking out' would be of little social value were it not from a position of independence of public and private power. But this is an elusive criterion in practice, since the requisite authority and independence would be hard to secure without the legal and administrative framework by which schools are provided and teachers employed, from the 'special relationship' within which teacher and learner mutually engage. Yet it is the second and third characteristics which encapsulate the core of our inherited beliefs regarding professionalism. The professional claims a special relationship and bond with clients, in view of which a public authority and freedom to speak and act independently is conferred.

Empirical confirmation (Hughes *et al*, 1985) that these essential features of professionality are accurately reflected in the working lives and experiences of teachers is amply and convincingly provided in Nias' (1989) study of primary teachers talking about their work. Her accounts and commentary offer a richly elaborated expression and exemplification of the centrality of this relationship and bond with learners, within teachers' sense of their professional role. She concludes:

> For a number of historical, philosophical, psychological, and cultural reasons, teachers in English primary schools are socialised (from their pre-service education onwards) into a tradition of isolation, individualism, self-reliance, and autonomy – in which high value is attached to self-investment and the establishment of a personal relationship with pupils. The teacher as a person is held by many within the profession and outside it to be at the centre of not only the classroom but also the educational process.
>
> (Nias, 1989, p 202)

Teaching and personhood

This suggests that the autonomy traditionally thought to be enjoyed by teachers and claimed by them as a fundamental requirement of the educational process is a necessity, not a privilege, a condition, not merely a desirable enhancement of the educational process itself. Crucial here is the question whether the nature of this process is to be retained in its traditional form, as a moral enterprise entailing the establishment and maintenance of a personal relationship between teacher and learner, whose requirements are prior to the technical needs inherent in the pursuit of prespecified cognitive, physical and aesthetic achievements. Freedom to think, act, question, discover, feel and express in ways which both manifest and contribute to the formation and maintenance of personal identity (a 'self') are the practical attributes of 'autonomy'. Autonomy is necessary for 'selfhood', which is acquired and sustained through freely transacted relationships with others. Without a framework of autonomy, actions within relationships cannot be authentic; their authoring would emanate from elsewhere, from the coercive interpretation and enforcement of relevant rules by others in positions of power. Thus, of 50 teachers in mid-career interviewed by Nias, 'forty-two believed that to adopt the identity of "teacher" was simply to "be yourself" in the classroom' (p 182). Being oneself was exemplified by those interviewed as 'being whole', experiencing a unity and coherence between their experience and actions as individual persons and their lives as teachers. And so, as teachers, they strove to create 'wholeness' in the lives of their pupils and resisted pressures to fragment, separate or subject the activity and experience of pupils to externally imposed criteria and procedures. The indissolubility between teacher and pupil as 'selves', and the nature of the educational process itself, are also revealed in these accounts. Teaching is seen fundamentally as 'establishing relationships with children'. The authenticity of the teacher as a 'self', the inalienable claim of the pupil on the attention of this responsible 'other', the wholeness of the learning experience in a context where teacher and learner 'belong' to the school as a community of free persons, constitute the essential purposes and preconditions for professional practice.

Autonomy and regulation

But there is another side to the practice of relationships. Freedom is necessary but not sufficient. The separate identity of the 'other', though requiring freedom in order to emerge authentically, requires orderliness, similarity, regularity, if it is to emerge and be definable as an identity at all. Manifestations of 'I-ness' which are repeatedly dissimilar are only with great difficulty reconcilable with the concept of identity adopted here. A teacher who acts in ways radically dissimilar, from day to day or lesson to lesson, to an extent that the reason for such differences is fundamentally inaccessible, and often unintelligible, to pupils, will be unable to teach, in the sense that teaching and learning have already been defined as a process mediated through personal relationships. To be able to know someone and act trustingly and effectively with them in a relationship presupposes experience of their identity, in actions of sufficient orderliness that we can attribute meaning to those actions and thereby construct, however tentatively and provisionally, their identity as a person. Regularity (of practice) contributes to identity as crucially as autonomy (of conditions).

What links these two constituents of action in social settings is the dynamic requirements of control within social relations. Without the means and possibility of control, social organisation could not exist. Regularity in social life arises from efforts by 'identities' to secure one particular outcome rather than another in a process not yet complete (Taylor, 1991, pp 105–6). In part it is their emerging identity (sameness over time) which transforms the irregularity of contingent circumstances into the orderliness discernible in events, yielding patterns of meaning from what might otherwise have been meaningless disorder (White, 1992). Patterns which obtain general social approval and enactment in practice may be termed rules. Organisations exist to make these patterns of effective, authentic practice durable and dependably recurrent, through the observance of tacitly or explicitly formulated rules. A question arises whether the position of teachers, given the changes which have taken place in both their conditions of employment and the social context in which they now commonly work, leaves them with the necessary and right kind of authority to imbue their organisation with a learning ethos, as well as with the individual and collective autonomy to sustain a personal learning relationship with pupils. Structural and technical changes in the form and realisation of social life in most countries of the world bring with them profound threats as well as potentially novel opportunities.

The threat of late modernity

The most radical and pervasive of these threats is the challenge to all sources of authority, characteristic of the late modern era. Giddens (1992, p 176) has characterised this period as marked by 'the sequestration of experience and the transformation of intimacy', as individuals pursue the search for significant personal experience in their private rather than their public lives. Within the private sphere universal moral codes no longer provide guidance for behaviour founded upon traditional sources of authority, as the period has witnessed the overthrow of externally derived regimes of truth and value (Smart, 1993; MacIntyre, 1981, p 71). All definitions, even of reality itself, are now contested (Bauman, 1987, p 129). For individuals, however, a code of practice is still sought, to guide behaviour and support individual decisions; but it is increasingly one against which personal actions will be assessed primarily for their contribution to a person's desired emotional life.

This divergence of private and public leaves professionals more exposed than ever between the shifting fluidities of personal *mores* and the remote, depersonalised, functional moralities, implicit in the exercise of central authority. Whilst it is the former which are formative for the individuals in their care, it is the latter which give legitimacy and a resource base from which teachers exercise their social role. A dilemma is exposed even at the point where their authority as experts is relied upon. Increasingly, as we have seen in the first part of this chapter, the authority derived from expertise rests less on personally manifested qualities of individual behaviour (reliability, integrity, sincerity, capability) than on the objective, publicly observable and auditable evidence. Yet integral to the learning process is the capacity to distinguish good from bad, beauty from its surrogates, meaning from nonsense, reality from appearance and truth from falsehood. And the role of the teacher is inseparable from the social task of maintaining these individual human capabilities in prevailing social and political conditions. This presents teachers with a new kind of personal and professional dilemma.

Learning is a morally grounded enterprise, hence the condition of personal and professional autonomy as necessary for learning to take place. The professional, in such an enterprise, enjoys a *locus standi* derived from commitment to serve the interests of the other. And this is the justification for the teacher to be freed from some of the normal social constraints in matters directly affecting the interests of the individual learner, to whom the 'duty of care' is owed. Many social developments of the late twentieth century bring with them new ethical challenges not always revealed clearly in the writings of the better-known protagonists of postmodernism. Bauman (1993) presents his critique with unusual intensity, clarity and humanity: in conditions of late modernity, morality and rationality may be irreconcilable.

> From the perspective of the 'rational order', morality is and is bound to remain irrational. For every social totality bent on uniformity and the soliciting of the disciplined, co-ordinated action, the stubborn and resilient autonomy of the moral self is a scandal. From the control desk of society, it is viewed as the germ of chaos and anarchy inside order; as the outer limit of what reason (or its self-appointed spokesmen and agents) can do to design and implement whatever has been proclaimed as the 'perfect' arrangement of human cohabitation. (Bauman, 1993, p 13)

This stark formulation reveals the bare roots of a dilemma between reason and goodness which should be definitive for the teaching profession.

Prospects

Resolution of the inherent conflict is impossible. Teachers must ground their role and responsibilities in the needs of the moral 'self', lest both they and their pupils become the compliant, functional objects of external control. The apparent coherence of the dominant ideology conceals both the existence and the social implications of the dilemma. Rarely confronted within the narrow limits of contemporary public and political discussion of the future of education in Great Britain, such questions arise from a secular shift in social thought and practice which is more widely acknowledged and discussed in theoretical terms; of a conflict between individuals and organisations, variety and uniformity, pluralism and common entitlements. Hargreaves (1994) has revealed the contrived nature of the collegiality required to realise new organisational practices in education, designed to increase the readiness of teachers to implement curriculum reform in ways desired and specified by central authorities. Morris (1990) has shown, in the case of school-centred innovation strategies attempted in Hong Kong, that they develop 'a mechanism which stresses hierarchy, control, conformity and accountability' (p 36). Busher and Saran (1994), in their examination of 'models of school leadership', point to the conflict between the authority derived from expertise in a discipline (professional) and the 'task' authority derived from organisational position (functional). This is similar to the conflict noticed earlier in the case of medical and paramedical professionals within a managerialised health service. Social workers and other caring professions are also similarly affected (Davies, 1995). But how useful is this dichotomy, even though its force and effect in teachers' perceptions and attitudes is real and verified? Is it a conflict[3] (Webb, 1994, p 74) to be acknowledged and worked with, or resolved by redefining the nature and implications of professionalism?

Redefinition must escape the self-interested limitations inherent in inherited conceptions of professional autonomy. It should not be seen as a zero-sum entity, enjoyed in a privileged domain, in which power is exercised to effect freely chosen outcomes (Barber, 1992). Teachers will enjoy the kind of autonomy which benefits learners if they are able and committed to act supportively upon the conditions and processes of individual learning. Such support, and the role within which learning provision is institutionalised, should respect and be receptive to the independently formed interests of the learner. Whilst decisions concerning what is taught, to whom and at what social cost are properly made within a collective, representative framework, teachers need to retain control of how such agreed social learning objectives may be achieved so that the integrity, freedom and potentiality of the individual learner can be protected, sustained and realised. Teacher autonomy is, foundationally and properly defined, for the benefit of learners and the moral condition of social life in future generations.

Notes

1. The ugly local face of consumerism in action is vividly conveyed in the account of one primary headteacher in the sample interviewed by Webb (1994, p36):

   There's a lot more aggression now amongst parents – I mean it's symptomatic of the way society is now in general. People are far more well-informed of their rights … and they think it gives them *carte blanche* to come in and be rude and obnoxious and to try and make me organise the school around their own child.

2. It is retained within the DfE specifications for teacher education courses as a required 'competence' with a robustly instrumental orientation. Teachers in preparation must understand the conditions of learning, and learning failure, as causative. They are to 'exploit, in all their teaching, opportunities to develop pupils' and to 'devise goals and tasks and monitor and assess them' (DfE, 1993, sections 2.2.3 and 2.5). In other words they are to be part of a system in which the teacher is to fulfil a crucial manipulative function and must be efficient. There is little room here either for teacher and pupil autonomy or for a mediating relationship.

3. Evidence that this conflict lies at the heart of the cultural and organisational changes now taking place in primary schools may be examined in Webb (1994, p 76):

   In all the schools in the sample [50], teachers reported varying degrees of increased co-operation with colleagues and described the contexts and ways in which they were working together. A number of factors can be seen to be combining to break down the private individualist culture of primary schools and replace it with one characterised by openness, trust and co-operation… However, equally strong, if not stronger, forces appeared to be combining to promote directive management styles by headteachers, which undermine the feasibility of teachers working together collegially to formulate policies and promote continuity of practice.

References

Arnot, M and Barton, L (eds) (1992) *Voicing Concerns: Sociological Perspectives on Contemporary Educational Reforms*, Triangle Books, Wallingford.

Barber, M (1992) *Education and the Teacher Unions*, Cassell, London.

Bauman, Z (1987) *Legislators and Interpreters: On Modernity, Post-modernity and Intellectuals*, Polity Press, Cambridge.

Bauman, Z (1993) *Postmodern Ethics*, Blackwell, Oxford.

Boulding, K E (1973) *The Economy of Love and Fear*, Wadsworth, Belmont, California.

Busher, H and Saran, R (1994) 'Towards a model of school leadership', *Educational Management and Administration* 22, 1, pp 5–13.

Davies, C (1995) *Gender and the Professional Predicament in Nursing*, Open University Press, Buckingham.

Department of Education and Science (DES) (1983) *Teaching Quality, Cmnd 8836*, HMSO, London.

DES (1987) *Teachers' Pay and Conditions Document*, HMSO, London.

Department for Education (DfE) (1992) *Circular 9/92*: Initial Teacher Training (secondary phase), HMSO, London.

DfE (1993) *Circular 14/93*: The Initial Training of Primary School Teachers: New Criteria for Courses, HMSO, London.

Downie, R S (1990) 'Professions and professionalism, *Journal of Philosophy of Education* 24, 2, pp 147–59.

Eagleton, T (1991) *Ideology: An Introduction*, Verso, London.

Education (No. 2) Act (1986) HMSO, London.

Education Reform Act (1988) HMSO, London.

Education Act (1992) HMSO, London.

Education Act (1993) HMSO, London.

Eraut, M (1993), 'The characterisation and development of professional expertise in school management and in teaching', *Educational Management and Administration* 21, 4, pp 223–32.

Feinberg, W (1991) 'The public responsibility of public education', *Journal of Philosophy of Education* 25, 1, pp 17–25.

Fischbach, G D (1992) 'Mind and brain', *Scientific American* 267, 3 pp 24–33.

Gellner, E (1983) *Nations and Nationalism*, Macmillan, London.

Giddens, A (1992), *The Transformation of Intimacy: Sexuality, Love and Eroticism in Modern Societies*, Polity Press, Cambridge.

Graham, D and Tytler, D (1993) *A Lesson For Us All: The Making of the National Curriculum*, Routledge, London.

Hargreaves, A (1994) *Changing Teachers, Changing Times: Teachers' Work and Culture in the Postmodern Age*, Cassell, London.

Hughes, M, Ribbins, P and Thomas, H (1985) *Managing Education: The System and the Institution*, Holt, Rinehart & Winston, London.

The *Independent* (1994a), 11 November 1994, p 1.

The *Independent* (1994b), 14 November 1994, pp 1, 2.

The *Independent* (1995a) 'English teachers try to maintain test ban', 3 January, 1995, p 7.

The *Independent* (1995b), 27 January 1995, p 4.

Jonathan, R (1990) 'State education service or prisoner's dilemma: the hidden hand as a source of education policy', *British Journal of Educational Studies* 38, 1, pp 16–24.

Leadbetter, C and Mulgan, G (1994) 'Lean democracy and the leadership vacuum', *DEMOS*, 3, pp 14–25.

MacIntyre, A (1981) *After Virtue: A Study in Moral Theory*, Duckworth, London.

Morris, P (1990) 'Bureaucracy, professionalization and school centred innovation strategies', *International Review of Education* 36, 1, pp 21–41.

Nias, J (1989) *Primary Teachers Talking*, Routledge, London.

Ranson, S (1994) *Towards the Learning Society*, Cassell, London.

Smart, B (1993) *Postmodernity*, Routledge, London.

Strain, M (1993) 'Education reform and defamiliarization: the struggle for power and values in the control of schooling: towards a postmodernist critique', *Educational Management and Administration* 21, 3, pp 188–206.

Strain, M (1995) 'Autonomy, schools and the constitutive role of community: towards a new moral and political order, *British Journal of Education Studies* 43, 1, pp 4–20.

Taylor, C (1991) *The Ethics of Authenticity*, Harvard University Press, Cambridge, Mass.

Thompson, G (1993) 'Network co-ordination' in Maidment, R and Thompson, G (eds) *Managing the United Kingdom*, Sage, London, pp 51–74.

Times Educational Supplement (*TES*), (1995a), 'Shephard's letter leaked in full', 20 January 1995, p 2.

TES (1995b), 10 February 1995, p 3.

TES (1995c), 17 February, 1995, pp 5–6.

Tomlinson, J (1993) *The Control of Education*, Cassell, London.

Webb, R (1994) *After the Deluge: Changing Roles and Responsibilities in the Primary School*, ATL Publications, London.

White, H (1992) *Identity and Control*, Princeton University Press, Princeton.

Chapter 4

Changing Conceptions of a Profession
Eric Hoyle

Introduction

There has been virtually a century of debate about the idea of a profession. It is a debate which is so well known that it need not be rehearsed yet again here. Suffice it to say that the main protagonists have been those who believe that there is a distinctiveness about a profession which is centred on knowledge, judgement, ethics and self-government, and those who believe that *profession* is an ideological term deployed to enhance power, status, remuneration and freedom from accountability. This largely academic debate perhaps reached its peak in the 1960s and 1970s which happened to correspond to the apotheosis of the professions themselves (for summaries of this debate see Hoyle, 1980; Downey, 1990; Avis, 1994).

In *The Rise of Professional Society*, Perkin (1989) charted the growth of the professions from the nineteenth century. It was a growth which accelerated considerably with the concomitant extension of the welfare state in the period following the Second World War and the great professionalisation of personal services – the 'personal service society' as Halmos (1970) termed it. There were reservations about some of the characteristics of this professionalisation even amongst staunch supporters of the welfare state. Ultimately it was not this 'internal' critique of the professions but the New Right policies of successive Conservative governments which led to what Perkin (1989) termed, in the title of his final chapter: 'The decline of professional society'.

The New Right policies which have had such an impact have not, of course, been specifically and explicitly articulated in the terms of the earlier debate about the professions. Their implications for the professions have been the by-product of their focus on the market, the consumer, deregulation and freedom of choice, and the more recessive but still important focus on the politicisation of accountability through direct or indirect centralisation. In terms of the earlier debate, the effect of these policies could be termed *deprofessionalisation*. Nevertheless if the language of the debate about the professions were to be used by those responsible for these policies it might be argued that their effect was not so much deprofessionalisation but to make those occupations commonly termed professions more truly professional in relation to the needs of their clients.

An emerging concept of a profession is perhaps conveyed by a particular connotation which is now given to *professional* as noun or adjective. To be 'professional' is to have acquired a set of skills through competency-based training which enables one to deliver efficiently according to contract a customer-led service in compliance with accountability procedures collaboratively implemented and managerially assured.

This condensed, and intentionally overstated, summary conveys a number of changes in terms of practice, training, control, etc which can be explored in terms of shifts along a series of dimensions which can be presented in summary form as follows:

From	To
Profession	Professional
Knowledge	Skill
Education	Training
Effectiveness	Efficiency
Conception	Delivery
Status	Contract
Clients	Consumers
Influence	Compliance
Responsibility	Accountability
Leadership	Management

Figure 4.1 *Trends in the teaching profession*

These dimensions are discussed below and are necessarily treated in an over-simplistic form. This summary will be followed by a discussion of some of the implications of this for the future of teaching as a profession.

Emerging concepts

From profession to professional

The idea of a profession encompassed a number of real or alleged virtues. A professional was a member of a profession. Members were professional in so far as their practice incorporated these virtues. However, over time, and increasingly so in both common usage and in political discourse, *professional* both as a noun or an adjective has become somewhat uncoupled semantically from *profession*. In common usage the variations in the connotation of professional have become very wide and in some instances, eg ruthlessness, are wholly inimical to the original connotation. In political discourse professional has come to connote skill, efficiency, reliability, compliance and a no-nonsense anti-intellectualism.

Some of these elements are quite congruent with the idea of a profession. For example, all professionals are presumed to have a high degree of skill. But it is the emphasis which signals a change. Skill is given priority over knowledge, compliance over judgement, etc. In fact, most of the shifts discussed below in some way characterise a shift from profession to professional. To be a professional is to be an efficient deliverer of a predetermined product (Ribbins, 1990).

From knowlege to skill

Although professional practice is essentially concerned with the exercise of a particular skill it has been traditionally argued that although professional practice is in large part routine there are also those elements of uncertainty wherein the practitioner must rely on experience coupled with recourse to a body of valid knowledge. The knowledge base of teaching has, of course, long been questioned – often by teachers themselves as well as by external critics. Whilst critics concede that teachers must have a necessary level of content knowledge if they are to be effective, they have doubts about what theoretical knowledge they need.

Whilst there are different kinds of theoretical knowledge entailed in teaching, these are usually undifferentiated by critics but just as likely to engender their scorn were they to be differentiated. Pedagogical theory, the theory of teaching and learning, is usually dubbed 'airy fairy' or 'trendy'. Teaching is seen as an atheoretical craft. Curriculum content is seen as relatively unproblematic and, since its determination is the function of government through its nominees, curriculum theory as such is regarded as unimportant for teachers.

Education theory, using the term in this context to refer to such issues as the nature of the educational enterprise, its functions in relation to individuals, families, communities and society, is again not seen as being of any concern of the teacher except, perhaps, as a vehicle for what 'society' expects of them.

Thus theoretical knowledge is seen largely as having the instrumental function of ensuring the efficient delivery of a predetermined curriculum. Hence the growing emphasis on skill and the discrete competences which are held to characterise it.

From education to training

It is often rightly argued that the dichotomy between education and training is false. However, the broad distinction can be usefully deployed in this context to indicate the trend in policy which gives priority in the preparation of teachers to skill acquisition over understanding. This is in line with the shift from knowledge to practice with its underlying doubts about the relevance of theory to practice. It is argued that one does not need a knowledge of the theory of the internal combustion engine in order to drive a car.

As the preparation of teachers moved from the school to the training college in the nineteenth century, the relationship between education and training became problematic. The education of entrants entailed increasing their knowledge of the subjects which they were to teach. However, this subject component came to constitute a higher education for training college students who were often there only because, for various reasons, they were unable to enter universities. Thus there was a constant tension between subject-for-teaching and subject-for-personal-education, which was not a problem for those entering teaching as university graduates.

The education components of the course expanded beyond a concern with the skills of teaching to a fuller understanding of the education process. This became more pronounced as the minimum length of the course expanded from two to four years in the decade of the 1960s and the final award became a degree. There was a change in nomenclature from 'training college' to 'college of education' which symbolised that this institution was now providing a professional education.

The reaffirmation of training over education is seen particularly in the policies which have moved the preparation of teachers towards a school-based pattern. The shifts which have occurred have not yet, in fact, gone as far as members of the present government (and particularly their advisers) would have wished. The link with higher education, and hence the possibility of student teachers experiencing a professional education as well as skill training,

62

has remained. However, the creation of the Teacher Training Agency which has replaced the Council for the Accreditation of Teacher Education is symbolic: the full significance of the return to the use of 'training' rather than 'education' on the education–training relationship has yet to emerge.

The trend from education to training is not confined to teaching. In some other occupations it is now possible for individuals to achieve a professional level by two routes. One is through the conventional process of higher education and professional training. The other is via the competency-based, skill-training route provided by National Vocational Qualifications, the highest level of which, level 5, is considered to be significantly above first degree level (Smith, 1995).

From effectiveness to efficiency

These old stagers are as relevant now as perhaps they have ever been in their history. The relationship between them is complex and a full elaboration is not possible here. Essentially, effectiveness entails achieving an end and efficiency minimising the misuse of resources. Effectiveness might not be too difficult to achieve if resources are unlimited, but because they *are* limited, efficiency must always be a factor in the equation. The problem is one of balancing the two principles, of cost effectiveness.

A single example will suffice. A teacher has to decide what percentage of a class of 20 to enter for a particular examination. Some will almost certainly pass, some will almost certainly fail; the chances of passing of those in the middle is uncertain. If the best 10 only are entered and all 10 pass, this constitutes 100 per cent efficiency. If all 20 are entered and only 15 pass, this constitutes only 75 per cent efficiency. But 5 more students have passed than otherwise would have been the case and therefore a 50 per cent increase in effectiveness will have been achieved.

The shift has been from effectiveness to efficiency in the work of all professions. Increasingly, efficiency is being assessed in terms of performance indicators which are concerned with short- rather than long-term outcomes. Short-term efficiency may lead to long-term ineffectiveness and even long-term inefficiency. If the escape rate is an efficiency indicator for a prison it may be in the interests of the prison management to keep inmates in their cells 23 hours a day in order to reduce escapes and thereby increase efficiency. But if such a regime reduces prisoner education and leads to a high degree of recidivism it is neither efficient nor effective in the long term.

The professions are concerned with effectiveness. The quest for effectiveness gobbles up resources and a shift towards efficiency may well be necessary in a time of growing expectations. The problem is to achieve efficiency without undermining effectiveness. One difficulty for professionals is that the demonstration of efficiency gains in the context of quality assurance and accountability is time consuming and may lead to decreased effectiveness if it reduces the time available for their core task – of teaching, for example. Much has been written about the intensification of the teacher's work in terms of deprofessionalisation – or, as some writers have it, proletarianisation – of the teacher's work (Densmore, 1987). Whilst some of this is directly about teaching, much also covers non-teaching activities concerned with demonstrating efficiency.

From conception to delivery

Despite the somewhat misleading reproductive connotation of this subtitle it is retained because it is widely used in the literature, particularly by those writers who represent teaching and other middle-class occupations as being proletarianised (Ozga and Lawn, 1981). Whether or not this is a useful way of conceptualising changes in the class structure of advanced societies, some of the separate elements in the alleged process are nevertheless worthy of consideration since they are important and are not only a feature of alleged proletarianisation. From conception to delivery is one such process.

Basically it refers to the fact that the span of responsibility in many middle-class occupations has been reduced and subdivided in such a way that whereas the professional identified a problem, conceived a solution and undertook the implementation there is now a division of labour whereby those who implement solutions have not necessarily conceived them.

In education this entails a disjunction, putting it over-simply, between devising and implementing a curriculum and merely teaching it. In Britain it is the National Curriculum and particularly its associated testing which has troubled teachers to the point of a refusal nationally to conduct tests in 1993. The reasons for this surprising mobilisation are complex but it would perhaps be reasonable to infer that one aspect of this refusal was teachers' rejection of their limited role in relation to the delivery of the curriculum and their assessment of it.

From status to contract

These famous terms will be deployed here in a somewhat more limited way than was intended by the jurist Maine (1985), who used them to describe a fundamental shift in social relations. In this context they are used to indicate that whereas the status of certain occupations as professions was regarded as a guarantee that they could be trusted to do their best by their clients this trust has been withdrawn and contracts are increasingly used as an alternative.

It is again not difficult to see why the excesses of some professionals in putting their own interests ahead of those of their clients and 'working the system', ie the welfare state, should have led to a loss of trust and more towards detailed job specifications and contractual obligation. However, such excesses were more prevalent in medicine and law than in education. Moreover, in education contractualisation has been a greater characteristic of further education than the schools' sector.

There are perhaps certain ironies in the attempt to have teachers work to contract. It has long been recognised that the teacher's work is never done. Moreover, the nature of teaching is such that perhaps the most effective aspects of it are just those which cannot be delivered to contract. The requirement that teachers should be engaged in variously defined ways for 1265 hours per year led to a reduction in the amount of time which teachers spent in non-teaching activities, to which some people – probably fancifully alas – attribute the decline in the country's sporting prowess. A further irony is that, notwithstanding the move towards contract, teachers are increasingly being expected to involve themselves in endless out-of-hours meetings without recompense or time off in lieu.

From clients to consumers

Professionals have clients. The expectation inherent in the idea of a profession is that they will do their best by their clients in terms of their judgement about their needs. The market, of course, puts the customer in the saddle and increasingly those needs are defined by the customers supported by a raft of 'charters'. The radical left critique of the professions held that they tended to treat their clients as objects to which things had to be done largely without their involvement; perhaps this had some weight and there was a case for giving the client a greater involvement and certainly a wider choice.

The idea of customer choice and customer redress is central to the operation of the commercial market. It also has a greater place in the operation of markets for professional services and the breaking down of monolithic provision and the increase of redress have undoubtedly had a positive impact on client attitudes towards professional practice. But there are limits to this process. To make consumers the sole arbiters of what and how the professions should function would be to undermine the expertise which is central to the idea of a profession. The problem in relation to education is compounded by the fact that there are different sets of clients whose expectations are different and perhaps in competition.

From influence to compliance

Most commentators on the relationship between teachers and the state argue that the consensus which prevailed from the 1940s to the mid-1970s has been broken and that state control has now become more visible and explicit (eg Grace, 1987). Implicit in the idea of a profession is its relative independence from the state. An independent profession acts as a flywheel in a democratic society protecting immediate clients from the swings and roundabouts of the competing ideologies of successive governments. The established professions such as medicine and law have historically managed to sustain independent bodies of self-governing professionals which have had a considerable influence on shaping relevant government policy on the basis of collective expertise. These leading professionals have also had separate bodies such as the British Medical Association which have performed trade union type activities.

The teaching profession has never been able to establish an independent professional body. Scotland has a General Teaching Council but efforts to establish a counterpart for England and Wales have not yet succeeded in achieving government recognition. Nevertheless, when the professions were at the height of their powers in the 1960s the teaching profession exerted considerable influence on government policy and became part of what Manzer (1970) called 'the sub-government of education'. This influence was turned into compliance under successive Conservative governments.

The fact that the teaching profession was represented by trade unions led in part to their displacement from a position of influence given Conservatism's strongly anti-union stance. But more generally successive governments treated all professional advice as being self- rather than client-interested and dismissed the protestations of what was presented as a unitary establishment of educationists resistant to change, and left-wing dominated to boot. On matters of educational policy ministers took the advice of a number of policy units and quangos, which they themselves had created and whose membership they had nominated.

Thus the teaching profession has become largely reduced to compliance with government policies. The great exception was the previously mentioned teachers' refusal to carry out tests in the summer of 1993, led by an alliance of all teacher unions. Ironically, although the tests were opposed on professional grounds, the action was granted legitimacy by the courts on the grounds of the excessive workload which testing caused – a traditional union 'conditions of work' issue.

From responsibility to accountability

The 'accountability movement' is generally held to have begun with James Callaghan's Ruskin College speech of 1976. Its emergence was a recognition that the teaching profession as a whole and its individual members had become too autonomous. The accountability that existed in education – essentially peer accountability if one took education as a whole, including teacher education, advisory services, HMI, etc – was not functioning effectively in the interests of any group of clients. From this point, and increasingly after the election of a Conservative government in 1979, the accountability movement gained such strength that it dominated the massive amount of educational legislation which was enacted over the ensuing 20 years.

Relatively few observers would deny the bracing effect on education of this movement which brought into powerful combination political, legal and market forms of accountability at the expense of professional forms. However, despite the undoubted advantages of increased accountability (see Eraut, 1992, for a valuable discussion), the movement has had a downside which includes the problem of hyper-accountability, whereby a disproportionate amount of professional time was spent on accountability measures at the expense of the core function of teaching. But perhaps a more fundamental shift has occurred from responsibility to accountability.

A distinction between these two concepts was made in the following terms by Hoyle and John (1995):

> For the purpose of the argument, *responsibility* is given a different conno-tation from *accountability*. It is conceptualized as being a broader principle. To accept the need for, and to respond to, the processes of accountability is to be responsible. In general terms, accountability entails meeting the requirements of a set of procedures designed to assure the various clients of a profession that the accounting units (eg individual teachers, depart-ments, schools, etc) are meeting appropriate standards of practice. Respon-sibility entails a more voluntaristic commitment to a set of principles governing good practice, and the realization of these through day-to-day professional activities. These principles include *inter alia* the recognition of and compliance with the requirements of accountability, but responsi-bility reaches the parts which accountability cannot always reach since they are more fundamental. And, because they are more fundamental, at times they could be in conflict with governmental requirements of accountability.

The danger of undermining responsibility is that it can encourage a cynical and ritualistic response to accountability procedures. The message has often been conveyed over the past 25 years that teachers are professionally untrustworthy, which is a reason for installing tight accountability procedures. One doesn't really need recourse to labelling theory to indicate the unfortunate consequences of this view.

From leadership to management

'School management' (both the process and the term itself) is relatively new in British education. Before the emergence of the term 'management' in this context in the late 1960s the term 'administration' – imported from the USA – was used by those who wrote about the topic in academic terms, otherwise 'leadership' was used to describe the activities of the head. The reasons for the emergence of concern with management are complex, although the creation of large comprehensive schools was undoubtedly a factor, as was the growing range of social and welfare tasks ascribed to schools.

The conceptualisation of educational problems as management problems arose from growing demands for accountability, not least market accountability, from the late 1970s. This was not a belief which applied to education alone. It is seen, perhaps *a fortiori*, in the National Health Service. Given the huge allocations of resources to education and health it must be right that these are used efficiently – as well as effectively – and this is a quintessential management function. The problem is not that of management but of managerialism – a culture of which the central belief is the general organisability of institutions and the priority of financial outcomes.

Because of the strong professional leadership tradition in Britain – professional leadership here meaning educational leadership – the excesses of managerialism are not yet widespread. Moreover, as far as one can tell, management development continues to focus on the key function of educational leadership – the promotion of effective teaching and learning in cognitive, aesthetic, social and moral domains – with, rightly, specific skill training in management techniques included as appropriate. However, the dangers of what one might call 'professional managerialism' are ever present and there is a need to reaffirm the importance of educational leadership.

Commentary and conclusion

This chapter has sought to identify some of the changes which have been affecting all the professions but the teaching profession in particular, deploying for the purpose ten dimensions. One must now pose the question of whether or not these changes can, when taken together, constitute a fundamental reconceptualisation of a profession and whether any such reconceptualisation has greater advantages than disadvantages for clients.

The rise of professional society reached its apogee in the 1960s in terms of the influence of the professions on social life generally. There is little doubt that this influence has declined. However, there is no sign of any decline in the number of occupations which are becoming 'professions' according to such external criteria as qualifications, professional bodies, codes of conduct, etc. This is a function of an increase in the personal service occupations. It might be noted that, ironically, there has been an increase in the number of people employed in the consultancy professions whose duties include the assurance of quality and general accountability of the other professions.

From the 1970s one began to see the emergence of the accountability movement. In education this was marked by the Ruskin College speech and the great debate in education. We do not know how the professions would have changed under a continuing Labour administration. We do know that successive Conservative governments have sought to control the influence of the professions, render them more financially accountable and deliver services according to the wishes of consumers or, where these are difficult to determine by market forces, the views and values of a central government claiming to act as a proxy for them. Thus, at the heart of the new concept of a profession is the notion of efficient and skilful delivery.

There can be little doubt that these changes have had beneficial consequences for consumers of professional services in that professionals have been deprived of a number of devices which they had earlier been able to deploy to protect themselves against charges of incompetency, inefficiency, treating clients with disdain and detachment and so forth. There have also been efficiency benefits to the economy.

Whether these gains outweigh the losses will depend upon one's view of the culture of the professions before the 1980s. There is little doubt that the idea of a profession was idealistic. The professions have always been characterised by a degree of self-interest which has belied their alleged commitment to clients. There is little doubt that in the strictures of the political left the idea that a profession is little more than an ideology supporting self-interest carries some weight. The question is one of degree.

On the issue of whether the changes noted in this chapter are likely to have a beneficial effect or otherwise the jury is still out. The changes have perhaps not yet brought about a fundamental shift in the culture of the professions and there is perhaps still time to reaffirm some of the older notions of the professions as indicated by the 'left-hand' list of components in Figure 4.1. Perhaps the key players in this process are headteachers who can resist the managerialisation of their own roles in favour of educational leadership. They can encourage a professionality amongst their colleagues which values autonomy along with collaboration, knowledge and reflection as well as skill, a genuine commitment beyond the confines of a contract and the thrust of managerial sanctions, and a responsibility which is deeper than a superficial compliance with accountability procedures. In short, despite the many lapses from the ideal there was much of value in the idea of a profession which is worthy of protection.

References

Avis, J (1994) 'Teacher professionalism: one more time', *Educational Review*, 46, 1, pp 63–72.

Densmore, K (1987) 'Professionalism, proletarianization and teachers' work' in Popkewitz, T. (ed) *Critical Studies in Teacher Education*, Falmer Press, Lewes.

Downey, R S (1990) 'Professions and professionalism', *Journal of Philosophy of Education* 25, 2, pp 147–159.

Eraut, M (1992) *Developing the Professions: Training, Quality and Accountability*, University of Sussex Press, Brighton.

Grace, G (1987) 'Teachers and the state in Britain: a changing relation' in Lawn, M and Grace, G (eds) *Teachers: The Culture and Politics of Work*, Falmer Press, London.

Halmos, P (1970) *The Personal Service Society*, Constable, London.

Hoyle, E (1980) 'Professionalization and deprofessionalization in education' in Hoyle, E and Megarry, J (Eds), *World Yearbook of Education 1980: The Professional Development of Teachers*, Kogan Page, London.

Hoyle, E and John, P (1995) *Professional Knowledge and Professional Practice*, Cassell, London.

Maine, H S (1985) *Ancient Law*, Holt Rinehart & Winston, London.

Manzer, R A (1970) *Teachers and Politics*, Manchester University Press.

Ozga, J and Lawn, M (1981) *Teachers, Professionalism and Class*, Falmer Press, Lewes.

Perkin, H (1989) *The Rise of Professional Society*, Routledge, London.

Ribbins, P (1990) 'Teachers as professionals: towards a re-definition' in Morris, R (ed) *Central and Local Control of Education after the ERA 1988*, Longman, Harlow.

Smith, P (1995) 'NVQ peril for the professions', *Times Higher Educational Supplement* 24 February 1995, p 12.

Chapter 5

Teacher Union Perspectives on the Management of Professionals
John Beresford

Introduction: two models of management

The inspiration for this book is the contention that teachers, in response to government legislation since the 1980s, have had to broaden the focus of their activities: 'Well-understood pedagogical responsibilities have been widened to include administrative and, in some cases, managerial duties' (Busher and Saran, 1990). They have had to become, using Hoyle's term, 'extended professionals' (Hoyle, 1975).

Government legislation over the past 15 years relating to the management of schools has tried to marry two models, a rational-economic model and a human relations model. Much of recent teacher union activity has been addressed to restraining the domination of the first model over the second.

My contribution to this volume is to look at how the six teacher unions have responded to these changes. My main sources have been the unions' own organs of communication with their membership as well as those publications that bring the six unions' views together, for example the reports of the School Teachers' Review Body (STRB). Using these sources, union views will be explored on the issues of professionalism, collegiality versus hierarchy, control versus imposition and the National Curriculum.

This chapter argues that two models of management operate within the English education system. This duality profoundly influences union attitudes and pronouncements. We need to return to the high inflation economy of the 1970s in order to trace the impetus which generated the amalgamation of these two models. This high inflation occasioned a fundamental review of policy and management structures in British industry, one major outcome of which was a move away from roll-forward to cash-limited budgets. Where businesses had been content with a planning process which merely added an inflation element to the previous year's budget, costings were now made prior to, rather than after, transactions (Sizer, 1989). Cash-limited budgets were not only controlled but scrutinised in order to promote cost effectiveness. It was clear to industrial giants like Philips that such control and scrutiny could best be exercised at the managerial level where costs were incurred, that is at the local plant level (Beresford, 1993).

High inflation generated a similar review in the public spending sector. The fundamental review of education policies and structures undertaken after Callaghan's Ruskin College speech of 1976 was just such a response. It coincided, fatally or fortuitously according to your political standpoint, with similar calls (largely on philosophical grounds) from the right wing of the Conservative Party (Cox and Dyson, 1969a; Cox and Dyson, 1969b; Cox and Dyson, 1970; Cox and Rhodes Boyson, 1975). The Taylor report on school management (1977) suggested a similar response to funding problems in education to the response being employed in industry:

> We consider that a more effective use of resources would be secured by locating decisions with the users in the schools and that this in turn would foster a sense of responsibility in heads and senior staff and help ensure that all the various interests involved in the running of the school were engaged in a constant examination of the school's needs and ways of meeting them effectively and economically. (Taylor 1977, p 67)

Government departments themselves were being encouraged to develop along these lines (Treasury and Civil Service Committee, 1982).

A number of tentative local pilot schemes in site-based management of schools mushroomed in Cambridgeshire and Solihull. Government interest occasioned a review of such schemes and the subsequent report (Coopers and Lybrand, 1988) effectively provided the blueprint for future local management legislation and implementation (Education Reform Act, 1988).

The structure set in place after the 1988 Act changed the locus of policy making in education. Formerly councillors and education officers at town or shire halls controlled the allocation of budgets and therewith a major share of the formulation and implementation of educational policy. Under local management (LMS) head office (town/shire hall) helped its business units (schools) to draw up their operational strategies (school development plans). An arm of central management (the inspectorate) audited the quality of the schools' strategic thinking. Schools were allocated micro-budgets from the local authority's macro-budget (Year Nought of the education committee's medium-term plan) and the micro-budget was managed by local budget holders (heads and governing bodies) with accountancy back up (LMS support team members).

This juxtaposition of management accountancy and school management terms highlights the industrial origins of LMS. The freedom for schools has, however, been further modified by other legislation which has created a set of parameters and accountabilities to regulate these new powers under LMS. These restraints, not the least of which is to deliver a curriculum which has been imposed on schools, are responsible for the uneasy alliance of two models of management: one formerly referred to as scientific, but now more commonly known as rational–economic, and the other a human relations model. This amalgam characterises school management today and is responsible for a number of tensions currently being addressed by the teacher unions.

Models of scientific management presented the work process as a set of discrete and prescribed activities undertaken by individuals who had been rigorously trained in the process. They were models characterised by the close supervision of process workers, the regular checking of the quality of work produced and a tight control and measurement of the inputs into the process. Levels of pay in these models reflected levels of production and were seen as the main motivating force for process workers.

Writers on educational management and headteachers had little interest in these scientific/rational–economic models before LMS was implemented. The idea of prescription in education ran counter to the perceived professional autonomy of the teacher. There were no agreed sets of discrete activities to follow and no tradition of close supervision of teacher activities. The budgetary information necessary for tight financial monitoring was not present at school level. In short, a rational–economic model was alien to most educationalists' perception of what happened in most schools.

Educationalists were more attracted by the human relations models which emerged as critiques of the rational–economic approach to management. These models recognised that workers did not work in isolation, but that they interrelated with fellow workers, supervisory staff, management and the technology with which they worked. The models acknowledged the workplace as part of a larger community, as a social system which interacted with groups and other systems outside, for example in the market-place or in the political arena. There was also a recognition that workers, supervisors and management held allegiances to groups and systems outside the workplace (Drucker, 1988;

Vroom and Deci, 1989). These descriptions of the work process as involving individual and group interaction and the emphases on motivation, leadership style and implementing change by consent matched more closely what was felt to be taking place in schools (Peters, 1976; Archer, 1981; Whitaker, 1983; Day *et al*, 1985).

School management today contains features of both models. The rational–economic model demands quantifiable inputs (age-weighted pupil units), quantifiable outputs (examination results) and other performance indicators (levels of truancy). There is regular scrutiny of school operations (central budgetary control, Office for Standards in Education (OFSTED) inspections, annual parents' meetings with governors and parental consultation). All of these controls are embodied in legislation of the past 15 years. Also embodied in the legislation is the recognition that, through their accountabilities, school management must address the interests of other groups. Heads are accountable to governors, governors to local authorities (or the Department for Education (DfE) in the case of grant-maintained schools), teachers to parents. Headteachers are contractually obliged to consult with interested bodies over the running of their schools (DfE, 1994, para 31).

The tension implicit between these two contrasting models of management is best illustrated in the discussion paper on primary school organisation by the 'three wise men' (Alexander *et al*, 1992). In the paper a rational–economic model is proposed, where primary schools are called upon to assess what is necessary in resource terms to operate effectively, and then match that assessment to the resources available. The paper proposes different modes of delivering the National Curriculum and challenges the traditional method of using one teacher attached to a single class. One of the three, as chief inspector, further rehearsed the theme in his annual report (OFSTED, 1995). An alternative human relations model would see a school adopt historical funding patterns, satisfying some of the goals of different groups within the school community, sometimes at the expense of the organisational goals of the school (Davies, 1989; Strain, 1990). The willingness of various school governing bodies to set an illegal budget (and not make teachers redundant), in response to the government's unwillingness to finance the 1995 teachers' pay award, is just such a response.

Teacher union views of professionalism

The views of the six teacher unions about teacher professionalism clearly favour a human relations model of teacher management and are more noteworthy for their similarities than for their differences. While the unreserved support of the Professional Association of Teachers (PAT) for a General Teaching Council remains contentious, few of the other teacher unions would disagree with its views on the main concerns of teachers and their representatives:

> The fundamental ingredient of professionalism is service to those in receipt of education. Firstly the control of teacher quality. Career development, appraisal, membership of the profession, in-service and post qualification courses should be a professional responsibility... Secondly the profession should be self-governed with appropriate machinery for ensuring accountability. The third element is the determination of salaries and conditions of service.   (PAT, undated)

The NUT would perhaps add a fourth element, laying stress on the physical and economic environment within which this professionalism is asked to operate: 'To meet the children's needs we need well resourced schools. We need school buildings that are properly maintained and are safe and healthy places in which to work' (NUT, 1994).

The Secondary Heads' Association (SHA) and the National Association of Head Teachers (NAHT) restrict their membership to heads and deputies. The NAHT 'recognises the central role of heads and deputies ... in the effective management of schools and colleges ... and ensures that their concerns are clearly and forcefully expressed' (NAHT, undated). The Association of Teachers and Lecturers (ATL; before 1993, the Assistant Masters' and Mistresses' Association or AMMA) excludes heads and deputies from full membership: 'When members seek ATL's help in a dispute involving their heads or principals, we will not be compromised by trying to represent both parties' (ATL, 1994).

Finally the National Association of Schoolmasters/Union of Women Teachers (NAS/UWT) believes that this professionalism is synonymous with, and can only be achieved through, effective trade union practices: 'Education and trade unionism ... are the two chief concerns of NAS/UWT' (NAS/UWT, 1992a). 'Protection of the individual can only be achieved through the collective process of responsible trade unionism' (NAS/UWT, 1992b). This 'responsible trade unionism' involves the likely expulsion of members who do not respond, for example, to executive calls for industrial action, a policy unique amongst the teacher unions.

These subtle distinctions between the teacher unions have their origins often in the distant past and have been explored and explained elsewhere (see, for example, Barber, 1992). From the extracts above the differences are clearly in the nature of each union's membership and in the tactics used to best represent their members' interests. Views on teacher professionalism are less contrasting. This is further borne out by the report jointly produced by the teacher unions, the School Management Task Force, the DfE, the Society of Education Officers and National Association of Education Inspectors, Advisers and Consultants, entitled *Effective Management in Schools* (DfE, 1993). Staff in 57 schools were asked three main questions:

- What is an effectively managed school?
- What do teachers and headteachers think constitutes effective school management?
- What criteria do teachers use when they are assessing the quality of management in their school? (DfE, 1993, p 2)

From these we can derive our own question: what are the school management conditions under which the teacher unions suggest that effective professionals should operate?

The report describes a model which tries to reconcile the rational–economic approach to management favoured in government legislation with the human relations style historically favoured by teachers. So while goals of academic achievement and good pupil behaviour are paramount, cordial as well as professional relationships amongst staff are seen as important elements in the school ethos. The working atmosphere is 'purposeful', but also 'relaxed' (DfE, 1993, p 2). Aims and policies are clearly presented, but are developed collaboratively by all staff rather than being the sole preserve of a hierarchical senior management team.

Headteacher and senior management responsibilities, accountabilities and functions are clearly delineated, but a large part of management effectiveness derives from an ability to support, motivate, consult and lead. Monitoring, co-ordinating and networking structures are in place, but they are adaptable and class teachers share in major decision-making about them. Teachers talk to each other about professional matters and strive to improve on their practice. Good relations with other systems are an integral part of effective professionalism in an effectively managed school: teachers enjoy good relations with parents, the local community and governors. 'There is a sound relationship between school and LEA' (DfE, 1993, p 6). Change is successfully managed through collaborative decision-making.

Tensions: collegiality versus hierarchy

The tensions in this model are not hard to find. They provide the focus for many of the concerns of the teacher unions in recent years. First, the collegiality of much of the management in effective schools runs counter to the hierarchical, incentive-based wage structure operating within teaching at present. It is also at odds with the government's desire to reward effective teachers. Second, school ethos and curricula have had to develop in the face of the external imposition of a National Curriculum and national performance indicators. These have raised teacher concerns about the quality of the National Curriculum as well as the workload involved and whether resources in schools are sufficient to meet these external demands.

The movement towards a salary structure more in keeping with this collegial approach in effectively managed schools has largely been led by the NAS/UWT, ATL, PAT and the NUT. The two other unions have been less enthusiastic. In their submissions to the STRB between 1992 and 1994 SHA, though accepting the need to establish common criteria for all discretionary payments and incentive allowances to teachers, have favoured a long, single and flexible pay spine in order that financial rewards can be allocated in smaller packets and to more staff. NAHT argued in 1992 for 'a differential pay award for heads and deputies ... in order to recognise the immense and ongoing changes in our members' jobs' (NAHT 1992). In 1993 it called for an entry grade, an extended standard scale with local flexibility to use incremental enhancements and discretionary scale points and a management scale that would embrace heads, deputies and those teachers with major managerial responsibilities.

NAS/UWT have consistently advocated an entry grade and a principal teacher grade, along which most teachers would progress, subject to performance review and which, like the NAHT management scale, would include heads and deputies. There would be no incentive allowances or discretionary payments. The NUT has wanted a short scale that recognised experience and responsibility, with no discretionary payments. AMMA's proposal for a higher teacher scale, along which teachers progressed after performance reviews, differs from NAS/UWT's with its retention of incentive allowances for extra responsibilities. PAT has proposed a separate spine for class teachers and managers, with movement from one to the other by application for advance. The present structure with a 17-point spine for classroom teachers and a separate one for heads and deputies represents what NAS/UWT has described as 'a substantial move towards collegiality' (NAS/UWT *Report*, February 1993).

The salary structures proposed in particular by NAS/UWT and ATL also represent a half-way house between collegiality and the out-and-out performance-related pay structure favoured by the government. The work of the STRB since 1992 represents an effort, on its part also, to reconcile the two. In 1992 it had no doubts 'that moves towards properly designed performance-related pay arrangements would be right in principle: providing better rewards for the best teachers and clearly offering worthwhile incentives to motivate all teachers to improve their performance' (STRB, 1992, para 62).

The STRB seemed prepared to accept union concerns about threats to collegiality and tentatively suggested that any scheme should recognise whole-school efforts in adding value to their pupils' education. 'Demonstrable benefits of collegiate action would be rewarded, not undermined' (STRB, 1992, para 70).

It recognised the inadequacy of raw test scores in assessing the performance of individual schools and called for the development of other performance indicators to measure school improvement. It stressed the need for extra funding and for new local funding mechanisms to transfer performance-related pay to schools' budgets (STRB, 1992, paras 69–77).

A joint submission from the teacher unions went along with these suggestions. It stressed the need for clear national criteria for any performance indicators used, for the system to be strictly separate from teacher appraisal, for extra resources to be allocated and for pilot schemes to be set up (STRB, 1993, para 140). In other words the teacher unions seemed in sympathy with STRB's efforts to reconcile the government's rational–economic approach to teachers' pay with a human relations approach to school management.

The DfE, however, would have none of it. Any performance-related pay scheme had to address individual teachers' performances, to reward 'good teachers in poor schools, but not poor teachers in good schools' (STRB, 1993, para 136). There would be no additional funding (para 133). The STRB reiterated its view that 'the present emphasis on rewards for responsibility detracts from the need to encourage excellence in classroom teaching' (para 73).

However its advocacy of a pay system it had tried but failed to reconcile with teacher union views had lost much of its conviction: 'It is evident that such arrangements can form part of an overall culture for driving an organisation towards its goals with the active support of the staff involved' (para 141).

The STRB noted, in its Third Report (STRB, 1994, para 102), the continuing reluctance of schools to reward excellent teachers. It also reported on the very small feasibility and pilot studies that had been undertaken in the past year and were ongoing. More significantly, a subject which had filled 17 paragraphs in its 1992 report and 18 in 1993 merited only eight in 1994. Whilst the notion persists in 1995, a method of funding acceptable to employers, unions and the STRB has still not been found (STRB, 1995, paras 113–17).

Control versus imposition

The imposition of the National Curriculum effectively took away from teachers a large element of control over what they taught. Their feeling of loss was exacerbated by their minimal involvement in its creation. A further bone of contention was that there was little leeway for local flexibility in its implementation. Teacher union criticisms were over two issues: the perceived lack of any attention paid to teachers' views by the government, particularly in the areas of assessment and testing, and the lack of any government appreciation for the differing needs of different schools. So, although the main thrust of the Dearing Report (1993) and the resultant revamped National Curriculum were to reduce the workload for teachers, the two documents were also a response to concerns about the quality of the curriculum offered.

Teacher unions missed few opportunities prior to the Dearing Report to criticise the National Curriculum and its related activities. Hence AMMA and SHA both questioned the House of Commons working party about the appropriateness of various tasks in the Music and Art curricula (AMMA, 1992; SHA, *Headlines*, February 1992). NAHT's complaint about the move away from teacher assessment at GCSE level provoked a response from the DfE, highly distrustful of such dependence: '[There is] a problem of securing reliable and publicly credible results from the marking, conduct and, especially, moderation of coursework' (NAHT *Bulletin*, February 1992).

The Secretary of State for Education, in response to NAHT reservations about the quality of Key Stage One testing, left teachers in no doubt as to his preferred sources of advice. 'I have been guided and still am by my professional advisers [Schools' Examination and Assessment Council (SEAC) supported by National Foundation for Educational Research (NFER)]' (NAHT *Bulletin*, April 1992).

The same headteachers' union was highly critical of the new Orders in English produced in 1993: 'It is difficult not to notice that the new elements thrust into the English Orders – standard English, phonics, grammar and spelling – are all hobby-horses of a relatively small group with a strong political bias' (NAHT *Bulletin*, September 1993).

Teacher union submissions to Sir Ron Dearing's review urged not only a slimming down of the National Curriculum, but a curriculum more appropriate to the professionally conceived needs of children. The NAS/UWT, for example, suggested that only the Maths, Science and English Orders should operate at Key Stage One (NAS/UWT *Report,* July 1993). The PAT suggested that 'reading, writing, doing sums and learning to do what you are told are entirely proper priorities in Key Stage One' (*Professional Teacher*, June 1993), that Modern Languages should be taught at Key Stage Two and that a wider range of options than those intended by government should be available at Key Stage Four. The ATL wanted the National Curriculum to terminate at Key Stage Three and for assessment to be ongoing in schools, with a system of standardised monitoring.

The joint submission of the unions suggested a framework in which the National Curriculum could be reviewed (ATL *et al*, 1993). They argued, in particular, for a slimming down of the non-core subjects to manageable proportions, for future revisions to embrace professional input from teachers and to address the balance of the whole curriculum rather than be introduced subject by subject. Hence the Dearing proposals were largely seen by the teacher unions as a long overdue injection of teachers' views into the National Curriculum. 'The Government has been forced to recognise teachers' professionalism and has made far reaching changes to the curriculum' (NUT *News*, November 1994); 'The National Curriculum should be a framework to support teachers' professional judgement, not a statutory prison of pedantic rules and regulations' (ATL *Update*, December 1994).

SHA and NAHT, in their joint proposals for a revised National Curriculum, called for greater use of the locality of the school (NAHT *Bulletin*, December 1992). This call for government recognition that schools' needs should be reflected in their curricula won some acknowledgement in the Dearing proposals. Twenty per cent of teaching time could now be used at the discretion of schools in support of the National Curriculum. This recognition of local needs was a key point in NAHT's criticism in 1993 of the new draft orders for Technology: 'The existing orders allowed more flexibility to explore "cultural" questions which many young people from different backgrounds would be motivated to pursue' (NAHT *Bulletin*, May 1993).

A battle is currently (1995) being fought over the government's insistence that a daily act of worship be held that is broadly Christian in content, an insistence which the NAHT finds 'dogmatic and insensitive' to the needs of many communities and schools.

Managing the National Curriculum

The ability of the teaching profession to meet the demands of the National Curriculum has also been the subject of much teacher union attention. The general level of teachers' pay is seen as important, both to retain and motivate teachers in service and to recruit new entrants. Most of the unions in 1992, for example, seemed to the STRB to want a pay increase 'unconstrained by statements of what might be afforded' (STRB, 1992, para 22). They pointed to high wastage rates amongst teachers in their twenties (para 45) and the NUT submission in subsequent years confirmed this trend towards a profession predominantly staffed by teachers over 40 (STRB, 1993, para 44; 1994, para 41). Good quality graduates were not being retained, which often resulted in secondary pupils being taught by non-specialist teachers (STRB, 1992, para 49; 1993, paras 33 and 34). The difficulty of recruiting in London (STRB, 1994, para 36) led to an increase in the London allowances in 1994. Concerns were also expressed about funding for training of both teachers (STRB, 1993, paras 144 and 166) and headteachers (STRB, 1994, para 126), though the STRB's response on each occasion was to leave decisions to local managers and governors. Arrangements for the induction of teachers under new initial teacher training arrangements introduced by the 1994 Act also exercised the minds of the unions. ATL, NUT and SHA called for the funding of an 80 per cent teaching load and NAS/UWT and PAT for support during induction (STRB, 1993, para 159), a call to which the STRB responded (para 162) with its own request for a review, which it had to repeat in 1994 (STRB, 1994, para 142). It was prepared to pre-empt the findings of such a review with a recommended amendment to the Teachers' Pay and Conditions Document, giving newly qualified teachers 'access to adequate support in the first year of professional life', and extending that access to returners to the profession (para 143).

Workload

The main reservation about teachers' ability to cope has, however, been primarily about the workload involved. A significant number of union-led surveys have looked at teacher workload, teacher morale and teacher stress. An AMMA survey of secondary teachers showed working weeks ranging from 52 to 58 hours and concluded that 'the government is exploiting the goodwill and professional commitment of an overstretched workforce in order to keep the secondary raft afloat' (AMMA *Update*, January 1992).

The association's annual assembly called for 'an end to the plethora of ill-considered documents contributing to the growing incidence of stress-related illness amongst teachers' (AMMA *Update*, May 1992).

A survey on morale undertaken with NAHT and SHA later in the year revealed 19 per cent of teachers were ready to retire or leave the profession within five years. Thirty-three per cent of all teachers were dissatisfied in their present position as a result of 'unmanageable workloads, stress and overwhelming levels of paper work and record-keeping' (AMMA *Update*, September 1992). A further AMMA survey on Key Stage One teachers showed one in three working on average over 55 hours a week and one in ten over 60 hours.

By the early months of 1993 a movement of protest over Key Stage Three English workload had grown into one of general discontent about testing and assessment arrangements throughout all the Key Stages. The NAS/UWT decided to ballot its members on a boycott of such arrangements (NAS/UWT *Report*, February 1993). The subsequent 'yes' vote (March 1993) and the ruling of the Appeal Court, (that such a boycott was a legitimate trade dispute about workload), galvanised both the NUT and the ATL into undertaking ballots to join the NAS/UWT in its action. Their members also voted in favour of a boycott. The subsequent response of the DfE to employ supply staff and markers for future testing led both the NAS/UWT and ATL to withdraw from the action. The NUT eventually withdrew on the promise of a 'full and thorough review of the school tests for 7, 11, and 14 year olds in 1995' (NUT *News*, January 1995) by the Schools' Curriculum and Assessment Authority.

The PAT questioned its membership on class size and non-contact time (*Professional Teacher*, April 1993), reviewed the available literature on stress and drew comparisons between hours worked by teachers and by better-paid professionals (*Professional Teacher*, December 1993). The two headteacher unions largely stayed out of the debate, though NAHT did offer counselling advice on stress to its members (NAHT *Bulletin*, November 1994).

Workload has featured prominently in union submissions to the STRB to amend conditions of employment (STRB, 1992, para 46; STRB, 1993, para 54). More teachers, particularly returners, needed to be recruited to staff the delivery requirements of the National Curriculum (STRB, 1992, para 39; STRB, 1993, para 36). There have been annual calls to address the issues of class size and non-contact time (STRB, 1992, paras 121 and 122; STRB 1993, para 163; STRB, 1994, para 145), which have finally led the Review Body to ask the Office of Manpower Economics to undertake its own survey of teacher workload (STRB, 1994, para 148). The survey of working hours covered 4000 teachers in primary, secondary and special schools. It showed an average working week for both primary and secondary full-time teachers of about 49 hours, a slight rise in non-contact time in the primary sector, and a slight decline in such time in secondary schools. The STRB noted that 'there is evidence that workloads are increasing generally for professional groups and that teachers are part of that broad trend' (STRB, 1995, para 153).

So whilst acknowledging an ongoing pressure on school resources, the Review Body saw no need at present to interfere in the processes of local management. 'We hope that the effective managing of teachers' workloads will be treated as a priority by headteachers and governing bodies' (STRB, 1995, para 155).

Concern has also consistently been expressed, particularly by the NAHT, about the imprecise nature of deputy heads' duties. This lack of precision had resulted in deputies being given an unrealistic workload, particularly in primary schools. Calls for a more precise definition (STRB, 1992, para 121; STRB, 1993, para 158) ultimately bore fruit (STRB, 1994, para 137). The Review Body has largely dismissed issues of morale as more affected by 'the quality of life in school' and 'a more positive portrayal of the teaching profession in the media' than anything within its own control (like pay) (STRB, 1993, para 54).

The future

The thesis of this chapter has been that a debate, initiated by the Labour Party, led the Conservative Party to impose a rational–economic management model upon a system which had been accustomed to a human relations approach. Much of the effort of many of the teacher unions in the 1980s and 1990s has been directed towards reconciling these two approaches. The indications are that the task of reconciliation will continue to be daunting.

The government continues to be set upon the strict enforcement of cash-limited budgets at national and local levels. The acceptance of the 1995 pay rise for teachers, which the government refused to fund fully from central coffers, suggests a shift to local affordability as an important factor in future pay settlements. Notwithstanding the result of the next general election, it suggests a development towards a structure of pay parameters within which workers are urged to negotiate at local levels, like nurses were in 1995. This is a short step from local wage bargaining, be it at local authority or at school level. It is small wonder that teacher unions are directing their collective attention to national levels of funding for education, as well as the mechanism for transferring that funding to localities (through standard spending assessments (SSAs)); to what Doug McAvoy, the NUT General Secretary, called 'the cost of meeting teacher professionalism in schools' (at the Education Show, Birmingham, March 1995).

The continuing squeeze on education budgets is leading to a gradual casualisation of the teaching force. According to the STRB 10.1 per cent of teachers were on part-time contracts in 1991 (STRB, 1992), 10.4 per cent in 1993 (STRB, 1994) and some 50,000, or nearly 11 per cent, in 1994 (OFSTED, 1995). Peter Smith, General Secretary of the ATL, forecasts a future workforce dominated by female (cheaper) teachers on fixed-term contracts (Birmingham, March 1995). The bureaucratic demands of the rational–economic model show no signs of relenting. Should the trend in teacher employment continue, a decreasing number of full-time teachers will be taking on an increasing number of responsibilities.

The difficulties experienced by many teachers in managing current change have led to an increase in the numbers retiring prematurely due to infirmity and, according to one NUT Regional Officer,[1] to a general expectation among teachers that retirement will take place long before the age of 60 is reached. This suggests a younger workforce in the future, both for reasons of economy and wear and tear. It also suggests that the government may need to restructure teachers' superannuation in a future where few are likely to achieve the 40 years' service necessary to draw a full pension.

While a five-year moratorium has been declared on developing the National Curriculum, the battle over the delivery of Key Stage Two is likely to continue. OFSTED, as it did in this year's annual report (OFSTED, 1995), will continue to question the ability of non-specialists to deliver what it deems to be specialist subjects. Primary schools will no doubt continue to argue that the traditional system of one teacher teaching mainly one class should persist, particularly with the present funding imbalance between primary and secondary pupils. This may result in the further modification of Key Stage Two to accommodate tradition rather than legislation to address teaching methods.

In terms of the management models addressed above, the rational–economic one has made considerable inroads into the English education system. The costs of the system are in check, both through government fiscal policy and a natural wastage of older, more expensive process workers. These more expensive workers are being replaced by cheaper ones, sometimes on part-time or fixed-term contracts. The specifications within the process, though the National Curriculum has been modified somewhat by Dearing, are still firmly in place, as are the quality controls in the system. Some of the accountabilities are currently being put under severe strain but they still retain the force of law and can ultimately only be tested in the lawcourts. The outputs or outcomes of the system, such as GCSE examination results, are improving year on year. The system would appear to be efficient and cost effective.

I have tried to suggest that there has been a human cost for the changes in teachers' conditions of work. The rational–economic model has been bureaucratic and burdensome. It has threatened the school social and management systems which were based upon traditional methods of teacher delivery. It has questioned these traditional methods in terms of teaching effectiveness and cost effectiveness. It has made its inroads swiftly and has demoralised many of the workforce. In seeking to provide an effective model of management it has effectively caused management problems. It is here to stay in one form or another, whatever the hue of government. It has ensured an ongoing role for teacher unions to counter its worst excesses and to try to establish a more compatible relationship with its more humane bedfellow.

Note

1   I am grateful to Alan Williams, of the NUT East Anglian Regional Office, for his help and advice with this article.

References

Alexander, R, Rose, J and Woodhead, C (1992) 'Curriculum organisation and classroom practice in primary schools', a discussion paper, Department of Education and Science, London.

Assistant Masters and Mistresses Association (1992) *Update*.

Archer, M S (1981) 'Educational politics: a model for their analysis' in Broadfoot, P, Brock, C and Tulasiewicz, W (eds) *Politics and Educational Change*, Croom Helm, London.

Association of Teachers and Lecturers (ATL) (1993–4) *Updates*.

ATL (1994) *ATL and Secondary Schools*.

ATL, National Association of Head Teachers, National Association of Schoolmasters/Union of Women Teachers, National Union of Teachers, Professional Association of Teachers and Secondary Heads Association (1993) *A Framework for Reviewing the National Curriculum*, published by the six unions.

Barber, M (1992) *Education and the Teacher Unions*, Cassell, London.

Beresford, J (1993) 'Towards "a community of aim"? Some aspects of the LFM primary pilot scheme in Cambridgeshire', unpublished MPhil thesis, University of East Anglia, Norwich

Busher, H and Saran, R (1990) 'Teacher morale and their conditions of service: a report on field work', paper given at British Educational Management and Administration Society (BEMAS) Annual Conference, 14–16 September, University of Reading.

Coopers and Lybrand (1988) *Local Management of Schools*, HMSO, London.

Cox, C B and Dyson, A E (eds) (1969a) *Fight for Education. A Black Paper*, HMSO, London.

Cox, C B and Dyson, A E (eds) (1969b) *Black Paper Two: The Crisis in Education*, Critical Quarterly Society, London.

Cox, C B and Dyson, A E (eds) (1970) *Black Paper Three*, Critical Quarterly Society, London.

Cox, C B and Rhodes Boyson (eds) (1975) *Black Paper 1975: The Fight for Education*, Dent, London.

Davies, B (1989) 'Economics and budgeting: budgetary and economic perspectives and their applications in local management of schools' in Fidler, B and Bowles, G (eds) *Effective Local Management of Schools*, Longman in association with BE-MAS, Harlow.

Day, C, Johnston, D and Whitaker, P (1985) *Managing Primary Schools: A Professional Development Approach*, Harper & Row, London.

Dearing, R (1993) *The National Curriculum and its Assessment: Final Report*, School Curriculum and Assessment Authority, London.

DfE (1993) *Effective Management in Schools*, Summary, HMSO, London.

DfE (1994) *School Teachers' Pay and Conditions Document*, HMSO, London.

Drucker, P F (1988) *Management*, Heinemann, London.

Education Reform Act (1988), HMSO, London.

Hoyle, E (1975) 'Professionality, professionalism and control' in Houghton, V *et al* (eds), *Management in Education 1*, Ward Lock, London.

National Association of Head Teachers *Bulletins* 1992–4.

National Association of Schoolmasters/Union of Women Teachers NAS/UWT (1992a) *Report*, March.

NAS/UWT (1992b) *Report*, April.

NAS/UWT *Reports*, 1992–4.

National Union of Teachers (NUT) (1994) *Your Union – Your Future: NUT Future Teachers' Guide*, NUT, London.

NUT *News*, 1992–January 1995.

Office for Standards in Education (OFSTED) (1995) *The Annual Report of Her Majesty's Chief Inspector of Schools*, HMSO, London.

Peters, R S (ed) (1976) *The Role of the Head*, Routledge & Kegan Paul, London.

Professional Association of Teachers (PAT) (undated) *Brief Note for Prospective Members*.

PAT *Professional Teacher*, 1992–4

School Teachers' Review Body (STRB) (1992) *First Report, Cm 1806*, HMSO, London.

STRB (1993) *Second Report, Cm 2151*, HMSO, London.

STRB (1994) *Third Report, Cm 2466*, HMSO, London.

STRB (1995) *Fourth Report, Cm 2765*, HMSO, London

Secondary Heads Association (SHA), *Headlines*, 1992–4.

Sizer, J (1989) *An Insight into Management Accounting*, 8th edn, Penguin, Harmondsworth.

Strain, M (1990) 'Resource management in schools: some conceptual and practical considerations' in Cave, E and Wilkinson, C (eds) *Local Management of Schools: Some Practical Issues*, Routledge, London.

Taylor, T (1977) *A New Partnership for Our Schools*, HMSO, London.

Treasury and Civil Service Committee (1982) *Efficiency and Effectiveness in the Civil Service, Cm 8616*, HMSO, London.

Vroom, V H and Deci, E L (1989) *Management and Motivation: Selected Readings*, Penguin, London.

Whitaker, P (1983) *The Primary Head*, Heinemann Educational Books, London.

Chapter 6

Teacher Professionality and the National Curriculum: Management Implications
Keith Foreman

Reform by 'brute sanity'

One of the most telling sentences in W O Lester Smith's *Education: An Introductory Survey*, published in 1957, was 'No freedom that teachers in this country possess is as important as that of determining the curriculum and methods of teaching.' (Smith, 1957, p 161). It was a freedom jealously guarded by the profession. For many teachers it was part of their professional heritage. Thirty years later that freedom was summarily removed by a Secretary of State buoyed up by a large parliamentary majority and much criticism of teachers for taking strike action in the mid-1980s. The introduction of the National Curriculum under the Education Reform Act of 1988 was a deliberate demonstration of government virility. There was no serious attempt to consult or placate. The *initiation* and *implementation* of the National Curriculum ignored the findings of extensive research into the successful management of educational change, which is usually founded on an initial policy decision with new structures and materials put in place. But to these, most crucially, must be added action to ensure that front-line implementers have the skills, commitment and understanding to implement new practices (Fullan, 1989, p 147).

First, whilst its sponsors may have had a clear and rational vision of the National Curriculum, they assumed that all they had to do was spell out its merits and everyone would be strongly motivated to put it into action. As

George Bernard Shaw put it: 'Reformers have the idea that change can be introduced by brute sanity.'

Second, the Secretary of State decided to rush through the planning process to get to the 'action stage'. 'Its requirements were promulgated with only a derisory show of consultation' (Becher, 1989, p 53). Though there had been discussion about the content and shape of the curriculum by HMI and the Department of Education and Science (DES) since 1977, there was no attempt to enlist professional support. Clearly, central government was out to win back some of the managerial power which had earlier been ceded to the local authorities and professional teacher interests.

Third, it was assumed that positional power, in this case that of the Secretary of State, would ensure success because legislation would provide sanctions sufficiently powerful to deter any opposition. In fact, the provisions of the Act soon had to be changed to make it workable, and the opposition to testing led to a boycott of the tests in 1993.

Fourth, the Secretary of State, in his speech on the second reading of the Bill in the House of Commons on 1 December 1987, argued that the need for reform was a consequence of poor standards, on the evidence of international comparisons, and a school system which 'has become producer dominated' (Haviland, 1988, p 2). But the 'producers' were mainly the teachers, the very people on whom the government would have to rely to make the National Curriculum work. Government pressure was then applied with minimum support (in terms of resources and training). Yet, 'a combination of pressure and support... are [the] two important balancing mechanisms, and success [in implementing change] is usually accompanied by both... Pressure without support creates alienation' (Fullan, 1989, p 147). In this case, there was indeed pressure without support (Barber, 1994).

Fifth, the system was significantly overloaded with changes. The National Curriculum was one of several innovations forced upon the education service in the short space of two years. Others included local management of schools (LMS), staff appraisal and development through Grants for Education Support and Training and a series of measures to make schools more accountable. In the eyes of government critics there was no apparent co-ordination, no overall strategy. The disenfranchised partners (LEAs and teachers) were, for both political and educational reasons, deeply opposed.

The management implications of the National Curriculum can, therefore, be considered in two ways. First, the effect of the government's action upon teachers' sense of their professional status in the management of the nation's schools, and especially of the curriculum and its teaching. Second, the impact on the management of schools which were required to 'deliver' a flawed and over-prescriptive government initiative.

Control of the curriculum

Much early criticism of the National Curriculum articulated by the teachers' unions resulted from the view that the government had taken away control of the *what* and, to a degree, the *how* of the school curriculum. For a period in the 1960s and 1970s there was indeed considerable freedom for schools to determine what they taught. The end of the 11-plus for grammar school selection and the Plowden Report (CACE, 1967) freed the way for primary schools to experiment with a variety of 'child-centred' approaches. The class teacher was largely in control of what went on in the classroom. For secondary schools, the move to comprehensive education was not accompanied by a national debate on the nature and purpose of a comprehensive curriculum. The Schools Council, set up in 1964, failed to produce a solution though it generated widespread debate, produced the Certificate of Secondary Education for less academic 16-year-olds and many innovatory approaches. Secondary schools were much influenced by 16-plus syllabuses (GCE, CSE and then GCSE) produced by the examination boards. However, mounting evidence of serious differences in what schools offered their pupils led to increasing national concern. In his 1976 Ruskin College speech the Prime Minister, James Callaghan, argued that it was time to examine the case for a core curriculum (Chitty, 1993, p 8).

The debate about a core curriculum

The concept of a core curriculum was first discussed in a green paper 'Education in schools: a consultative document' (DES, 1977). It was followed by 'A framework for the school curriculum' (DES, 1980) and 'The school curriculum' (DES, 1981). The last recommended English, Mathematics and Science for all, with the LEAs and teachers determining how much time should be given to them.

HMI rejected this subject approach. They argued for whole school curriculum planning centred around eight 'areas of experience'. Their chief concepts were *access* and *entitlement*. For a growing body of teachers this was a welcome approach and a number began to implement a curriculum appropriate to comprehensive primary and secondary schools (Chitty, 1993, p 10).

Thus, it was generally agreed that, in a democracy, the state should define the broad framework – but not the detail – of the curriculum for its schools and its teachers. As late as 1985 the Government stated that 'It would not ... be right for the Secretary of State's policy for the range and pattern of the 5–16 curriculum to amount to the determination of national syllabuses for that period' (DES, 1985, p 11).

Initiation and implementation

A core national curriculum was first announced by the Secretary of State for Education and Science, Kenneth Baker, on the London Weekend Television programme 'Weekend World' on 7 December 1986. He saw it as a key component in a series of measures to secure greater central control of the education system in the interest of the pupils, far too many of whom were, in his words, 'aimless and drifting'. There was widespread surprise – even among his Cabinet colleagues who had not been consulted – followed by immediate, widespread criticism. Keith Joseph, for instance, a former Secretary of State, described Baker's core curriculum as 'far too rigid' (the *Guardian,* 19 April 1988). Stuart Sexton, Director of the Education Unit of the Institute of Economic Affairs, saw it as a 'straitjacket' (*The Times*, 9 May 1988).

Baker ignored these critics and, more or less, everyone else. He issued a consultation paper to all schools in July 1987, with comments required by September – a period coinciding with the schools' summer holidays. For many heads and teachers it was an insulting charade. He proposed a National Curriculum for all pupils aged from 5 to 16 years based on ten subjects (English, Mathematics, Science, History, Geography, a Modern Foreign Language, Art, PE, Technology and RE) which bore remarkable similarity to the 1904 and 1935 Regulations for Secondary Schools. He dismissed accusations that he had merely recreated a traditional, secondary grammar school syllabus list wholly inappropriate for the schools of the late twentieth century. Despite the brief consultative period 20,000 replies were received, not one of which according to Julian Haviland was in favour of the particular version proposed (Haviland, 1988, p.viii). With minimum delay the Bill was introduced and became the 1988 Education Reform Act.

The original framework was soon transformed into a structure of great complexity. A National Curriculum Council (NCC) was created with members appointed by the Secretary of State. Subject committees of experts working independently produced vast lists of contents, soon to prove excessive and unmanageable. Attempts by the NCC to co-ordinate them on the basis of whole school curriculum planning were resisted by the DES.

To appease the right wing of his party the Secretary of State also announced a new structure for assessment to be controlled by another quango, the Schools' Examinations and Assessment Council (SEAC). His brief to the task group on assessment and testing stated that he expected assessment, including testing, to fulfil diagnostic (or formative) and summative purposes and 'purposes mainly concerned with publicising the work of the education service ... in the light of pupils' achievements' (DES, 1988). These conflicting expectations proved, in the end, to be unachievable. The task group's report recommended ten Levels of Achievement and Standard Assessment Tests (SATs). It was a compromise which gained few supporters. The right saw the tests as being far too elaborate and costly. Teachers found SATs complex and time consuming. SATs also challenged the professional role of teachers as assessors of children's progress. But opposition only led to the announcement that SATs had priority. To many teachers this was a serious denigration of their professional role. Priority for SATs was not formally reversed until 1994 – by another Secretary of State attempting to improve relations with teachers.

The professionality of teachers

'Professionality' is here taken to mean 'the knowledge, skills and values deployed (by teachers) in day to day practice' (Hoyle, 1992), to which one might add teachers' 'perceptions and feelings'. Knowledge in this context might refer, in common-sense terms, to the prescribed content of the individual subjects of the National Curriculum and to the content of previous teaching which it made redundant. It might also include information and experience about how to manage classrooms. Gaining subject content knowledge was to be the pre-eminent activity of pupils through the new curriculum, a mechanistic and nineteenth-century view of what was the central purpose of teaching which many teachers found difficult to accept.

Skills is taken to refer to the managerial and interpersonal skills necessary for teachers to impart or help pupils construct subject knowledge effectively, and values to the principles and beliefs of teachers which govern their teaching and underpin curriculum design and structure in individual schools. The fear for many teachers was, with knowledge so defined and circumscribed, would their teaching skills also be proscribed and circumscribed? Some would have difficulty in accepting what they perceived to be the values underpinning the National Curriculum.

Perceptions and feelings also matter. As central government did not consult teachers about these in relation to the National Curriculum, many felt that their professional integrity had been undermined. Even if Sir Ron Dearing might claim 'my consultations have shown that the concept of a national curriculum has the broad support of the teaching profession' (Dearing, 1993), it does not follow that this particular National Curriculum, however amended or even re-invented, has the 'broad support' of the profession.

It may be argued that, in any profession, *being professional* means members having a degree of control over the work they do. It is this which allows them to claim professional status. Any reduction in this control deskills or deprofessionalises. Prior to 1988 the curriculum, in the sense of what should be taught, was influenced by a shifting balance between DES and HMI, examination boards, LEAs, professional subject bodies and schools, with teachers having a major influence over its delivery in classrooms. The National Curriculum swung the balance sharply in favour of central government. It now determined *what* should be taught and, though it contended that *how* it should be taught should remain the professional prerogative of teachers, it then erected a complex scheme of assessment which, until it was pruned, significantly undermined teachers' professional freedom over pedagogy.

Primary schools

The impact on teachers

The most serious effects of the National Curriculum were felt in the primary schools for, unlike secondaries, they had not been organised on a subject basis. The impact on primary schools has been well researched (see, for instance, Campbell *et al*, 1991; Campbell and Neill, 1994; Osborn and Black, 1994; Webb, 1994; Croll *et al*, 1994; Pollard *et al,* 1994). In addition, there have been numerous DES, Department for Education and Office for Standards in Education (OFSTED) reports.

In summary, they found teachers were working conscientiously (perhaps too much so, with potentially serious health implications) and for longer hours, but a higher proportion of their teaching week was taken up with preparation, professional development, administration and, above all, assessment. They felt that 'standards in most subjects were little affected' (Campbell and Neill, 1994, p 96) though improvements were noted in Science, Technology, History and Geography to set against deterioration in Reading, Art, PE, Music and RE.

In spite of hopes to the contrary, most teachers were spending a high percentage of time on 'basics', ie English and Mathematics. Some lacked subject expertise. There was some loss of spontaneity and open-ended enquiry because of subject content demands.

However, as teachers adjusted to the demands of the National Curriculum so they altered their work patterns to make it work and began to recognise benefits. For instance, some reported that they now worked more closely with colleagues in planning the curriculum. Others felt themselves to be more skilful in the way they assessed the learning of pupils.

Many schools did not feel overwhelmed by the curriculum changes. In spite of increases in the external direction of their work and constraints upon their professional autonomy teachers adapted National Curriculum requirements to fit their particular circumstances (Croll *et al*, 1994, p 338). Furthermore, the original demands of the National Curriculum were being steadily modified after 1988 and were becoming more acceptable, partly as a result of teacher pressure and teacher consultation organised by NCC.

The evidence from longitudinal research since 1988 shows, as might reasonably have been expected, that half a million teachers in 20,000 schools were divided in their feelings about the effects of the National Curriculum on their personal sense of professionalism. For instance, almost half the infant teachers in the survey by Professor Campbell (Campbell and Neill, 1994, p 93) felt that their own professionalism had been damaged. But 17 per cent – a substantial minority – thought it had been enhanced. The Primary Assessment Curriculum Experience (PACE) survey (Key Stages 1 and 2) did not support the view that all teachers felt deskilled or deprofessionalised (Pollard *et al*, 1994, pp 59–102).

Management implications

The management implications may be grouped under four subheadings.

Management and administration
Any judgement about the impact of the National Curriculum on school management has to see it in the context of other government reforms. Faced with greatly increased responsibilities and workloads many headteachers were doing less teaching – except in small schools. The time spent on administration and management tasks had increased greatly. Deputies also faced a more demanding role, frequently acting as curriculum leaders with responsibility for one or more subjects, and a year, phase or key stage. Many felt the need for more training.

Osborn and Black (1994, pp 23–4) found that whole school development planning was increasingly common, with elaborate systems being put in place to monitor and record children's progress. Headteachers were supporting their staff by monitoring and prioritising documents from outside, preventing interruptions and avoiding crisis management. Classroom assistants were being employed in greater numbers. Many schools were working more collegially to address whole school issues, ie enhancing the professional role.

Subject management
The subject demands of the National Curriculum were a major problem especially in smaller schools. Some schools were reaching the decision that it was impossible to teach all the requirements (Webb, 1994, p 23). Conscious agreements were being made about what to omit – a clear assertion of the professional role. Surveys showed that many schools were appointing subject co-ordinators and/or semi-specialists to lead in particular subject areas especially at Key Stage 2. They also promoted new resources, collated subject policies and led in-service education and training (INSET)

Following visits to 49 primary schools (OFSTED, 1995), HMI found that most teachers were still class teachers. In the broader sense of curriculum management, HMI were concerned to find 'systematic monitoring of pupils' progress in only two of their sample schools'. The time spent on individual subjects varied significantly, with English receiving between 15 and 30 per cent, Maths 13–25 per cent and Science 4–15 per cent of the teaching week.

Subject teaching has remained a contentious national issue polarised, simplistically, into child–centred group work versus didactic, whole class methodologies. Webb (1994) found that the National Curriculum appeared to be increasing teachers' awareness of the need for differentiation, 'mainly achieved through the outcome and time for completion of tasks, and the use of additional help in the classroom' (pp 52–3). Ability groups were being used especially in Mathematics and English.

Collaboration between schools
In tackling some of the problems posed by the National Curriculum there was evidence that more schools were forming clusters with neighbouring primaries and secondary schools for the purposes of assessment co-ordination, professional development and progression. Clearly, teachers were welcoming this confidence-building, external reinforcement as they became more exposed to parental, community or even OFSTED judgement. Such collaboration is perhaps evidence of what Hoyle and McCormick (1976, p 75) called 'extended professionalism'.

Subject expertise

There is ample evidence that lack of non-contact time posed serious problems for staff development and planning in many primary schools. For the most part teachers were having to work long hours to prepare themselves for lessons. Campbell and Neill (1994, pp 10–20) found that 'teachers in Years Five and Six reported working an average of 53.1 hours per week with 36 per cent working over 55 hours per week'. Much training was clearly being done in teachers' own time. Lack of adequate subject knowledge remains a major concern for HMI: 'Even after the Dearing Review, the National Curriculum will demand subject knowledge that some teachers do not possess' (OFSTED, 1995).

Secondary schools

The impact on teachers

Compared to the primary field, the research evidence on the impact of the National Curriculum on secondary teachers is sparse. There are no longitudinal studies of the kind promoted by teacher unions for primary schools.

Secondary schools were fundamentally in a more comfortable position than primary schools to meet the challenges of the National Curriculum because prior to 1988 they were invariably organised by subject department or faculty. Thus there were specialists in place to take on the development work, focusing on the Orders as they were delivered. Not surprisingly, there were subject teachers who were reasonably content with the new syllabuses and others who were openly critical. The main frustrations related to the delay in the delivery of the Orders so that departments found it difficult to plan ahead, the lack of time for adequate planning and repeated changes to national syllabuses and assessment requirements. The latter led to considerable scepticism about the value of planning when the chances were that the requirements would be amended before implementation.

In some curriculum areas, secondary teachers were confronted with the need to teach subjects for which they had not been trained. Technology, for instance, a 'new' subject, covered a range of craft specialisms. Campbell and Neill (1991, p 40) found instances of mismatch between academic background and current teaching requirements in their study of the workloads of secondary teachers. Biologists, for instance, might be required to teach Chemistry in balanced Science courses, with obvious implications for retraining.

Management implications

The major challenges for management in secondary schools may be grouped under five subheadings.

The choice of subjects

The challenge was to fit ten subjects with their associated attainment targets and programmes of study together with the cross-curricular skills, themes and dimensions into existing structures. Inevitably some staff were more pleased than others with the results of internal audits and revised curricular plans. Subjects like Humanities had to fight their corner against the requirements that 'traditional' History and Geography were to be taught. Ribbins found that most secondary heads in his survey considered the degree of prescription to be much higher than existed in the past, but 'only a few found it excessive and several argued that it was not necessarily a bad thing' (Ribbins, 1993, p 63). Heads of department were sometimes faced with the need to reconcile the new requirements with existing course materials involving significant investment. They also had to meet the objections, which they may have held themselves, about the precise need for all these changes. 'What, exactly, is wrong with what we are doing now?' 'Do we need all this planning and revision when groups of children have to be taught?' 'Are they getting a fair deal?' (eg Kyriacou and Wilkins, 1993).

Key Stage 4

From the beginning there was controversy about Key Stage 4, the last two years of compulsory schooling, where there were practical problems of fitting so many subjects and cross-curricular themes into a finite amount of time. More significantly, many teachers complained that it did not make sense to try to teach all the foundation subjects and RE to pupils of all abilities without serious risk of indiscipline. There was also the problem of the apparent abandonment of vocational courses and qualifications. It did not take long for industrialists and even ministers (Chitty, 1993, p 151) to voice their support for wholesale reform. Then Kenneth Clark announced in January 1991 that only English, Maths and Science would remain compulsory after 14. It was a significant reversal.

Curriculum organisation

One problem of a list of subjects which would be assessed under the National Curriculum was that those not included might be given lower status by parents and students. Many heads and senior staff were determined that Arts subjects, for instance, should not be downgraded, but the pressures of declining budgets and published league tables of examination results worked in the opposite direction. There was always the danger that budgets would be skewed in the direction of the core and foundation subjects, as Ball and Bowe (1992) found. With many schools experiencing a fall in real income as a result of the government's squeeze on public spending, the temptation to spend more on National Curriculum subjects was inevitable.

Assessment
Ball and Bowe (1992) found very negative attitudes towards the proposed assessment procedures at Key Stage 3. It is therefore not surprising that in the following year the main teacher unions, for once working together, led the refusal to implement national tests. Most of the impetus came from the secondary teachers who were traditionally more militant than their primary colleagues. This revolt led to the Dearing Review and a significant change of course. For the first time the government decided to consult the professionals on whom the success of the National Curriculum had always depended.

Teaching and learning
Until the Dearing Report reopened it, one effect of an imposed National Curriculum was to temporarily close down the debate about the secondary curriculum, which had been a feature of the comprehensive school in the 1970s and 1980s. School development plans now began to feature the improvement of teaching and learning styles, a concern linked to the need to demonstrate good performance through the published 'league' tables of National Curriculum, GCSE and A level results. Some teachers may not have found this interest in their personal practice too much to their liking. Many schools also began to produce whole school assessment, recording and reporting policies in an effort to encourage greater consistency and coherence of practice. Again, this could be a threatening exercise to departments wedded to their own ways.

The Dearing Report

In the Spring of 1993 Secretary of State John Patten, faced with a storm of protest over testing, invited the chairman designate of the Schools' Curriculum and Assessment Authority (SCAA) (formed to replace NCC and SEAC – which in many people's eyes ought never to have been created as independent bodies) to undertake a major review of the National Curriculum.

Sir Ron Dearing immediately began a programme of extensive consultation with teachers, holding a number of regional conferences. His interim report was published in July 1993 and his final report in January 1994. Its key points were:

- the existing National Curriculum for 5–14-year-olds to be streamlined to release a day a week (20 per cent of the teaching week) for schools to use at their own discretion;
- the reduction in curriculum content for this age group to be concentrated outside the core subjects of English, Maths and Science;
- for 14–16-year-olds, more flexibility to allow more schools to offer a wide range of academic and vocational options (with the prospect of a 14–19 continuum);
- the workload of teachers to be cut through National Curriculum simplification, and reduced testing and recording demands;
- the ten-level scale to be simplified and to run only until the end of Key Stage 3;
- all National Curriculum subjects to be reviewed in one go for September 1995;
- no further change to the National Curriculum for five years after this (Dearing, 1993).

The reports were greeted with relief by some teachers. Even the unions eventually decided not to oppose testing in 1995. Sir Ron stressed his wish to provide 'scope for professional judgement'. The *Observer* (13 November 1994) commented that 'professional responsibility is to be handed back to the teachers. Within a broad framework they will decide what goes on in the classroom. This is common sense.' But relief did not imply passive acceptance. The attacks on their professional role had left many teachers suspicious and distrustful.

Sir Ron Dearing's political role as the saviour of a government in deep trouble was apparent. In spite of a loosening of the reins, control of the curriculum, in the eyes of many teachers, still lay fundamentally with central government. For some teachers 'slimming' meant 'narrowing' or even 'impoverishing'. It was still 'a content and transmission driven curriculum' (Wright, 1994). The row over 'Standard English' and approved reading lists exemplified the extent of continuing prescription. 'We need a thoroughgoing debate on the philosophical basis of national curriculum English' (*TES*, 3 March 1995).

There was suspicion that a five-year moratorium on curriculum change would be meaningless. 'If the history of the National Curriculum over the last seven years has shown anything, it is the extraordinary complexity and difficulty inherent in constructing a curriculum and associated testing arrangements and getting it right!' (Wright, 1994). For some subject specialists there was little to praise. 'If you slim down the camel that a SCAA committee created while trying to design a horse, you get a slim camel rather than a horse' (*TES* National Curriculum Update, February 1995).

The problem of the Key Stage 4 curriculum remained unsolved. The Dearing Report gave no clear guidance on breadth and balance in the core programme, the place of vocational education post-16, the structure and accreditation of short courses and accreditation for those with learning difficulties. The 14–19 continuum was tabled, but many teachers and heads doubted the government's sincerity over academic and vocational 'pathways of equal status'. As John Dunford put it: 'The real problems [of Key Stage 4] were never addressed' (*TES*, 10 February 1995).

The impact of the National Curriculum on teachers: a survey

To find out how teachers perceived the impact of the National Curriculum on their professional status, Hugh Busher and I, in late 1994, conducted a small-scale survey by questionnaire of teachers working in 55 primary and 73 secondary schools in Derbyshire, Leicestershire and Nottinghamshire. Of the 128 in the sample (11 Key Stage 1, 44 Key Stage 2 and 73 Key Stage 3) 22 teachers volunteered and were selected for structured interviews. Sixty per cent were middle managers; 54 per cent were male, an unrepresentative sample of teachers in schools. Of the schools, 18 described themselves as serving rural, and 14 'inner city' catchments. The rest served a mixture of rural/urban and urban areas. In selecting for interview we concentrated our attentions on teachers of Design and Technology (D&T) because this was a 'new' curriculum area, and Mathematics, Science and English, the three core subjects.

Although, generally, the changes in the curriculum brought about by the National Curriculum were welcomed by teachers, the changes in teaching methods it has required and the increased administrative load it has brought with it were not. Many teachers thought they had suffered alienation as a result of its introduction.

The impact of the National Curriculum on teachers was explored under five headings.

Subject or topic knowledge

The National Curriculum has caused teachers a great deal of extra work in curriculum preparation. Although about 25 per cent of teachers said they had not introduced new materials as a consequence of the National Curriculum, over 50 per cent gave examples of introducing up to four new materials or topics. Primary schools, for example, were using new materials to meet subject requirements, notably in Science and Technology. At the same time, two-thirds of the sample reported that no materials had been made redundant. Most teachers had gained the content knowledge for these topics from private study, joint preparation with colleagues and school-based INSET. Not surprisingly, perhaps, less use was made of subject association documents and award-bearing INSET (long courses/higher degrees).

Despite the extra work, teachers expressed satisfaction with the new syllabuses which they had contructed. Over 50 per cent of respondents reported that schemes of work currently in use were, in their view, better than previous syllabuses; about one third thought they were not. Science teachers generally welcomed curriculum breadth which was 'more challenging'. Others resented topics being so detailed 'that schools have no time to develop aspects which pupils find of particular interest'.

Among the reasons given for improvement, the following featured prominently: 'It is more structured', 'I am made to teach in more depth', 'There is less chance of missing certain areas', 'Schemes of work have been developed collaboratively'. Others feared that: 'Too much work is subject-based knowledge rather than skills' and 'Some topics are removed from children's interests and experiences'.

Such changes had incurred considerable costs. Over half the respondents mentioned 'financial costs' (eg buying new equipment and materials) and 'time costs' (eg increased paperwork, preparation of new schemes of work and record keeping). One-third suggested 'teacher stress' (eg tiredness, pressure on family life) and 20 per cent 'costs to pupils' (eg less frequent contact with teachers, disruption to learning caused by the need for planning, assessing and recording, and neglect of children with special needs).

Teaching methods

Sixty per cent of teachers thought that the National Curriculum had changed their teaching methods. A clear majority of primary teachers stated that they now engaged less frequently in group work (practical and project work, investigations and individual support) and more frequently in didactic, whole class teaching. They were unhappy with this change because it meant 'less differentiation' of the curriculum and 'less opportunity for individual children to follow their own line of interest or development'. Those who thought things were improved said there was 'increased emphasis on Science teaching' and (in contrast) 'more attention to differentiation'. Subject specialists in secondary schools were more equally divided in the methods they now used, but most of them, too, were unhappy with the changes. English teachers were the least content. They perceived 'less scope for individual thought and expression' and 'less time for drafting and redrafting.' But scientists, too, were concerned at 'more rote learning.'

In contrast, those who were more optimistic mentioned 'increased level of appropriate work for individuals in Years Eight and Nine' (Science), 'investigational and practical approaches to teaching have been encouraged by the National Curriculum' (Maths), 'more individualised teaching' (D&T) and 'record keeping is more accurate and professional now' (English).

Most teachers claimed that they had developed their new teaching methods through private study and/or working with colleagues and school-based IN-SET. Cluster or family INSET, LEA-organised INSET, study of NCC/SEAC/SCAA documents and using pupil textbooks were also popular, but little use was made of award-bearing courses.

Assessment

A high proportion of teachers in the sample claimed that they were spending 'much more time than previously' on assessing pupils' work. As a consequence, primary teachers claimed that they were doing less 'talking to individual children', 'displaying pupils' work' and 'teaching'. Design and Technology teachers mentioned that they were giving less attention to individual projects. Scientists thought they were giving less time to 'expanding topics in response to pupils' interests' and English specialists were worried that they were giving less encouragement to 'creative work for pure enjoyment or self-expression'.

Changes in school management

Although it was clearly difficult for respondents to separate the effects of the National Curriculum on management practices from those of LMS and other reforms, some items emerged. The National Curriculum seems to have become embedded in the management processes of schools. Teachers explained that it was regularly an item on the agenda in department meetings or staff meetings (primary schools), and usually discussed at inter-school meetings. However it is, perhaps, still largely a matter of professional concern, being discussed much less frequently at governors' meetings and rarely, if at all, at parents' association meetings.

Primary teachers thought the National Curriculum had affected the culture of schools, emphasising bureaucratic processes (meetings, administration, supervision), organisational hierarchy (eg more work for subject co-ordinators) and more formal relationships with pupils. However, some Science teachers welcomed the development of 'more inter-departmental liaison'.

Primary and some secondary teachers resented the increased influence of central government over the curriculum, commenting on the 'constant readjustments and re-inventing the wheel' (Science). This has reduced their professional control over their work processes.

The professional status of teachers

Many teachers thought that they had lost status as a result of the National Curriculum. Only 10 per cent felt that it had improved the image of teachers in the eyes of the general public. Most were divided between those who believed their image to be diminished or unchanged – though some teachers differentiated between the public at large (much influenced by a still, if less critical media) and parents and governors, who had shown their support in the assessment issue in 1993. As for personal perceptions of their professional status only a small minority (5 per cent) thought that it had been enhanced by the National Curriculum; 25 per cent saw no significant change and well over 50 per cent thought it had been diminished.

Conclusion

The trends discerned in this small study in the East Midlands reflect generally the findings of earlier researchers. Most teachers felt that the National Curriculum impugned their professionality not so much because it was a National Curriculum *per se* but because it had been introduced without consultation and was perceived to be seriously flawed. Central government had deliberately ignored teachers but required them to make it work. The Dearing Report and its consultation helped to restore confidence in the professional role, but it was too overtly political to convince everyone. As one of our interviewees said, 'The money that has been wasted on getting the National Curriculum to this stage is criminal.'

The National Curriculum, very clearly, has put a high premium on leadership in schools. Where teachers were working collaboratively in planning and in assessment, they saw positive gains. Some teachers thought that it had enhanced, unintentionally perhaps, their professionality. As one of the teachers interviewed in our study said, 'The National Curriculum has had a terrifically positive effect because we have really got to think about why we are doing things... what we are teaching and why we are teaching it.'

The opposite view was eloquently stated. 'Professionalism is about control, knowledge, a sense of your own input, your own values and your own contribution. Whereas now we are passive recipients of what we will do, how we will do it and when we will do it.'

Very clearly the loss of control over the subject content of the curriculum and, to some extent, of its delivery remains, for many teachers, a significant curb on their sense of professionality – their knowledge, skills and values. However, in time, and with the benefit of a new generation of teachers whose careers began after the advent of the National Curriculum, teachers may see themselves, with Aspin *et al* (1994) more as 'modulators, adaptors and providers' rather than curriculum designers. Perhaps, too, they will identify with David Hargreaves' *new professionalism* which involves 'a movement away from the teacher's traditional authority and autonomy towards new forms of relationship with colleagues, with students, and with parents' (Hargreaves, 1994).

References

Aspin, D, Chapman, J and Wilkinson, V (1994) *Quality Schooling*, Cassell, London.

Ball, J and Bowe, R (1992) 'Subject departments and the implementation of National Curriculum policy: an overview of the issues', *Journal of Curriculum Studies* 24, 2, pp 97–115.

Barber, M (1994) 'Power and control in education, 1944–2004', *British Journal of Education Studies* 42, 4, pp 348–62.

Becher, T (1989) 'The National Curriculum and the Implementation Gap', in Preedy, M (ed) *Approaches to Curriculum Management*, Open University Press, Milton Keynes.

Campbell, R, Evans, L, Neill, S and Packwood, A (1991) *Workloads, Achievements and Stress: Teacher Time In Key Stage One*, Assistant Masters and Mistresses Association (AMMA), London.

Campbell, R and Neill, S (1991) *The Workloads of Secondary School Teachers*, AMMA, London.

Campbell, R and Neill, S (1994) *Teacher Commitment and Policy Failure*, Longman, Harlow.

Central Advisory Council for Education (CACE) (1967) *Children and their Primary Schools* (The Plowden Report), HMSO, London.

Chitty, C (1993) 'The school curriculum: from teacher autonomy to central control' in Chitty, C (ed), *The National Curriculum: Is It Working?*, Longman, Harlow.

Croll, P, Abbot, D, Broadfoot, P, Osborn, M and Pollard, A (1994) 'Teachers and education policy: roles and models', *British Journal of Educational Studies* 42, 4, pp 333–47.

Dearing, R (1993) *The National Curriculum: The Final Report*, Schools' Curriculum and Assessment Authority, London.

Department of Education and Science, DES (1977) *Education in Schools*, DES, London.

DES (1980) *A Framework for the School Curriculum*, DES, London.

DES (1981) *The School Curriculum*, DES, London.

DES (1985) *Better Schools*, HMSO, London.

DES (1988) *National Curriculum: Task Group on Assessment and Testing: A Report*, DES, London.

Fullan, M (1989) 'Managing curriculum change' in Preedy, M (ed) *Approaches to Curriculum Management*, Open University Press, Milton Keynes.

Hargreaves, D (1994) 'The new professionalism: the synthesis of professional and institutional development', *Teachers and Teacher Education* 10, 4, pp 423–38.

Haviland, J (1988) *Take Care Mr Baker*, Fourth Estate, London.

Hoyle, E (1992) 'An Education Policy for Tomorrow', paper presented to the British Educational and Management Administration Society Annual Conference, 12–13 September, University of Bristol, Bristol.

Hoyle, E and McCormick, R (1976) *Innovation and the Teacher*, Open University Press, Milton Keynes.

Kyriacou, C and Wilkins, M (1993) 'The impact of the National Curriculum on teaching methods at a secondary school', *Educational Research* 35, 3, pp 270–77.

Office for Standards in Education (OFSTED) (1995) *Primary Matters: A Discussion on Teaching and Learning in Primary Schools*, OFSTED Publications, London.

Osborn, A and Black, E (1994) *The Changing Nature of Teachers' Work: Developing the National Curriculum at Key Stage 2*, National Association of Schoolmasters/Union of Women Teachers, London.

Pollard, A, Broadfoot, P, Croll, P, Osborn, M and Abbot, D (1994) *Changing English Primary Schools?*, Cassell, London.

Ribbins, P (1993) 'Telling tales of secondary heads: on educational reform and the National Curriculum', in Chitty, C (ed) (1993) *The National Curriculum: Is It Working?*, Longman, Harlow.

Smith, W O L (1957) *Education: An Introductory Survey*, Penguin, Harmondsworth.

Webb, R (1994) *After the Deluge: Changing Roles and Responsibilities in the Primary School*, Association of Teachers and Lecturers, London.

Wright, N (1994) 'Dear, dear Dearing', in *Curriculum* 15, 2, pp 57–67.

Part Two
The Institutional Focus

Chapter 7

Leadership and Professional Development: Developing Reflective Practice
Christopher Day

Introduction: making a difference

Most of my professional life has been spent as a teacher, teacher of teachers, schools adviser and researcher. Throughout these roles, and in my current leadership roles in my own university, I have been concerned with making a difference to the lives of pupils, students and colleague professionals. Early on I learned that 'being a professional' meant more than acquiring and using subject knowledge and pedagogical skills, that teaching children is more than the transmission of knowledge, that the quality of the 'interconnectedness' between teacher and learner is central to successful teaching and learning, and that issues of motivation and self-esteem must be managed alongside the formal curriculum of the school. I learned that teaching was an intellectually and emotionally demanding occupation, requiring the exercise of rational and non-rational decision-making and judgement. I learned, in relation to this, that I could not develop (passively) the children or adults with whom I work. I could only provide opportunities for their development (actively). Development, ultimately, is in the hands of the individual.

It took me many years to learn that I was in the business of managing change, that my success could to some degree be measured against the kind and quality of leadership which I brought to this, and that I too was a learner. As a result of interaction with these experiences and others my life also has been influenced, perhaps through a poem, a book, the teachings of a great teacher, the practice model of a respected friend or colleague, or students themselves. I have learned that what I am as a person should not and cannot always be entirely separated from what I am as a professional. The one is nested in the other, the two are interdependent, two parts of one whole. I want, therefore, in this chapter to examine the proposition that leadership is about making a difference in the quality of the lives of colleagues and that in order to achieve this a key role of headteachers is to create the conditions that encourage professional learning (a natural process which is often unplanned, unremarked and undocumented), and enhance professional development (which I will define as planned accelerated learning). A key element in these processes is reflection.

The purpose of schools is to make a difference to the lives of children. This provides the core value context in which leadership responsibilities and those of teachers are located; and it serves as a reminder that it is necessary at times to revisit moral purposes, perhaps answering along the way the question posed by the Chorus in T S Eliot's *The Rock*:

Where is the wisdom we have lost in knowledge?
Where is the knowledge we have lost in information?

Education is viewed universally as vital to the economic and social well-being of most if not all countries in the world; and school effectiveness research tells us that schools represent an important value-added component to the education of children and young people (Rutter *et al*, 1979; Mortimore *et al*, 1988). In a sense schools mediate the view of society which the children whom they educate will form, help prepare them for the world of work and are dedicated to their individual welfare. Schools have instrumental, social and moral purposes. They provide access to knowledge – though increasingly their more important contribution lies in fostering skills of inquiring, selecting, process-ing and making informed critical judgements about the worthwhileness of particular knowledge content within individual and collective personal and social value frames. Indeed, the school

is the only institution in our society specifically charged with providing to the young a disciplined encounter with all the subject matters of the human conversation: the world as a physical and biological system; evaluative and belief systems; communication systems; the social, political and economic systems that make up the global village; and the human species itself.

(Goodlad, 1990, p 49)

Vitally, schools have moral purposes too:

> The school is the only institution in our nation specifically charged with enculturating the young into a political democracy ... (even one without a Queen!) ... Schools are major players in developing educated persons who acquire an understanding of truth, beauty and justice against which to judge their own and society's virtues and imperfections ... This is a moral responsibility. (Goodlad, 1990, pp 48–9)

Despite the rhetoric espousing the importance of schools, or perhaps because of it, in recent years governments throughout the world have demonstrated increasingly a lack of trust in their efficacy, effectiveness and ability to discharge these weighty responsibilities. Throughout Europe, the USA and Australia government-inspired and imposed systemic reforms in subject matter teaching; in standards, curriculum, teaching and student assessment; in the governance of schools; and in the monitoring and inspection of teaching standards, have challenged teachers. Often, since these reforms are not always congruent with teachers' prior experience, established beliefs and present practice, predictably, their commitment is not always fulsome. It is not surprising, therefore, that externally imposed innovation often saps commitment (Louden and Browne, 1993).

In 1991, reporting a cross-national study of 'What it means to be a Teacher' in French and British primary schools, Broadfoot and Osborn (1991) concluded that 'current attempts to impose nationally generalised solutions and directives on primary teachers ride roughshod over what our evidence shows to be the real influences on teachers' professional motivation and practice'.

They observed not only 'a sharp drop' in morale but predicted also that:

> teachers will be exerting themselves to the utmost to find ways of continuing to apply what they consider to be the best approach to teaching ... [in order to] ... protect children's education from the reductionist influence of some aspects of the National Curriculum, to preserve the joy and warmth of the teacher–pupil relationship, and to find ways of resisting the temptation to engage in more didactic forms of teaching. (Broadfoot and Osborn, 1991, pp 86–7)

In other words, longstanding views of professionalism, whether implicit or explicit, will not be easily changed by central policy initiatives. The principal's role is to support and nurture the professionalism of teachers.

Reflective practice

Reflective practice is defined as continuing conscious and systematic review of the purposes, plans, action and evaluation of teaching in order to reinforce effectiveness and, where appropriate, prompt change. There are eight key strategies through which headteachers who put service first may make a difference in the opportunities for teachers to engage in reflective practice: investing in continuing professional development; promoting reflective practice; investing in the school's culture; knowing, communicating and sharing philosophy; developing a moral commitment; being the right kind of leader; developing critical communities; promoting personal development profiles.

Investing in continuing professional development

Leadership in matters of professional development in the 1990s and beyond is likely to continue to be framed in part by external visions of what a school should be, and these will not always match those held by teachers in schools. The challenge to leadership created through systematic externally generated innovation has been compounded by the parallel decentralisation of responsibility for implementing policy to school level. Earmarked resource allocation favours the use of short, one-off solution-oriented training options or awareness raising in-service days designed to disseminate specific sets of knowledge, ideas, practices or curriculum materials. In England and Wales legislation has ensured that a minimum of five days each year are committed to professional development. Cowan and Wright (1990) surveyed the use of 110 of these and found a lack of coherence and continuity, lack of follow through and an expressed feeling of cynicism, frustration and dissatisfaction among teachers. More recently Newton and Newton (1994) conducted a similar survey in 99 primary and 94 secondary schools from five local education authorities. They found that most primary school events were concerned with an awareness-raising information-giving, related to preparation for classroom teaching. They were characterised by immediacy and largely determined by current events.

The tendency over the last decade to regard development as training which may be achieved in short, sharp bursts and which must be directly related to policy implementation is increasing (Gilroy and Day, 1993). Studies in Australia, England and Sweden indicate that both teachers and administrators may favour an emphasis on technical rationality in professional development programmes (Sachs and Logan, 1990; O'Donohue *et al*, 1993). If this trend remains unchecked the consequences may be the downgrading of headteachers as autonomous, responsible and accountable professionals to headteachers as mere functionaries. The trend which I have identified may have the effect of deskilling headteachers and teachers as professionals (with a responsibility for the moral purposes of education) and reskilling them as technicians (with a responsibility for uncritical delivery of knowledge and skills).

If local patterns of resource allocation which tend to favour the training model persist or become the only route to professional development for most teachers, then, according to Australian researchers:

> Rather than developing reflective practitioners who are able to understand, challenge and transform their practice, in-service education in its current form encourages the development of teachers who see their world in terms of instrumental ends achievable through the recipes of 'tried and true' practices legitimated by unexamined experience or uncritically accepted research findings. (Sachs and Logan, 1990)

Teachers' professional development will thus be restricted.

Promoting reflective practice

Research to date concerning teachers' development shows that they have not generally taken an active part in the production of knowledge about their own teaching – indeed there has been a tension between so-called scientific knowledge (theory) and professional or practical knowledge (practice). In a sense teachers have been disenfranchised. They are perceived as basing their practice on their professional, practical knowledge and experience: 'Teachers are cut off, then, both from the possibility of reflecting and building on their own know-how and from the confusions that could serve them as springboards to new ways of seeing things' (Schon, 1992, p 119).

Important issues, therefore, are how practice can become reflective, and by what means the teacher may be supported over time in developing reflective teaching practice at different levels (Day, 1993). It is equally important to recognise that, to date, much learning through reflection has been private. Conditions of service and the organisation cultures in many schools do not allow for regular professional dialogue about teaching which goes much beyond anecdotal exchange and the trading of techniques. Conscious reflection in the classroom is limited for most teachers who develop repertoires and routines to an implicit level (Clark and Yinger, 1977). Furthermore, opportunities and motivation for professional discourse about teaching with colleagues will be limited according to both the culture of the school (Little, 1990; Schein, 1985) and the rhetoric/reality roles played by teacher as educationist and teacher as practitioner (Keddie, 1971). These and the privacy norms which, even now, are characteristic of the professional serve to undermine or diminish the capacity for teacher learning and sustained professional development (Rosenholtz, 1989; McLaughlin and Marsh, 1979). These problems of educational discourse make it difficult for teachers to understand and review their own knowledge base without support. Experience itself, then, is limited as a source of development.

Single and double loop learning

Self-renewal as an underpinning purpose of professional development is essential because, in changing times, our existing mental maps or frames may 'cease to fit the territory' (Pascale, 1990, p. 13). Yet research tells us that teachers working alone in classrooms are likely to operate on models of restricted professionality. Once they have developed a personal solution to any problems of teaching which they perceive – and this is usually achieved without any systematic assistance from others – it is unlikely that this solution will again be significantly questioned (Day, 1985). Argyris and Schon (1974), who investigated the work of people in several professions, including teaching, nearly 20 years ago characterised this 'normal' world of learning as 'single loop' in which 'we learn to maintain the field of constancy by designing actions that satisfy existing governing variables'. In other words teaching becomes a means of control, not development. More importantly, it is embedded in the many training courses for teachers which teach self-reliance and self-sufficiency, and in school cultures where the sharing of problems and issues may be seen as signs of weakness.

Since that time Donald Schon in particular has described teachers as needing also to engage in 'reflection on action' in order to review their teaching from a distance. Others add the need for teachers to engage in reflection 'about' the action (Fullan and Hargreaves, 1992). Argyris and Schon (1974) stress the need from time to time to move to 'double loop' learning in which intentions and practices in teaching are raised to an explicit, publicly accessible level; and others advocate action research as a powerful means of achieving this. My own research through extended classroom observation, analysis and evaluation of in-service professional development in primary and secondary schools over a number of years provides empirical support for the widespread existence of single loop learning and the benefits to be derived through reflection on teaching (Day 1981, 1985, 1990, 1993).

The term 'reflective practitioner' has become a buzz word in the education of teachers and needs to be unpacked. There is a continuum within which there are levels of reflection which require more, or less, thoughtful exploration by teachers (Elliott, 1991; Grundy, 1994). Reflective and non-reflective practitioners do not exist as two fundamentally irreconcilable groups. I have noted elsewhere that reflection is a necessary but not sufficient condition for learning. Confrontation by self or others must occur. It is the headteacher's role to ensure opportunities for this to be effective. These others must be skilled, trusted colleagues who are knowledgeable about and experienced in reflection in, on and about the action and who are supported within a culture of collaboration and a leadership which is prepared to deal positively with the very real constraints of time and the control ethos of bureaucracy (Day, 1993).

Investing in the school's culture

How, then, may headteachers contribute to the professional development lives of teachers, the greatest asset of the school? Crowther and Postle (1991) left no doubt about the importance of their role as leaders of professional development: 'if teachers are to perform the highly complex and responsible roles that will be required of them in Australia's short-term future, their own ongoing education must be revamped in terms of the value placed upon it, the approaches used, and the assumption of responsibility for it' (p 1).

The report concluded by highlighting the importance of the principal's role in this.

> To the extent that principals insist that professional growth be viewed as an ongoing, long-term process, teachers will feel a sense of security and personal identity that will contribute to their sense of professional worth. On the other hand, where principals fail to demonstrate leadership in these areas, the perceptions of teachers regarding professional development tend to be marked by a degree of futility and cynicism.
>
> (Crowther and Postle, 1991, p 96)

Grundy has suggested that educational improvement should not be regarded solely as the responsibility of the individual teacher, that 'the responsibilities of "the school" for improving the educational opportunities afforded to its students must also be understood as being greater than the aggregated responsibilities of the individual teachers who are part of the unit', that 'we need to understand that responsibility for the quality of education is… a matter for the school, not just for the individual teacher' (Grundy, 1994, p 24). She refers to the work of Baker and Proudfoot (1989) in New South Wales schools in Australia. They found that:

- the culture of the school is a key factor which influences student outcomes;
- structures which support interactive social relationships... can create a sense of ownership and commitment;
- the dynamics of school improvement involve a process of change at individual and organisational levels;
- leading and managing change is a developmental, reflexive process involving knowledge of alternative models of schooling, technical skills and expertise, intuition and experience.   (cited in Grundy, 1994, pp 26–27)

There are clues here which point to the key areas with which headteachers must be concerned. In setting the scene or creating the conditions for professional development they are in the business of shaping and working with school culture, creating structures in which teachers and children can learn effectively, and managing change. Moreover, they will be expected to call upon knowledge, skills, intuition and experience in order to achieve this. This is no small challenge for those who already may feel frayed around the edges as a result of persistent and increasing demands made upon them over the years at a time when, for some, energy levels may be declining and health, family and a sense of mortality are increasingly important factors in their consciousness.

Knowing, communicating and sharing philosophy

A prerequisite for effective headship must be the possession of a personal professional philosophy which some have called vision. Writing about his own personal philosophy, Chris McDonnell, headteacher of a primary school of 350 pupils and 15 staff in a semi-rural residential area 25 miles north of Birmingham, and a teacher of 26 years standing, had this to say:

> Schools, I believe, are about people... It is the formation and nourishment of this 'community of interest' I regard as pivotal to the task of the head of a school... A school, and especially a primary school, is a focal point for a community that may have little else in common. Families who happen to live in the same area, but who do not necessarily mix socially or through occupation, come together as their children start school. This is their new shared ground where, for a specific reason (the supported education of their children), they come day by day and begin to form new relationships. The head, therefore, has to foster and support such growth... The signals sent out by a school to its local community determine very quickly the perception that community has of the experience we call 'education'. We can reinforce a stated aim of supportive education, with parents and teachers

116

exercising a partnership role, or we can drive a deep wedge between home and school and from our particular standpoints view each other with deep suspicion. My perception of the task the head's role demands, therefore, goes beyond mere concern for academic progress. Because children bring to school each day the cultural fragment that, for them, is home, the joys and strains of family relationships, the comfort or hardship of their homes, I find it difficult to see how their circumstances can be ignored if the school is to be a co-operative agent with their parents in their education. We are not filling stations, in spite of recent legislation. The concern a head has for the pastoral needs of pupils and their families should also be shared by the staff of the school, for it is they who, day to day, put into daily practice the agreed philosophy of the school. A head can dream of an educational Nirvana from within the confines of an office, and there the dream remains unless it is translated effectively into good classroom practice by the teaching staff… The time spent chatting with staff (very often about matters far removed from education) is not wasted: it is part of the relationship web that enables professional exchange to take place in an effective and meaningful manner ... Unless both pupils and staff come to school in the morning with an understanding that each is valued first and foremost as a person, the quality of the experiences of that day will be diminished. The value of the person must be recognised by the society in which that person operates. The resulting alienation when such value is not recognised can give rise to frustration and resentment for the pupil, and disillusionment in the teacher. Both learner and teacher are engaged in an interactive partnership, the quality of which determines the success of the classroom experience.

(Mortimore and Mortimore, 1993, pp 5–7. Reprinted with permission from Paul Chapman Publishing Ltd)

This lengthy extract illustrates the importance to leadership of self-knowledge, of clarifying what is important, of continuing to revisit and retell core beliefs and values. It is a recognition that leading involves interaction of the head and heart.

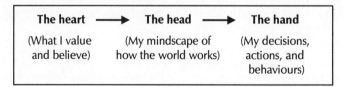

The heart ➝	The head ➝	The hand
(What I value and believe)	(My mindscape of how the world works)	(My decisions, actions, and behaviours)

Figure 7.1 *Interaction between the head and the heart of leadership (Sergiovanni, 1992, p.8)*

Visions must be created, communicated and maintained. They are socially constructed. They are not abstract. Vision is part of the daily life of the school, the result of a process.

Vision is a central theme of school improvement and school culture studies world-wide over recent years (Pettigrew, 1979; Bormann, 1983; Wilson and Corbett, 1983; Herriott and Firestone, 1984; Hallinger and Murphy, 1985; Louis and Miles, 1990), but it is only relatively recently that this has come to be seen as an important aspiration of headteachers and teachers.

A recent research study of professional culture in nine primary schools in Belgium found that 'a vision is not created by leaders but is developed collectively through action and reflection' (Staessens and Vandenburghe, 1994, p 193).

The researchers were also able to identify high and low vision schools.

High and low vision schools

High vision

● High degree of self-awareness	● High degree of awareness of common goal
● Communication about vision sharing	● Principal as team member who supports activities leading to shared vision
● Daily interventions by principal to reinforce expectations and creation of shared vision	● Continuous reflection and assessment (dailiness as a strategy to increase the perceptions of vision, Manassee, 1985)
● Conflicts not experienced as negative	● Platforms for reflection on vision make it easier to respond to externally imposed innovation

Low Vision

● Communication with principal superficial, marked by conflict sometimes	● Principals' expectations unknown
● Principals not considered as team member etc	

Figure 7.2 *High and low vision schools (based on Staessens and Vandenburghe, 1994)*

The everyday conditions of schooling often mean that headteachers spend a disproportionate amount of time coping with the immediate demands of their job. Yet if they lose sight of why they are doing it they may have an unclear view of what is really important to them. This applies equally to classroom teachers. Personal mastery goes beyond competence and skills. It involves continual clarification and questioning of purpose and learning to see current reality more clearly.

> Organisations intent on building shared visions continually encourage members to develop their personal visions. If people don't have their own vision, all they can do is 'sign up' for someone else's. The result is compliance, never commitment. On the other hand, people with a strong sense of personal direction can join together to create a powerful synergy toward what I/we truly want. (Senge, 1990, p 211)

Developing a moral commitment

Eraut argues convincingly that 'it is the moral and professional accountability of teachers which should provide the main motivation for their continuing professional development.' He suggests further that being a professional practitioner implies:

- a moral commitment to serve the interests of students by reflection on their well-being and their progress and deciding how best it can be fostered or promoted;
- a professional obligation to review periodically the nature and effectiveness of one's practice in order to improve the quality of one's management, pedagogy and decision-making;
- a professional obligation to continue to develop one's practical knowledge both by personal reflection and through interaction with others.

(Eraut, 1993)

The task of contributing to the shaping of what people become morally – and this applies equally to lecturers in higher education – attracts many whose motives are idealistic (Goodlad, 1990) and altruistic (Lortie, 1975). Thus, 'many teachers have a moral vision, a moral sense, and a moral motive however mixed up they may be in any individual person' (Sockett, 1993, p 14).

Teaching, then, has an essentially moral purpose in the sense that it is always concerned with the betterment or good of pupils (Noddings, 1987; Sockett, 1989, 1989a, 1993; Elbaz, 1992), just as headship is always concerned with the betterment or good of teachers. What is deemed as good will, of course, vary across cultures and individuals. What is clear, though, is that professional development opportunities must provide support for classroom pedagogy that goes far beyond the mechanics of teaching.

Yet increasingly the argument has been made that, with limited financial resources, professional development opportunities can only be supported centrally where they can be seen to relate directly to the needs identified nationally or by schools themselves. The net effect of this is that there has been a growth in school-based work and short courses designed for particular purposes despite the longstanding criticism that this will lead to parochialism (Henderson and Perry, 1981). There has been a decline in full-time students registering for courses in institutions of higher education. (These have themselves been criticised for not being sufficiently relevant to school need.) In those areas where there is a tradition of collaboration between higher education, schools and LEAs (which, for example, involves joint planning meetings to design in-service work, needs identification groups consisting of LEA, school and higher education representatives, visits to schools by higher education colleagues and vice versa) there have been moves towards more resource-led in-service training in which work is commissioned by schools whose role becomes that of purchaser. Contracts are put out to tender and 'value for money' in the limited short-term economical sense of numbers and costs may become the governing factor. However, in terms of the effectiveness of professional development:

> the real crunch comes in the relationship between these new programmes or policies and the thousands of subjective realities embedded in people's individual and organisational contexts and their personal histories. How these subjective realities are addressed or ignored is crucial for whether potential change becomes meaningful at the level of individual use and effectiveness. (Fullan, 1982, p 35)

It follows that all teachers should be encouraged to recognise their responsibilities as change agents in the classroom with moral purposes, and that these, collectively, shape the culture of the school:

> Cultures get changed in a thousand small ways, not by dramatic announcements from the boardroom. If we wait until top management gives leadership to the change we want to see we miss the point. For us to have any hope that our own preferred future will come to pass, we provide the leadership. (Block, 1987, pp 97–8)

Schein (1985) defined culture as 'the deeper level of basic assumptions and beliefs that are shared by members of an organisation, that operate unconsciously, and that define in a basic 'taken for granted' fashion an organisation's view of itself and its environment' (p 6). We sometimes call it ethos. It will affect and be affected by its leaders in particular and will therefore need to be actively managed in rational and non-rational ways. For example, whilst it is agreed that one characteristic of effective schools is goal consensus, the standard means of attempting to achieve this tend to be rational – discussions, formally documented statements, evaluation and review procedures. However, this is not enough. Hallinger and Murphy (1985) distinguish between cognitive goals (specific statements about desired results) and cathartic goals which concern the mission of the school, and describe the organisation's core or primary values. These non-rational goals act as a source of identification and motivation for staff, giving meaning to their work, binding them to the organisation (Staessens and Vandenburghe 1994, p 188). Thus, a vital function of leaders is to manage both rational and non-rational goals in their daily interactions with colleagues (management by wandering about is part of this).

Being the right kind of leader

A range of terms has been applied to leadership through the years. Some readers may identify with autocratic, democratic or *laisser-faire*, others will aspire to transactional, others to an educative approach – and still others to being transformative leaders. The official language of management outside schools leads us to believe that:

> Leaders are characters who single-handedly pull and push organisational members forward by the force of their personality, bureaucratic clout, and political know-how. Leaders must be decisive. Leaders must be forceful. Leaders must have vision. Leaders must successfully manipulate events and people, so that vision becomes reality. Leaders, in other words, must lead.
>
> (Sergiovanni, 1992, p 119)

Even some of the more recent literature, whilst admitting to the complexity of leadership, nevertheless remains within the old paradigm of leading from the front: 'The new manager... will not be a classical, hierarchically oriented bureaucrat but a customised version of Indiana Jones: proactive; entrepreneurial; communicating in various languages; able to inspire, motivate and persuade subordinates, superiors, colleagues and outside constituents' (cited in Beare, 1989, p 19).

The criticism that single-word descriptors or classifications of leadership fail to capture its complexity or the crucial role played by experience and intuition is supported in Australia by the work of Duignan (1987) and Duignan and Macpherson (eds) (1992) and through examples of research in elementary schools in America (Sergiovanni, 1992), Belgium (Staessens and Vandenburghe, 1994) and elsewhere. In England Southworth, reflecting on his experiences as a researcher in primary school projects over a five-year period, found that successful 'cultures of collaboration' rested upon four intersecting beliefs:

● individuals should be valued;
● since individuals are inseparable from the groups of which they are part, groups should be fostered and valued;
● the most effective way of promoting these values is by developing a sense of mutual security;
● fostering openness amongst staff.   (Southworth, 1993, p 75)

The majority of definitions of leadership have been based on: (1) a fallacy; (2) an omission; (3) a failure to recognise that changing organisational contexts will affect how leaders lead.

The fallacy is that good leadership is a cognitive process involving rational behaviour – characterised by school development plans and target setting. It is the separation of the head from the heart.

The omission is that of the central part that the moral dimension must play. Writing about teacher education and the teaching profession, John Wilson had this to say about classroom practice (which applies equally to leadership practice):

Moral qualities are directly relevant to any kind of classroom practice: care for the pupils, enthusiasm for the subject, conscientiousness, determination, willingness to cooperate with colleagues and a host of others. Nobody, at least on reflection, really believes that effective teaching – let alone effective education – can be reduced to a set of skills; it requires certain dispositions of character. The attempt to avoid the question of what these dispositions are by employing pseudo-practical terms like 'competence' or 'professional' must fail.   (Wilson, 1993, p 113)

Finally, leaders must now operate within a changing context in which the traditional dominant relationship between schools and the public is moving to one of more equal partnership. As schools move towards a more decentralised situation, independence and isolation (called by some, autonomy) are being replaced by co-operation, with an emphasis on school as community.

Developing critical communities

Professional development should present opportunities for teachers to escape being prisoners in their own classroom by combining action and reflection. One means of achieving less isolation is through the active encouragement of critical friendships which may be defined as practical partnerships entered voluntarily, based upon a relationship between equals and rooted in a common task or shared concern. They can be a means of establishing links with one or more colleagues from inside or outside the school as well as assisting in processes of learning and change so that ideas, perceptions, values and understandings may be shared through the mutual disclosures of feelings, hopes and fears. Critical friendships (I prefer this term to that of coach, since it is based upon co-equal relationships) can serve to decrease isolation and increase the possibilities of moving through stages of reflection to confrontation of thinking and practice. Reflection in itself will not necessarily lead to self-confrontation (Day, 1993a) and self-confrontation may need skilled support to be translated into new action. On one's own 'one will only see what one is ready to see, one will only learn what is on the edge of the consciousness of what one already knows' (Thompson, 1984).

In terms of the appraisal of classroom practice, for example, a critical friend may establish and sustain a responsive, mutually acceptable dialogue through which situations will be created in which the teacher is obliged to reflect systematically on practice.

The advantages of critical friends (from inside or outside the school) are that, providing they are skilled and trusted, they can:

1. lighten the energy and time loads for observation (enable teacher to carry on teaching, maintain his or her duties);
2. be used to check against bias in self-reporting, and to assist in more lengthy processes of self-evaluation;
3. offer, where appropriate, comparisons with classroom practice elsewhere;
4. move freely and see the curriculum in action;
5. focus in on an agreed issue or area of concern, eg small group task work;
6. contribute to policy development;
7. act as a resource which teachers, departments and schools may use at times appropriate to the needs which they perceive (based upon Day *et al*, 1990).

Collegiality, contract making, entitlements and critical friendships are all elements within professional development schemes which support teacher autonomy and reinforce a sense of responsibility by affirming confidence in teachers' professionalism.

In order to operationalise critical friendships, schools will have to engage in a form of contracting. This is not intended to be a legalistic process. Agreements (a softer, more humane word than contracts) are, of course, often made informally between teachers and increasingly now more formally under school development plans. Many teachers will have experienced the value of being able to share thoughts, practices and feelings with one or more trusted colleagues. The importance of agreeing contracts is such, however, that it may be necessary to document them for use as *aides-mémoire*. Written or at least explicit verbal contracts can do much to clarify mutual expectations as to goals and methods.

Promoting personal development profiles

The means by which visions as well as craft may be created, developed, reviewed and renewed will be the personal development profile, a learning contract between the teacher, the community and the school. It will guarantee for the community that the teacher will continue throughout a career to provide the knowledge, skills, commitment, care and vision appropriate to the needs of the pupils. It will guarantee for the school that the teacher will fully participate in maintaining its growth as a learning organisation; and it will guarantee for the teacher that both school and community will provide tangible support and genuine commitment and encouragement for his/her development.

Personal development profiles must be designed so that they foster the development of teachers as whole persons throughout their careers, recognising that, 'There is a natural connection between a person's work life and all other aspects of life' (Senge, 1990, p 307) and, therefore, that personal mastery in all aspects of life must be supported; recognising that teachers are not technicians, but that teaching is bound up with their lives, their histories, the kind of persons they have been, and have become. They will, therefore, contain but not be dominated by competences. Because profiles will be lifelong and because teacher development, like that of children, will relate to individual history as well as present circumstance, they will need to be based upon principles of differentiation, balance, and continuity and progression and a view of learning as interdependent as well as independent. They will allow, at different times in a teaching career, for the kinds of learning and development opportunities which might be predominantly focused upon the personal need (of the teacher as human being), and long-term professional need (of the teacher as a member of a learner community of professionals), as well as classroom practitioner and member of a particular school with needs. The creation of personal development planning support mechanisms over a career which involve opportunities for both the enhancement of job skills and the development of personal and organisational vision are not simply desirable for teachers in the twenty-first century. They are essential.

There are six principles which underpin the notion of personal development planning.

1. teacher development which supports teacher learning is lifelong, continuing if not continuous;
2. it must be self-managed and, at certain times, it will involve others – teachers cannot be self-sufficient;
3. it must be supported and resourced;
4. it will be in the interests of the teacher and the school, though not always simultaneously;
5. there must be an accounting process;
6. whilst every teacher has a right and responsibility to engage in development over a career, it must be differentiated according to individual need.

Conclusion

The one constant of leadership in the past, present and future is that working with people (big and small) is always at the centre of the job. So, in the end, the leadership that counts is the kind that touches people differently (Sergiovanni, 1992, p 120), a morally based leadership – a form of stewardship. This is the centrepiece of three interdependent leadership roles:

- designer: promoting systemic visions and values, supporting effective learning processes;
- steward: of the shared vision, the collective understanding of purpose which binds staff together;
- teacher: who helps teachers restructure their views of reality to see beyond the superficial conditions and events into the underlying causes of problems.   (Senge, 1990, p 12)

The leader within these roles is one who by skilled intervention, clear vision, the application of principles of social justice and a pragmatic recognition that the best way of learning is through motivation and commitment, influences others to achieve mutually agreed upon purposes for the organisation:

The principal for the next decade must remember that he or she is a person whose work as an educational leader is, first, foremost, and always with persons – persons who are physical, intellectual, spiritual, emotional, and sound beings ... As a person in a community, the principal of the 1990s and beyond will be concerned with several things. Recognising that communities and their occupants flourish in caring, nurturing environments, these principals will seek to utilise a caring ethic to guide their decisions and actions ... They will view teachers, students, parents, and others as colleagues, partners, co-learners, and (where possible) friends. And they will relish the challenge of working with these groups to [build] a community of learners in which all persons can flourish. (Beck and Murphy, 1993, p 195)

'Servant leadership', being a leader of leaders, brings stewardship responsibilities to the heart of the headteacher's role. It may involve, for some, 'letting go of outlived professional identities' in order to develop their schools into those with characteristics of shared decision-making; decentralised, school-based management processes; and greater professional autonomy expressed in redefined roles, rules, relationships and responsibilities (Bredeson, 1993). For some this will be a challenge. It will certainly create a particular set of conditions for professional development. In research from English primary schools, effective headteachers relied upon three professional attributes:

- they saw their work as being concerned with developing their staff. They were educators;
- they were patient-tenacious, assiduous, persistent in striving to see their beliefs put into practice across the school;
- they could synthesise and link ideas and information. (Southworth, 1993)

Leaders of professional development, then, work on both instrumental and expressive levels, recognising that 'management which adopts an unyielding approach and takes no account of human creativity is not only mechanical and inflexible but is also inappropriate for developing and improving schools' (Southworth, 1993).

Research internationally is unequivocal in telling us that effective leaders are those who make a difference in the professional development lives of colleagues who put service first. Such leaders are those who possess a personal philosophy which they communicate and revisit; and who dedicate themselves to building a collectively owned culture; such leaders communicate and daily reinforce the message that teachers count, and that their needs as professionals are complex, continuing, and demand the application of principles of differentiation, continuity and progression, coherence and balance over a career.

Such leaders know their staff as well as their pupils, and are receptive to their learning needs. Such leaders aim to build learning-enriched schools for staff as well as pupils. They bear the flag of the new professionalism of leadership which regards making a difference in the lives of colleagues as of paramount importance to improving the quality of life in schools.

References

Argyris, C and Schon, D A (1974) *Theory in Practice: Increasing Professional Effectiveness*, Jossey-Bass, New York.

Baker, R and Proudfoot, C (1989) *Change and Context: case studies of secondary schools*, New South Wales Department of Education, Sydney.

Beare, H (1989) 'Educational administration in the 1990s', paper given at the National Conference of the Australian Council for Educational Administration, University of New England, Armidale, NSW.

Beck, L G and Murphy, J (1993) *Understanding the Principalship: Metaphorical Themes 1920s–1990s*, Teachers College Press, New York.

Block, P (1987) *The Empowered Manager*, Jossey-Bass, San Francisco.

Bormann, E G (1983) 'Symbolic convergence: organisational communication and culture' in Putman, L L and Pacanowsky, M E (eds) *Communication and Organisations: An Interpretive Approach*, Sage, Beverly Hills, pp 99–122.

Bredeson, P V (1993) 'Letting go of outlived professional identities: a study of role transition and the role strain for principals in restructured schools', *Educational Administration Quarterly* 29, 1, pp 34–68.

Broadfoot, P and Osborn, M (1991) 'French lessons: comparative perspectives on what it means to be a teacher', *Oxford Studies in Comparative Education* 1, pp 69–88.

Clark, C M and Yinger, R J (1977) 'Research on teacher thinking', *Curriculum Inquiry* 7, 4, pp 279–304.

Cowan, B and Wright, N (1990) 'Two million days lost', *Education* 2 February, pp 117–18.

Crowther, F and Postle, G (1991) *The Praxis of Professional Development: Setting Directions for Brisbane Catholic Education*, Brisbane Catholic Education Centre, Brisbane.

Day, C (1981) *Classroom-based In-service Teacher Education: The Development and Evaluation of a Client-centred Model*, Occasional Paper 9, University of Sussex Education Area, Brighton.

Day, C (1985) 'Professional learning and research intervention: an action research perspective', *British Educational Research Journal* 11, 2, pp 133–51.

Day, C (1990) 'The development of teachers' personal practical knowledge through school-based curriculum development projects' in Day, C, Pope, M and Denicolo, P (eds) *Insights into Teachers' Thinking and Practice*, Falmer Press, London, pp 213–39.

Day, C (1993) *Research and the Continuing Professional Development of Teachers*, inaugural lecture, School of Education, University of Nottingham, November.

Day, C (1993a) 'Reflection: a necessary but not sufficient condition for professional development', *British Educational Research Journal* 19, 1, pp 83–93.

Day, C, Whitaker, P and Johnston, D (1990) *Managing Primary Schools in the 1990s: A Professional Development Approach*, Paul Chapman, London.

Duignan, P A (1987) 'Leaders and culture builders', *Unicorn* 13, 4, pp 208–13.

Duignan, P A and Macpherson, R J S (eds) (1992) *Educative Leadership: A Practical Theory for New Administrators and Managers*, Falmer Press, London.

Elbaz, F (1992) Hope, Attentiveness and Caring for Difference: The Moral Voice, *Teaching and Teacher Education* Vol.8, No.5/6, pp 421–32.

Elliott, J (1991) *Action Research for Educational Change*, Open University Press, Buckingham.

Eraut, M E (1993) 'Developing professional knowledge within client-centred orientation', unpublished paper, University of Sussex.

Fullan, M G (1982) *The Meaning of Education Change*, Teachers College Press, New York.

Fullan, M and Hargreaves, A (eds) (1992) *Teacher Development and Educational Change*, Falmer, London.

Gilroy, P and Day, C (1993) 'The erosion of INSET in England and Wales: analysis and proposals for a redefinition', *Journal of Education for Teaching* 19, 2, pp 141–57.

Goodlad, J (1990) *Teachers for Our Nations' Schools*, Jossey-Bass, San Francisco.

Grundy, S (1994) 'Action research at the school level: possibilities and problems', *Educational Action Research: An International Journal* 2, 1, pp 23–37.

Hallinger, P and Murphy, J (1985) 'Defining an organizational mission in schools', paper given at the annual general meeting of the American Educational Research Association, Chicago.

Henderson, E S and Perry, G W (1981) *Change and Development in Schools*, McGraw-Hill, London.

Herriott, R E and Firestone, W A (1984) 'Two images of schools as organisations: a refinement and elaboration', *Educational Administration Quarterly* 20, 4, pp 41–57.

Keddie, N (1971) 'Classroom knowledge' in Young, M F D (ed) *Knowledge and Control*, Collier-Macmillan, London.

Little, J W (1990) 'The persistence of privacy: autonomy and initiative in teachers' professional relations', *Teachers College Record* 91, 4, pp 509–36.

Lortie, D C (1975) *Schoolteacher: A Sociological Study*, University of Chicago Press.

Louden, L W and Browne, R K (1993) 'Developments in education policy in Australia' in Beare, H and Lowe Boyd, W (eds) *Restructuring Schools: An International Perspective on the Movement to Transform the Control and Performance of Schools*, Falmer Press, London.

Louis, S K and Miles, M B (1990) *Improving the Urban High School: What Works and Why*, Teachers College Press, New York.

Manassee, A L (1985) Improving conditions for principal effectiveness: Policy implications of research, *Elementary School Journal* 85, 3.

McLaughlin, M W and Marsh, D D (1979) 'Staff development and school change' in Lieberman, A and Miller, L (eds) *Staff development: New Demands, New Realities, New Perspectives*, Teachers College Press, New York.

Mortimore, P, Sammons, P, Ecob, R, Stoll, L and Lewis, D (1988) *School Matters: the Junior Years*, Open Books, Salisbury.

Mortimore, P and Mortimore, J (eds) (1993) *The Primary Head: Roles, Responsibilities and Reflections*, Paul Chapman, London.

Newton, D P and Newton, L D (1994) 'The infamous five: a survey of the use made on non-contact days', *British Journal of In-Service Education*, Triangle Press, Oxford.

Noddings, N (1987) 'Fidelity in teaching, teacher education, and research for teaching', *Harvard Educational Review* 56, 4, pp 495–510.

O'Donohue, T A, Brooker, R and Aspland, T (1993) 'Harnessing teachers' dilemmas for professional development: a Queensland initiative', *British Journal of In-Service Education* 19, 2, pp 14–20.

Pascale, P (1990) *Managing on the Edge*, Touchstone, New York.

Pettigrew, A (1979) 'On studying organizational culture', *Administrative Sciences Quarterly* 24, 4, pp 570–82.

Rutter, M, Maughan, B, Mortimore, P and Ouston, J (1979) *Fifteen Thousand Hours: Secondary Schools And Their Effects On Children*, Open Books, Wells.

Rosenholtz, S J (1989) *Teachers' Workplace: The Social Organisation of Schools*, Longman, New York.

Sachs, J and Logan, L (1990) 'Control or development? A study of in-service education', *Journal of Curriculum Studies* 22, 5, pp 473–81.

Schein, E H (1985) *Organizational Culture and Leadership: A Dynamic View*, Jossey-Bass, San Francisco.

Schon, D A (1992) 'The theory of inquiry: Dewey's legacy to education', *Curriculum Inquiry* 22, 2, pp 119–39.

Senge, P (1990) *The Fifth Discipline*, Doubleday, New York.

Sergiovanni, T (1992) *Moral Leadership*, Jossey-Bass, San Francisco.

Sockett, H (1989) 'Research, practice and professional aspiration within teaching', *Journal of Curriculum Studies* 21, 2, p 15.

Sockett, H (1989a) 'A moral epistemology of practice', *Cambridge Journal of Education* 19, 1, p 15.

Sockett, H (1993) *The Moral Base for Teacher Professionalism*, Teachers College Press, New York.

Southworth, G (1993) 'School leadership and school development: reflections from research', *School Organisation* 13, 1, pp 73–87.

Staessens, K and Vandenburghe, R (1994) 'Vision as a core component in school culture', *Journal of Curriculum Studies* 26, 2, pp 187–200.

Thompson, A (1984) 'The use of video as an observation tool' in Thompson, L and Thompson, A (eds), *What Learning Looks Like: Helping Individual Teachers to become more effective*, Schools Council Programme 2, Longman, Harlow.

Wilson, B D and Corbett, H (1983) 'Organisation and change: the effects of school linkages on the quantity of implementation', *Educational Administration Quarterly* 19, 4, pp 85–104.

Wilson, J (1993) *Reflection and Practice: Teacher Education and the Teaching Profession*, Althouse Press, University of Western Ontario.

Chapter 8

Values as Central to Competent Professional Practice
Bertie Everard

The importance and nature of values

> Values are at the heart of the human condition (both personally and corporately, and that includes organisations). They are the engines that drive our lives.
>
> (Stewart, 1990)

Values therefore lie also at the heart of education. John White describes early education as 'the formation of dispositions', its purpose being 'to shape the tendencies and propensities with which children are born into settled dispositions of certain sorts. We can think of this as bringing their actions under the sway of certain values' (White, 1990). Even in early education children are helped to make value judgements for themselves.

A value is a statement about how the person who holds the value sees the world. In one sense, values are closely linked with what people believe – beliefs being statements of personal conviction. In another sense, values relate to truth; they are self-evident, derived from insight, and in line with reason, honestly used. As such, values are inescapable: we do not choose them; they claim us. They involve a sense of inner obligation (Watson, 1987). Values help to inform our opinions, our professional judgements, and undergird our attitudes and predispositions. At the risk of intellectualising these relationships, it may be said that the values we espouse can powerfully influence our behaviour (response to any situation).

Collier (1993) defines values in terms of the tacit, often unverbalised driving forces or aspirations in people's lives which determine where they will direct their effort and energies, and to which in their inner selves they attach

131

the greatest value or importance – summed up in the biblical saying 'Where your treasure is, there will your heart be also.' Thus he differentiates between tacit valuations which are felt in one's bones and express some orientation at the core of one's personality and verbalised, abstract statements which arise from intellectual discussion and academic debate.

Collier (1994) also distinguishes between, on the one hand, values that form the basis of any civilised community and, on the other hand, forms of behaviour in which these basic values are expressed. The former, he says, would include truthfulness, dependability for one's word, moral courage, sense of fair play, law-abidingness, concern or respect for other individuals and concern for the common good. The latter are typified by the statement of comprehensive school values (Stewart 1990) reproduced in Figure 8.1 later on p 134.

Beck (1990) introduces the notion that values are grounded in human well-being, arising out of basic human needs and tendencies; they are inherent in human nature and the human condition, and are what ultimately make life seem good and worthwhile.

However defined, the importance of people developing a sense of, and a set of, values can hardly be overstated. Watson (1987) argues for an impressive commitment in schools to education in beliefs and values, amounting to some four hours a week. Values are an integral part of individual personhood and collectively of a culture (the web or fabric of customs, meanings, relationships and values that characterise a given community or organisation); both have a major effect on individual, organisational and societal behaviour. Two well-known studies, one from education and one from business, serve to illustrate this. Rutter *et al* in *Fifteen Thousand Hours* (1979) showed that the culture or ethos of a school, the 'hidden curriculum', has a greater effect on pupil behaviour than does the academic curriculum. Peters and Waterman in *In Search of Excellence* (1982) showed that American firms in the top league are values driven: the culture is a major determinant of behaviour leading to success.

These seminal studies have recently been further strengthened by a study undertaken by the NFER for the National Commission on Education (NEC) (*Learning to Succeed*, 1993). This confirmed that a school's ethos has a powerful influence on the effectiveness of teaching and learning:

> An ethos which is conducive to good morale and high expectations is not a matter of accident, but a product of good management at every level ... Headteachers, their senior staff and governing bodies have a crucial role in developing and communicating values which will encourage a sense of cohesion, shared purpose and commitment throughout the school.

> (NEC, 1993, p 153)

The Scottish Inspectorate has developed 'ethos indicators' to assess how well this is done.

Schooling as a way of imparting values

The shaping of values, whether through nurture by parents, the professional practice of the teacher, the leadership of the head (or indeed of a chief executive, sovereign, president or prime minister), is an exceedingly powerful instrument in human affairs. Schooling is the dominant means by which the state (through a framework of legislation, advisory circulars and the National Curriculum) and the local community (eg through education authorities and Standing Advisory Councils on Religious Education) deliberately set out to cause young people to learn certain values. Legislation such as the 1986 Education (No 2) Act, which prescribes the duties and composition of governing bodies, also influences the way in which it is decided what values are to be promoted and how.

The key provisions are enshrined in the 1988 Education Reform Act. Clause 1(2) states:

The curriculum of a maintained school satisfies the requirements of this section if it is a balanced and broadly based curriculum which –
(a) promotes the spiritual, moral, cultural, mental and physical development of pupils at the school and of society; and
(b) prepares such pupils for the opportunities, responsibilities and experiences of adult life.

Note that a school must by law promote the spiritual, moral and cultural development not only of pupils, but also (presumably mainly through them) of society at large. This is a challenging, value-laden responsibility for schools to take on. Although it is sometimes dismissed as mere rhetoric, Clause 1 is a valuable and meaningful philosophical statement, with important implications for professional practice in education.

In the past, the word 'instruction' was commonly used to describe the pedagogical process whereby societal values were imparted to children; they were expected, for example, to memorise the Ten Commandments. More recently schools have tried to shape children's values by relying more on an acculturisation process akin to osmosis. The school's values and aims are capable of both revealing and shaping the so-called hidden curriculum (see Figure 8.1 below).

Values in comprehensive schools

A comprehensive school will demonstrate through PERSONS and STRUCTURES that it is:

1. An extended COMMUNITY OF PERSONS where each member is accorded the RESPECT and DIGNITY which are the RIGHT of all persons and the opportunity to SERVE OTHERS.

2. Where the EQUAL VALUE of ALL PERSONS as PERSONS is recognised.

3. Where it is a PRIVILEGE and RESPONSIBILITY to accept each person and create ACCEPTING COMMUNITIES.

4. Characterised by a spirit of OPENNESS, PARTICIPATION and COOPERATION which recognises the need for AUTHORITY STRUCTURES and where CONFLICT and COMPETITION are experienced and managed as well as HARMONY and COLLABORATION.

5. WHERE there are OPEN, PERMEABLE BOUNDARIES with the WIDER COMMUNITY, local, national and international.

6. Where DIFFERENCE and DIVERSITY are WELCOMED and CELEBRATED within a COMMUNITY which works TOGETHER for the COMMON GOOD.

7. A JUST COMMUNITY where ACCESS, OPPORTUNITY and RESOURCES are seen to be available to ALL with EQUITY and where POSITIVE AFFIRMATION is exercised as some are DISADVANTAGED.

8. A CARING COMMUNITY based on FAIR, UNDERSTANDING COMPASSIONATE and LOVING RELATIONSHIPS.

9. Where RIGHTS and RESPONSIBILITIES have joint emphasis.

10. Where DEVELOPMENT is of the WHOLE PERSON – concepts, knowledge, understanding; attitudes; values; experiences; skills across a spectrum embracing the aesthetic, creative, economic, ethical, linguistic, mathematical, philosophical, physical, political, scientific, social, spiritual, technological for ALL.

11. Where there are HIGH EXPECTATIONS for ALL in the pursuit of EXCELLENCE.

12. Where there is a POSITIVE, CONSTRUCTIVE approach to ALL fostering SELF-BELIEF, a POSITIVE SELF-IMAGE and enabling EMPOWERMENT.

13. Where ALL are ENCOURAGED and able to have an ACTIVE RESPONSIBILITY for and PARTICIPATION in their LEARNING DEVELOPMENT.

14. Where FAIR, FULL, WHOLE-PERSON ASSESSMENT is the RIGHT of ALL.

15. Where there is a PARTNERSHIP with parents, industry and commerce and all who have a legitimate interest in the educational process.

16. Where the LEARNING EXPERIENCE is seen as one part of a process of LIFELONG DEVELOPMENT.

Figure 8.1: *Comprehensive values* (Stewart, 1990)

The management of an organisation's culture is not, of course, confined to schools. Industrial firms deploy sophisticated techniques to induce a culture that promotes safety, quality, customer service, cost cutting and improvement, which causes employees to value underlying aims significantly more than they naturally would (see, for example, Woodcock and Francis, 1989). The conscious shaping of a school's culture (and hence the values of those within it) has likewise become a clear management responsibility for the head and the governing body (Beck, 1990; Everard, 1992b).

The need for headteacher training

Heads, however, are ill equipped for this responsibility, according to the findings of the National Education Assessment Centre Project established in 1990 (Green 1993). Assessment of 100 heads showed them to be weak on 'educational values', ie not possessing a well-reasoned educational philosophy and receptive to new ideas and change, and lacking confidence in handling values issues. This was confirmed at a meeting with a group of HMIs in the summer of 1991. The project identified the need for heads and governors to explore values in relation to the doctrines of the great educators and to trends in our cultural traditions. Few heads had had any training in the area of educational values and the processes of valuing (ie reflecting on, identifying, articulating, and perhaps asserting and celebrating, values). Newly appointed heads in particular needed to be able to identify the prevailing values among the school's stakeholders – a process that might be called 'values mapping'. Moreover, there are at least 11 other values processes in which heads and teachers need to be competent, according to Everard (1990b):

- valuing;
- value-consciousness raising;
- values decision-making;
- values shaping;
- adaptation to changing values;
- connecting values to beliefs and behaviour;
- values reconciliation;
- values confrontation;
- measuring value;
- regulation by values;
- values competence development.

National competence standards and management practice

The recognition of the centrality of values in management is reflected in the draft national standards of occupational competence for senior management of all kinds (including school management), which contain functions and units that mention values specifically (Management Charter Initiative (MCI), 1994; my italics below):

B1 Charting the way ahead
Contribute to developing and communicating the mission, objectives, goals, *values* and policies of the organisation and its units.

B1.3 Values
Draw together *values* and policies which guide the way the organisation operates.

B1.4 Buy-in
Consult and negotiate with and generate support amongst management and other stakeholders for the organisation's mission, objectives, goals, *values* and policies.

C3 Culture
C3.3 Values in work
Consult and provide guidance on ways in which *values* are to be expressed in work and working relationships.

The above underlines the clear management responsibility to grasp the process of winning hearts and minds to stated values positions, to make the organisation more effective and above all to stand accountable to the organisation's stakeholders for its general direction.

Collier (1994) identifies three ways in which the head of an educational institution discharges this responsibility: (1) by coercion, (2) by establishing trust and (3) by managing innovation. It is impossible for a head to avoid exerting authority: there has to be a code of law or regulations, specifying sanctions and providing support for civilised values. Coercion, then, is unavoidable to some extent. It is necessary for the head to establish trust by habitually treating people in accordance with these values in personal contacts, formal meetings and on informal occasions. S/he needs to ensure that the system of law is appropriate, effectively promulgated, observed and periodically reviewed. It is important to establish a sense of shared purpose; as Brighouse (1985) puts it: 'The first ingredient of an excellent school, in which relationships are good and learning happens, is a shared value system.' To manage innovation, Collier argues, a head needs to ensure that in-house initiatives are carefully prepared, for institutions are often beset by conservatism, and innovation can strike at value systems in ways that require systematic management (as Everard and Morris (1990) explain).

Ethical responsibilities and values in education

The values-shaping process and its direction should be exposed to careful scrutiny. What values are learned in schools, and how they are inculcated, is not a matter to be left unobserved in the secret garden of the curriculum. Given the potential within a school or a university department of education for what some would regard as social engineering, it is important that there should be some checks and balances in the system. Parents, governors and inspectors all have a monitoring role, although it is not always exercised.

So potent can values education be (sometimes insidiously so) that many teachers are deeply concerned about it; some recoil from any situation in which the conscious shaping of values or beliefs could be construed as indoctrination or social conditioning, lest they be accused of interfering with someone else's personal liberty. They may be comfortable with exploring pupils' values, but not with changing them, which they would regard as tantamount to manipulation. This is one extreme.

Other teachers, and indeed education committees, hold different views. A Christian foundation running a school may see it as entirely right and proper – indeed a duty – for teachers to mould children's value systems and to inculcate particular beliefs, their authority to do so stemming from their religion (Roman Catholic Bishops' Report, 1983). LEAs have been known to seek to erode traditional middle-class values and to replace them with those of the working class or of ethnic minorities (Anderson (ed), 1982). A respected authority on local government, Professor Stewart (1986), writes of the primacy of the political process in determining what is taught in schools, clearly inviting education officers to be agents of political indoctrination if so instructed by elected members. Individual teachers may do so wedded to a particular set of values (eg social versus economic or socialist versus capitalist) which blind them to any merits in the opposing set. This is the opposite extreme.

However, it is a mistake always to think of such value sets as in direct opposition; they can be complementary and orthogonally related – like the warp and weft of a fabric. A strong fabric, like a healthy society, needs both sets of values; citizens have to hold the two sets in a single value system (Everard,1990b).

A code of ethics for teacher professional practice

One of the characteristics of professions is that they usually have a code of ethics or standards of professional practice which uphold the good standing of the profession in the eyes of the public at large. Engineers, social workers, psychologists, accountants, doctors, personnel managers all subscribe to such codes and expect their peers to judge their professional practice by the extent to which they comply with them. In the absence of a General Teaching Council (at least in England and Wales), there is no recognised national code for teachers or heads, although no one would deny that there is an ethical dimension to their practice.

The teaching profession as a whole is noted for collectively espousing certain human values; many of its members are strongly critical of the uncaring values which they think are espoused in business and they deeply deplore attempts to import these into schools. Words like managerialism are often used pejoratively. Teachers tend to regard themselves as bulwarks protecting the young against these questionable values (supposedly encouraged by the state and the media): eg materialism, individualism, consumerism, greed, acquisitiveness, competitiveness, hypocrisy and so on.

Such a 'holier than thou' stance rests on somewhat flimsy foundations; those who have spent substantial periods of their working lives in both industry and education have found that the common stereotypes of professional practice in each sector are often belied by the reality. Industrial managers can be just as caring as headteachers (Everard, 1986). It is not, therefore, a helpful manifestation of such practice for teachers to claim the moral high ground; nor is it a necessary ingredient of professional competence.

What is missing is a nationally accepted code of values to govern the professional practice of teachers and heads and of those who train them. Too many disquieting examples exist of unethical practice (Everard, 1982, 1990b). Not enough is done to define and promote ethical practice. The National Association for Values in Education and Training (NAVET)[1] was set up 'to explore and improve processes involved in education and training by providing opportunities to identify, clarify and apply values in an atmosphere of developing understanding and critical openness' – one of a number of organisations affiliated to the Values Education Council.[2] It is hoped that these bodies will eventually be able to define what constitutes ethical professional practice in dealing with values in an educational context.

Assessing professional competence within the context of values

It is beyond the scope of this chapter to describe in detail the far-reaching developments in the UK of competence-based assessment since about 1987. Readers unfamiliar with these developments are referred to sources such as Everard (1989, 1990, 1991, 1992a), Esp (1993) and Fletcher (1994).

At the time of writing (1995), some 85 per cent of the UK workforce is covered by National Occupational Standards of Competence and the Scottish and National Vocational Qualifications (S/NVQs) derived from them. This national initiative probably represents the biggest single reform of vocational education and training since the Statute of Artificers was enacted in 1563. Already some £75 million of public funds have been spent or earmarked to develop the standards. This UK initiative has been quickly adapted for use in other Commonwealth countries, especially Australia (where standards for teachers exist) and New Zealand (where a single authority regulates all qualifications, vocational, academic and professional).

Despite the many problems which might be expected to accompany such a major reform (Everard, 1990a), most employers and candidates have welcomed it, because it has made vocational qualifications much more relevant to good practice in the workplace. Essentially, performance standards represent a shift from an input-based educational model (filling empty vessels with knowledge and skills) to an output-based model (developing people who can perform in an occupation to the standards expected in employment). Assessment has shifted away from norm towards criterion referencing, which has helped students to answer such questions as 'What is expected of me at work?' and 'How am I judged?'

Contrary to media reports the reforms have not led to a diminution in the status of underpinning knowledge and understanding, where possession of this is essential to competent performance in an occupation. Indeed, such knowledge and understanding, together with the ability to apply it, is an important component of competence, especially at professional levels (Employment Department, 1994b). It would indeed be surprising if this were not so for the growing proportion of the workforce who are classed as 'knowledge workers'.

The ethical dimension and Sport and Recreation education

As noted earlier, another characteristic of professional work is its ethical dimension – the espousal and application of values that inform moral and ethical decisions (Mitchell, 1993). Since the Occupational Standards of Competence initiative was launched, much progress has been made in integrating values into definitions of professional competence and in developing ways of assessing their application. A state-of-the-art report on Ethics in Occupational Standards, NVQs and SVQs was published in 1994 (Employment Department, 1994a). It concludes that: 'there is an immediate need in the context of national standards development and NVQs and SVQs to fully incorporate the ethical dimension of competence in occupational standards.'

It also states that 'Ethical issues cannot be dealt with adequately if they are seen as just a bolt-on extra to what has already been achieved in the standards... The incorporation of ethical issues within occupational standards and in NVQs and SVQs is vital for the credibility of the standards.'

This has been recognised by most of the lead bodies, consisting of employer and employee representatives, which are responsible for developing national occupational standards of competence and related NVQs and SVQs for professional workers. Moreover, the National Council for Vocational Qualifications (NCVQ, 1995) now requires lead bodies to incorporate in national standards aspects of competence such as applying ethical judgements.

Two employment sectors which have pioneered the application of values to assessment of competence are the care sector (health and social services), which introduced a values base unit of competence, and Sport and Recreation. The latter includes outdoor education (OE), making OE teachers, sports teachers and heads of LEA outdoor centres the only educational professionals who can (so far) be assessed to national standards within a values context; consequently, this approach is particularly germane to the subject of this chapter.

The Sport and Recreation Standards have the ethical dimension built into the Performance Criteria (PCs) and Range Statements (RSs), with added emphasis in the Underpinning Knowledge (K) requirements. In addition, for each occupational subsector (such as the OE, training and recreation subsector and the playwork subsector), specific Values Statements were developed by respected technical experts from the subsector and endorsed by the Sport and Recreation Lead Body (SRLB) responsible for the Standards; these reflect the prevailing ethos of the subsector. They form the backcloth against which professional practice is required to be judged.

The cross-sectoral Values Statements for all those who manage facilities within the industry (including heads of OE centres) were developed by the author of this chapter from various sources, such as the Institute of Management's Code of Ethics; they are reproduced in Figure 8.2 (see end of chapter) and are offered as a model which could be readily adapted for use in school management.[3]

A lead body's values are specified as an aspect of knowledge and understanding, ie 'everything people need to have in their heads if they are to perform competently' (Employment Department, 1994b); as such, values can be a mandatory part of NVQs and SVQs. It is, of course, essential that in addition to *possessing* such knowledge of values, NVQ and SVQ candidates must demonstrate that they can apply it in everyday situations – hence the inclusion of values-related PCs in the Standards.

The Values Statements also have another use. The Standards make frequent reference to broadly defined aspects of competence, such as 'recognised good practice', 'appropriateness of activities' and 'socially acceptable ways'. To ensure consistency, candidates and assessors are expected always to interpret such phrases by reference to the relevant Values Statements.

Gaining accreditation for ethical practice

Before a centre can be approved for delivery of SRLB NVQs or SVQs, it must demonstrate that its S/NVQ staff:

1. have taken cognisance of the relevant Values Statements in submitting its written application;
2. comprehend the relevant Values Statements and can explain them, if necessary, to candidates. Because of the abstract language in which the values are expressed, this is particularly important for candidates with a limited command of language;
3. can envisage how good practice (and other such general phrases) can be distinguished from bad practice by reference to a set of values.

In the context of Values Statements it is important to assess not only whether candidates know the right thing to do (ie knowing what the relevant Values Statements are), but also whether they habitually do the right thing in the workplace (Employment Department, 1994a, p 38). In the NVQ system this is achieved by checking candidates' understanding and assessing their performance over a period of time in the workplace.

This performance encompasses:

- what the candidate does himself/herself;
- the candidate's willingness to challenge breaches by others (this is vital in safety matters);
- displaying the intention to apply the relevant values, even if prevented by others;

- heightened values awareness, and the influence of values on work practice;
- ability to analyse situations and courses of action in terms of values, so as to choose ethical behaviour;
- understanding the options available to a candidate facing ethical challenges or dilemmas.

Each of these points is reflected in the PCs, RSs and K specifications. Assessors have to take them into consideration in gaining valid and reliable evidence of performance. All the usual types of evidence can be used for assessing against Values Statements:

- observation of workplace performance;
- reflective accounts of work, recorded in portfolios;
- products of work (eg a centre code of practice);
- work-based projects, simulations and role play;
- case studies and assignments;
- evidence of prior achievement;
- witness testimony;
- oral questioning, including 'what if' interrogation;
- written examinations or tests.

It may be that a candidate's manager does not live up to the centre's code of conduct, and expects the candidate to behave likewise. However, tragedies have occurred because of yielding to this kind of pressure, so it is important to realise that NVQs and SVQs are based on, and are assessed to, *national standards*, not expediency. Hence, at the end of the day, assessors must be prepared not to accredit candidates who only conform to local practice or malpractice. If the assessor observes unethical behaviour that flagrantly infringes the relevant Values Statements, this must always constitute grounds for a decision that the candidate is not yet competent.

Two examples from an OE centre illustrate how Values Statements are applied in practice.

Example 1. A seasonal employee is being assessed against several OE units, including H7 (Arrange for meals and domestic facilities). Whilst the clients are out on a night expedition, he decides to inspect their bunk rooms (inspection of clients' facilities is a mandatory component of competence) and to record this activity in his portfolio. In doing so, however, he steals some money from a drawer, and is caught red-handed by his assessor. Can the assessor sign off the candidate as competent? Why?

Values Statement A7 states: 'Pay due regard to the law and avoid the abuse or misuse of their position'. This enables the general phrase 'good practice' used in the Standards, but not defined, to be specifically interpreted.

Example 2. A centre manager is being assessed for element P6.1 (Develop and improve teams through planning and activities). The candidate's portfolio contains no specific reference to any discussion with the teams about values, although there are several pieces of acceptable evidence of values application by the candidate in relation to other elements. Is the candidate competent? Why?

A Range Statement for the element refers specifically to 'values and ethical standards'. One of the relevant Values Statements reads: 'Ensure that the set of values that govern the conduct of the organisation as a whole extends to and includes the conduct of every member of it'.

Implications for management in education

These examples of the use of values in the assessment of professional competence have been explained at some length because they show the way in which the 'values competence' of teachers in general, and of heads in particular, could be assessed by a trained assessor in the S/NVQ process. Although the education and youth service is probably the largest constituency of the 15 per cent of the UK workforce for whom National Occupational Standards of Competence and associated S/NVQs do not yet exist, it is probably only a matter of time before teachers will have access to such accreditation. The Teacher Training Agency (1994) is already moving in this direction. Hence it is instructive to see how cognate professions are managing this process.

Moreover, despite the lukewarm attitude of the Department for Education towards S/NVQs for teachers, a number of schools and other agencies have been piloting the use of competence-based assessment for those educational professionals in school management occupations (Esp, 1993). The College of Preceptors uses the generic MCI national Standards (without adaptation to the school environment) and awards the associated generic S/NVQs. As noted earlier, these Standards do not have Values Statements, although some values are implicit in the performance criteria (and not always showing a good fit with the school culture) and others are likely to be incorporated when the Standards are revised in 1996. LEAs that have worked with the MCI Standards include Calderdale, Bolton, Tameside and Rochdale – some assisted by Manchester Metropolitan University. The NFER has contextualised the MCI

Standards for school management, but no S/NVQs have been developed therefrom, and no Values Statements have been added. NFER has used these Standards in the consortium of 14 LEAs known as School Management South.

Although all these pilot experiments with the MCI Standards have their enthusiastic proponents, it has to be noted that a significant group of high-tech industrial companies have decided not to adopt the generic MCI Standards, believing that different parts of their companies adopt different values and ways of doing things that make it virtually impossible to address development needs in a single and uniform way (see Esp, 1993, p 115).

It is partly for this reason that some schools (following ICI, who provided technical support), have opted for the American management standards, associated with the names of Boyatzis, McBer and Schroder. In this approach, the word 'competence' is used to mean 'an underlying characteristic causally linked to superior performance on the job' – as distinct from the UK definition:

> a description of something which a person who works in a given occupational area should be able to do. It is a description of an action, behaviour or outcome which the person should be able to demonstrate (NCVQ, 1995, p 22)
> [or] the ability to perform work activities to the standards required in employment. (MSC, 1988, p 5)

The American definition allows the introduction of competences that are clearly value laden, such as 'efficiency orientation', 'proactivity', 'perceptual objectivity' and 'positive regard'. Indeed, the application of the American model by the Secondary Heads Association (SHA) and Oxford Brookes University actually includes 'educational values' as a category of competence. The Cleveland LEA schools, guided by ICI, have also adapted the McBer framework of competences to fit the school situation, but have not followed SHA/Oxford Brookes in separately identifying a values component.

The University of East London has developed an assessment procedure for Heads, in association with the occupational psychology consultants, Saville and Holdsworth. Their model also uses the American approach, supported by the Occupational Personality Questionnaire (OPQ) psychometric test. Criteria for assessment include values such as 'people orientation' (sympathy, tolerance). One of the features of this research is the use of the OPQ questionnaire to ascertain differences in personality characteristics (some closely associated with values) between male and female heads, and between heads and a composite group of managers. Females were found to be more affiliative, democratic, caring, artistic, methodical and conscientious; males more rational, relaxed, tough minded, active and competitive. There were no significant differences between primary and secondary school heads. Compared with the general population of managers, headteachers appear to be more persuasive, controlling, democratic, artistic, change oriented and optimistic. It would have been more illuminating, however, to have compared heads with managers of professionals. However, the variance within the groups far outweighs that between groups (Jirasinghe, 1994).

Although it is not possible to include personal attributes as such in occupational standards, they can often be translated into S/NVQ language by expressing them as behaviours or outcomes. For example, flair and creativity can be described as a function beginning with the words: 'Instigate and recommend new ...'; a caring disposition can be described by a PC reading: 'Customers and clients are treated politely and in a manner which promotes goodwill and trust' (Mitchell, 1993).

Conclusion

To summarise, there is indubitably scope for the systematic assessment of competent professional practice in educational occupations within a values context. To enhance school effectiveness and improve the quality of pupils' learning experience it is important to attempt both formative and summative assessment of teachers and heads. Despite the difficulties inherent in the current UK approach to competence-based assessment it is practicable to assess a person's espousal and application of values in the S/NVQ process. It may be easier, however, to do so in the American approach. The two approaches are not mutually exclusive; a combination of them, perhaps supplemented by the use of psychometric tests such as OPQ and Cattell's 16PF test of personality, may lead to more accurate prognoses of satisfactory performance in furthering a teacher's career. Those managing professionals in schools are unlikely to be regarded in the future as 'professional' themselves if they do not attempt to follow the standards of competence initiative, and to ensure that values are embedded in the standards by which staff are assessed and helped to develop.

Value Statements from Sport and Recreation Industry

Facilities covered by this project, and the services they provide, are sited in a great variety of settings:

- in voluntary sports and youth premises;
- in multipurpose, usually public, leisure centres with hundreds of employees;
- in activity centres run by youth services, local education authorities and one- and two-person private partnerships;
- in private fitness and racket sport centres, golf courses, squash clubs and marinas;
- in public parks;
- in health suites or activity centres attached to hotels or holiday camps;
- in works' sports and social clubs;
- in personal, team or management development centres that use outdoor activities as a vehicle for learning.

Competent facility staff operate at all times by reference to a set of values that includes the following:

A: As regards himself or herself, all staff should:
1. display commitment, initiative, honesty, integrity and a proper sense of responsibility, honouring the trust reposed by clients, employers, colleagues and the general public;
2. uphold the good standing of management, education, sport and sportsmanship;
3. provide conscientiously a service of value to society, concerned with the development of quality in all matters, including the quality of life;
4. be conscious of values issues and resolve values conflicts by using a reasoned approach;
5. exercise responsible stewardship over all resources under their control: financial, material and human, striving always to turn them to purposeful account;
6. take active steps to improve his or her own personal competence;
7. pay due regard to the law and avoid the abuse or misuse of their position.

B: As regards the facility, the manager should:
1. ensure that the set of values that governs the conduct of the organisation as a whole extends to and includes the conduct of every member of it;

2. engender a spirit of openness, participation and co-operation but which recognises the need for authority structures and provides for conflict and competition to be managed;
3. give rights and responsibilities equal emphasis;
4. establish high expectations for all in the pursuit of excellence;
5. ensure consistently high standards of health, safety and psychological well-being for employees, volunteers and clients.

C: As regards those who work at the facility, the manager should:

1. ensure that the general principles of ethical conduct and their application in specific contexts are understood and taken seriously by all staff and volunteers;
2. seek to ensure that the consciences of others are never put at risk;
3. value staff highly, recognise them as a valuable resource and encourage and assist them to develop competence, self-esteem and potential;
4. develop internal relationships on the basis of mutual trust and reciprocal loyalty;
5. provide safe, congenial and healthy working conditions;
6. plan work and personal development jointly so as to provide maximum job satisfaction, challenge, opportunity and, as far as external circumstances permit, job security for those with a satisfactory record of performance;
7. develop and maintain a working climate in which improvements occur naturally and continuously without being enforced or imposed;
8. by leadership, co-ordination and personal commitment and example, achieve acceptance by all of the need to be effective and successful.

D: As regards clients and suppliers, all staff should:

1. ensure that the facility offers good value for money, reflected in the quality of service provided;
2. sustain and develop mutually beneficial relationships with clients and suppliers;
3. regard every client as an individual with the right to dignity, respect and consideration, and display a caring attitude at all times;
4. accept that racism, sexism and prejudice against people with disabilities or who suffer social and economic disadvantage, have no place in the facility;
5. encourage clients to accept responsibility for their learning and enjoyment.

E: *As regards the environment, resources and society, all staff should:*
1. communicate to the public truthfully and without intent to mislead by slanting or suppressing information;
2. interact with the community, its members and its institutions so as to increase understanding of the facility's aims and activities, and in so doing ensure that the facility is seen as an asset to the community and a good neighbour;
3. foster responsibly the amenity and well-being of the local community and contribute to meeting its needs;
4. minimise any adverse impact on the environment caused by the facility's operations;
5. take full account of the need for public safety;
6. respond to global environmental issues by economising in the use of energy and non-sustainable resources, by avoiding destruction of natural resources, by controlling pollution and by careful management of waste.

Figure 8.2 *Example of Values Statements from the Sport and Recreation industry, including outdoor education*
Source: SRLB (1992), Crown Copyright, 1992 (reproduced with permission of the Controller, HMSO).

Notes

1. Address: Dr W Robb, 85 Argyll Place, Aberdeen AB2 4HU.
2. Address: David Rouse, Centre for Values Education for Life, Faculty of Education, University of Central England, Westbourne Road, Birmingham B15 3TN.
3. One of the criticisms of the early frameworks of occupational standards for professionals, such as the Management and the Training and Development Standards, was that the underpinning values were not made explicit and were inadequately assessed. More recent Standards development for professionals such as accountants and architects is less open to such criticism.

References

Anderson, D (ed) (1982) *Educated for Employment?*, Social Affairs Unit, London.

Beck, C (1990) *Better Schools: A Values Perspective*, Falmer Press, Lewes.

Brighouse, T (1985) 'Conference address' cited in Watson, B (1987) *Education and Belief*, Blackwell, Oxford, p 1.

Collier, G (1993) 'Learning moral judgement in higher education', *Studies in Higher Education* 18, 3, pp 287–97.

Collier, G (1994) 'Authority and institutional values', Address to National Association for Values in Education and Training (NAVET) Annual Conference, Westhill College, Birmingham.

Employment Department (1994a) *Ethics in Occupational Standards, NVQs and SVQs*, Technical Report No 22, Research and Development Series, Pendragon Press, Papworth Everard.

Employment Department (1994b) *The Place of Knowledge and Understanding in the Development of National Vocational Qualifications and Scottish Vocational Qualifications*, Competence and Assessment Briefing Series No 10, Pendragon Press, Papworth Everard.

Esp, D (1993) *Competences for School Managers*, Kogan Page, London.

Everard, K B (1982) 'Higher education: should industry be concerned?' in Anderson, D (ed) *Educated for Employment?*, Social Affairs Unit, London.

Everard, K B (1986) *Developing Management in Schools*, Blackwell, Oxford.

Everard, K B (1989, 1990, 1991, 1992a) 'Training Notes', *Management in Education* 3, 2, p 14; 4, 2, p 19; 5, 2, p 29; 6, 3, p 31.

Everard, K B (1990a) 'A critique of the MCI/TA/NCVQ competency approach as applied to education management', *Educational Change and Development* 11, 1, pp 15–16.

Everard, K B (1990b) *Values, Beliefs, Education and Training and Developing Competence in Dealing with Values*, NAVET Occasional Paper.

Everard, K B (1992b) A *Guide to Handling Some Values Issues*, NAVET Occasional Paper.

Everard, K B and Morris, G (1990) *Effective School Management*, (2nd ed) Paul Chapman, London.

Fletcher, S (1994) *NVQs, Standards and Competence: A Practical Guide for Employers, Managers and Trainers*, (2nd ed) Kogan Page, London.

Green, H (1993) 'Leadership, values and site-based management', *NAVET Papers* 8, p 13.

Jirasinghe, D (1994) 'Management competencies for headteachers: a job analysis of tasks and occupational personality characteristics', PhD Thesis, University of East London, Dagenham.

Management Charter Initiative, (MCI) (1994) *Draft Overview of the Senior Management Standards*, MCI, London.

Manpower Services Commission (MSC) (1988) *The Development of Accessible Standards for National Certification: Guidance No.3. The Definition of Competences and Performance Criteria*, MSC, Sheffield.

Mitchell, L (1993) 'NVQs/SVQs at higher levels: a discussion paper' given at the 'Higher Levels' Seminar, October 1992, *Competence and Assessment Briefing Series No 8*, Employment Department, Sheffield.

National Commission on Education (1993) *Learning to Succeed*, Heinemann, London.

National Council for Vocational Qualifications (NCVQ) (1988) *The NVQ Criteria and Related Guidance*, NCVQ, London.

NCVQ (1995) *NVQ Criteria and Guidance*, NCVQ, London.

Peters, T J and Waterman, R H (1982) *In Search of Excellence*, Harper & Row, New York.

Roman Catholic Bishops' Report (1983) *Signs and Homecomings*, Geoffrey Chapman, London.

Rutter, M, Maugham, B, Mortimore, P and Ouston, J (1979) *Fifteen Thousand Hours*, Open Books, Shepton Mallet.

Sports and Recreation Lead Body (SRLB) (1992) *Leading the Way in Vocational Qualifications: A guide to the proposed framework*, SRLB, London.

Stewart, J (1986) *In Search of the Management of Education*, Local Government Training Board, Luton.

Stewart, N (1990) 'Shared values', *Educational Change and Development* 10, 2, pp 1–3.

Teacher Training Agency (1994) *Draft Framework: Headteacher Managerial Tasks and Competences*, Department for Education, London.

Watson, B (1987) *Education and Belief*, Blackwell, Oxford.

White, J (1990) 'The aims of education' in Entwistle, N (ed) *Handbook of Educational Ideas and Practices*, Routledge, London.

Woodcock, M and Francis, D (1989) *Clarifying Organizational Values*, Gower, Aldershot.

Chapter 9

Developing Teachers as Extended Professionals
Hilary Constable

Introduction

This chapter reports on school development planning in England and Wales, and on the implications this has for teachers' professional development, through a case study of a faculty of science in a secondary school. Development planning has become increasingly emphasised in England and Wales as a means of helping teachers handle multiple concurrent demands for change within existing resources. This chapter considers within-school efforts to plan for development in science education and the implications this has for extending professionality. It is clear that school development planning brings to the surface a great deal more than mechanistic planning practices. There are many skills and awarenesses to be identified from the detail and texture of teachers' work.

In the 1990s in the UK there is no choice. The multiple demands on teachers mean that, generally speaking, all teachers must take some responsibility for each other's professional development. The case study to be reported shows teachers in the process of making shifts in their professionality. The main story concerns the way the head of faculty develops his own capacities as he sets out to develop the capabilities of the faculty staff. It illustrates the way a shift of emphasis exposes the skills which teachers have and use, and challenges previous practices and conceptualisations. It is essential in this climate that teachers' learning is taken seriously. Ironically the consideration of teachers as learners may be the point at which ideas of extending professionality grate and clash most with managerial ideas of development in schools.

The context of school development

The introduction of the National Curriculum followed a period when schools were seen by many outside education to be failing to meet the needs of society. A package of measures was introduced by central government to bring about changes designed to improve standards. An important thrust was to be the mobilisation of a combination of self-management and market forces. These were intended to produce significant improvements in the quality of state education. The stated rationale for the reforms included an intention by government to make schools operate in a market where the best schools would attract the most pupils. This was intended to allow parents to exercise choice, thereby ensuring good schools would continue to recruit pupils at the expense of poorer schools. This would move the control of education away from teachers and bureaucrats to parents as consumers. Funding would follow the pupils: that is, the budget of a school would be determined by the number of pupils who enrolled. Teachers would produce well-educated pupils and the definition and minimum specification of the pupils would be given by the National Curriculum. Bowe *et al* (1992, p 65) identify five main driving and interrelated factors behind these changes:

- choice – via open enrolment;
- diversity – via a range of schools;
- competition – schools would compete to be chosen by parents;
- funding to follow students;
- schools to take charge of their own budgets, tying each school directly to market forces.

Clearly teachers are not in the foreground of such ideas about educational development. Nevertheless they are the means by which change will happen and, as teachers are animate and sentient, the ways in which they respond will be the essence of any real educational change. Joyce and Showers (1988), from the USA, specifically in the context of raising pupil achievement through staff development, make the point thus:

> The school has its impact in three ways: one is what is taught, the second is in how it is taught, and the third is in its social environment. Teachers and administrators need to be engaged in the continuous study of all three, continually increasing knowledge of academic content, models of teaching, and models for school environments and how to create them.
>
> (Joyce and Showers, 1988, p 4)

This includes the way teachers behave towards each other and the attitudes they display towards learning: 'The social climate of the school and the attitudes and patterns of behaviour it promotes greatly influence the process of education' (Joyce and Showers, 1988, p 6). If this is true for pupils, then it is true for teachers. Teachers are part of the social climate for each other. The attitudes to learning held by them are part of the learning environment for pupils. The consequences of this in the context outlined by Bowe *et al* (1992) cannot help but be fascinating.

An important aspect of the reforms has been the multiple nature of the changes. Schools were to be responsible for performance and were much more visibly and directly accountable than previously. The consolidation of responsibilities previously distributed between schools and local authorities at the level of the school, together with the substantive reforms in curriculum and testing, made a large demand on teachers in schools. Schools needed to manage multiple demands, but at the same time the management of schools was targeted for reform. For the most part heads and senior management teams were seen both as objects of change, being expected to change their culture and practices, as well as agents of change to bring about certain other and substantive changes in curriculum, assessment and pedagogy.

School development planning

The School Development Plans project, sponsored by the Department of Education and Science, was designed to support and facilitate these changes (Hargreaves *et al,* 1989). The project itself was, however, another dual change: both a means of managing change but also a change in itself (Constable, 1994). Local education authorities had the responsibility for implementing these changes. Commonly, as in this case, they used the School Development Plans project materials for staff development, first with headteachers and then with senior managers and middle managers in schools. A point which is significant in its absence from both the documentation and provision was that the changes were to be carried out on the existing resource base.

Extending professionality

In the early 1970s Hoyle (1972) and Stenhouse (1975) presented models of the development of professionals. Both writers identified a 'wider view' as

153

characteristic of extended professionals. Hoyle claimed that extended professionals see their work 'in the wider context of school, community and society' (Hoyle, 1972, p 3). Stenhouse saw things differently and argued that the essence of extended professionality was: 'The commitment to systematic questioning of one's own teaching as a basis for development; the commitment and the skills to study one's own teaching; the concern to question and to test theory in practice by the use of those skills' (Stenhouse, 1975, p 144).

Hoyle and Stenhouse were thought provoking because their analyses argued that teachers' professionality was complex. Although viewing extended professionality differently, they acknowledged the problematic nature of teachers' professional development. This exposed simple ideas of progression from class teacher to head of department to headteacher as significantly limited in planning for teachers' professional development.

Since then few analyses have been so thought provoking, despite considerable efforts to characterise the work and professional development of teachers. The apparent exception to this is the work of Schon (1983, 1987). Eraut's (1994) incisive critique of Schon's position draws attention to the as yet unresolved challenge of characterising professionality and more especially its development. Eraut's (1988) analysis of management knowledge for teachers proposed six categories: knowledge of people; conceptual knowledge; situational knowledge; process knowledge; knowledge of educational practice and control knowledge. These categories can be seen in operation in the case study. However it is in Eraut's argument that the paramount need for teachers is to bring 'routine behaviour and intuitive thinking under some kind of critical control' (Eraut, 1994, p 156) that a more substantial and contemporary guide can be found to both the analysis of professional development and its research.

The challenge

The faculty of science in this case study was part of a school which had approximately 1450 pupils and 90 teaching staff. It consisted of the head of Science and 12 other teachers. Five teachers had promoted posts. Eight of the 12 teachers had responsibilities beyond their own classroom such as assessment, pupils with special educational needs, equal opportunities, resources, health and safety, co-ordination of Key Stage 4, co-ordination of Key Stage 3, and liaison with primary schools (pupils aged 5–11 years). Two of the teachers were newly qualified. As might be expected, the challenges facing the science faculty replicated those for the whole school, in that some concerns related to substantive matters whereas others were concerned with changing the management of these matters.

There was a structural and procedural framework within which the head of faculty worked. All teachers in the school were required to attend meetings of their faculty which normally took place every four weeks after the close of afternoon school. The science faculty met instead more frequently for a shorter period at lunchtime every two weeks. All the heads of faculty in the school met together once a week and met also with the head and deputies of the school and heads of upper and lower school. In the year in question the science staff were able to use two of the five days a year set aside for staff development for faculty concerns and priorities.

The substantive matters essentially consisted of a series of demands for the school and the faculty in the implementation of the National Curriculum and national assessment. In addition policies had to be implemented regarding such matters as safety, equal opportunities and pupils with special educational needs, as well as liaison with phases of education before and after the secondary school. Further to these a national requirement for teacher appraisal had to be implemented.

In this science faculty, as in others, the matters which required attention had a number of sources. Most originated at a national level, but others came from within the school or from the local education authority or internally from within the faculty. Inevitably there was significant interaction amongst these, so faculty concerns were specific manifestations of matters which, in their general form, were shared with science departments in other schools throughout the country. A list of national and local authority priorities for science education was assembled by the local authority inspector for the heads of science as a reminder of their targets for the school year 1992–3. This contained 14 separate items, listed in Figure 9.1, none of them small and some as large as 'Key Stage 4 courses in Science (double award and Science award) start for Year Ten'.

The purpose of faculty development planning was, as with whole school development planning, to find ways for staff to respond to these multiple concurrent demands. In addition to the national, local and school level demands, the head of faculty, given the pseudonym Mr Smithson, had professional concerns which were specific to the faculty. One was the current teaching materials for each of the Key Stages of the National Curriculum: some of these in Key Stage 3 had been recently devised and tried out only once. The head of faculty, together with staff, had devised new units of teaching material during the previous two years in response to early versions of the National

---

Science Development Plan

Major requirements
1. New Science orders take effect from 1 August 1992.
2. Key Stage 3 assessment becomes statutory for Y9
   (children with first reported result in summer term 1993).
3. Key Stage 4 courses in Science (double award and Science award) start with Y10 children.
4. GCSE courses for Y10 children taking the combination of Biology, Chemistry and Physics start. Existing GCSE syllabus to be used for this cohort only.
5. Sunderland LEA/Science Policy Statement in place.
6. Development of post-16 Science courses with suitable guidance provided to Y11 children.
7. Consideration of Science provision and assessment for children with special educational needs.
8. Appraisal.

Other requirements
1. Review of Key Stage 3 provision to date to take account of:
   * impact of New Orders;
   * trial assessments in summer 1992;
   * teaching and learning styles, including CASE
   * cross-curricular issues.
2. Review of Key Stage 4 options, to take account of:
   * new syllabuses;
   * syllabuses in Biology, Chemistry and Physics from September 1993;
   * uptake of courses to date.
3. Liaison developing closer links with:
   * feeder primary/junior schools;
   * post-16 providers;
   * other secondary schools.
4. Health and Safety issues. A need to consolidate, monitor and, as appropriate, modify practice with particular reference to:
   * ionising radiation;
   * COSHH (health and safety rules);
   * electricity at work;
   * pressurised containers.
5. Departmental management issues to include:
   * department review and planning;
   * finance, resources, accommodation, technicians, staff development and deployment.
6. Induction of newly qualified teachers (NQTs).

What is required to July 1993
1. Science department/faculty development plans for 1991/2 1992/3 1993/4 (to include financial plan).
2. Science department/faculty handbook or portfolio with details of:
   * staff, structures, procedures, timetable;
   * schemes of work for each Key Stage;
   * accommodation;
   * resources;
   * INSET;
   * Science policy statement.

Policies on health and safety, A/R/R, teaching and learning styles, cross-curricular equal opportunities, community links, liaison, review and other areas (some policies may be in the process of development).

Figure 9.1: *Local education authority: science development plan*

Science Curriculum. The new materials had demanded a considerable amount of effort from staff both in devising the materials and in teaching them. A review of the materials and their implementation was needed. In Key Stage 4, published materials had been introduced in the faculty as a support but, in Mr Smithson's opinion, had rapidly come to define the limits of teachers' aspirations. He identified a need to review the ways in which teachers could become more creative and flexible. A third problem lay in the area of differentiation – the ways in which teachers attempted to match general curriculum demands to different levels of pupils' achievement and ability in the year group and also in the same class. Mr Smithson saw as pressing concerns: the current teaching materials for the Key Stages 3 and 4 of the National Curriculum; the introduction of Standard Assessment Tests (SATs) for 14-year-old pupils; differentiation of the curriculum – the ways in which teachers attempted to match general curriculum demands to different levels of pupils' achievement and ability; and general issues of health and safety at work, equal opportunities and pupils with special educational needs. These shaped his view of the list from the science inspector.

It can be seen that, by any standards, the number of issues was large and the time available limited; and the head of faculty had concerns which went beyond managing time. At best he wanted staff morale to be high with commitment to implementing changes and to taking a share of the work involved. At worst he wanted to avoid staff feeling demoralised and defeated by the impact of apparently constant changes and modifications to the curriculum and assessment. For these reasons he wanted staff to have some control and ownership of the work of the faculty. In view of the number of changes raining on the department from outside, this would not be easy, because the imposed changes risked leaving staff feeling that it was not worth making the effort to respond since each initiative was apparently superseded by new ones, possibly leaving them worse able to cope with the next changes which were demanded.

Mr Smithson had the job of managing motivation and morale of staff on a time scale longer than one year. To achieve this he wanted to introduce medium- and long-term planning or at least some approximation to them. He wanted plans to cover the medium term to give some sense of orderly progress and to allow prioritisation of demands for change to have a practical face. He also wanted to build on previous efforts of the staff in the department. This included encouraging staff to exercise the responsibilities they held within the department and establishing a systematic programme of development. This programme was intended to allow staff to gain ownership of change, to draw on their expertise and to share out the work to be done. Mr Smithson wanted all the faculty staff to be involved in the development work, that is not merely to participate in doing part of the work, but to feel some sense of involvement (Constable *et al*, 1988).

The response

An important resource for the head of faculty was the school programme of faculty staff meetings and development days. Mr Smithson needed to make good use of these. Accordingly he took into account a number of organising ideas in planning the programme for the year: the structure of the programme in terms of the annual cycle of meetings, the distribution of time between development and maintenance, the selection of substantive matters for attention and the participation and involvement of staff. It had been common for the agenda of the fortnightly meetings to fill up with matters which concerned the maintenance, rather than the development, of faculty functioning or the implementation of whole school policies. Common items were administrative matters concerning school rules, pupil behaviour, care of equipment, ordering and use of resources and pupil records and reports.

As there was rarely time to think ahead in terms of the work of the science faculty Mr Smithson decided to dedicate some meetings specifically to development work. First an estimate of the size of this resource was made. A count of how many meetings could realistically happen in the year was made – half the number of weeks in the school year, together with realistic reductions for emergencies and for the beginning and end of the school terms and year. A roughly equal division was made between administrative and maintenance matters on the one hand and development issues on the other.

This process helped Mr Smithson envisage the year and shape the programme. It would be necessary in each year to attend to some significant development matters, to keep all other matters under reasonable control and to review the year's work and plan for the following year. He decided to organise the work into phases: first the implementation of the present plan and then preparation for the plan for the next school year together with input into and from the whole school plan.

The selection of substantive items from the many pressing concerns was a further crucial issue. All the items had a claim to attention. The identification of a matter as a priority put off others until a later date and perhaps implied a lesser importance, not necessarily a message the head of faculty wished to give.

There was also a balance to be struck here between always appearing to be starting something new and giving attention to the same area repeatedly. Abandoning work risked demotivating staff who had worked hard to produce and introduce materials. These were important considerations as the tendency was for the many demands to fragment attention and effort rather than to consolidate it.

One of the faculty-specific concerns which offered the opportunity for this was to review the current teaching materials for each of the secondary Key Stages of the National Curriculum. For Key Stage 3 the head of faculty, together with staff, had devised new units of teaching material during the previous two years in response to early versions of the National Science Curriculum. Each of the teaching units had been prepared by one or two members of staff and had been used by most of the teachers in the faculty. The new materials had demanded a considerable amount of effort from staff both in devising the materials and in teaching with them. A review of the materials and their implementation was needed. In Key Stage 4, published materials had been introduced in the faculty as a support but, in Mr Smithson's opinion, had rapidly come to define the limits of teachers' aspirations. He identified a need to review the ways in which teachers could become more creative and flexible.

The choice by the head of faculty of the review and revision of modules of teaching material for pupils in Key Stage 3 built on work done by staff over the last two years, allowing an element of continuity as well as a close look at an innovation which had really only just got started. It built on two of his concerns – the work of the pupils in Key Stage 3 and differentiation. A start had been made on using the new units in teaching, but staff needed to review them in terms of how they worked in practice, and in particular how they met the needs of pupils of different abilities. It was expected that additional activities would need to be prepared for pupils with the least and the most ability. The choice also allowed the inflection of the curriculum development from the previous concern with preparing materials for a new curriculum to differentiation – allowing both consolidation and change. Mr Smithson had been concerned that the work on these new teaching units should not be abandoned or left suspended.

The way the head of faculty managed the review further supported his aim to involve staff. The review of each unit of the Key Stage 3 materials was to be led by the member of staff who had prepared the teaching material. The review sessions were structured to involve staff explicitly in supporting the development of other teachers. This was the first time some staff had had experience of leading sessions for other members of teaching staff. In preparing these sessions the deputy head of science commented that she had not previously thought of the preparation of staff development sessions in such a strategic way, nor had she previously given so much attention to their detailed preparation.

It was planned that the review sessions should start with each teacher privately making notes on what, from their experience of working with the materials from the unit under review, had worked well for them and what had not worked so well. The teachers then reported to the group on what had worked well and only when this was complete was a shift made to those items which had not worked so well. This order of procedure was chosen deliberately to give the designer of each unit some praise and positive feedback and to engage all staff in making a positive contribution. Following this there was a discussion of additional activities for pupils which different members of staff had tried, and proposals for further ones were made. The head of faculty deliberately started the series of meetings by reviewing the unit he had designed – as a means of demonstrating the approach he wanted to be taken, as well as showing his good faith by exposing his own work to scrutiny first.

Having introduced a more structured plan for the use of staff meetings and started the review of the teaching materials for the modules in Key Stage 3, by the middle of the school year the head of faculty was able to look forward to the next year and start to consider possible priorities for it, as well as looking back and reviewing the processes and procedures he had introduced.

Outcomes

Increasing control in a shifting environment

Whilst Mr Smithson made no claims to have solved all the problems involved in development planning for the faculty of science, he could point to a number of achievements. He had grappled with the multiple concurrent demands on him, and with his staff had imposed some order on them. They had not only tackled some of the pressing substantive concerns for the faculty but had also started to introduce some procedures which enabled them to deal with change. He had been faced with issues bound up with school development planning: first as an innovation to bring about innovation, second as a simplified scheme to deal with messy reality and third as an attempt to deal with conflicting values. Constable (1994) discusses these arenas of tension in more detail and in the imagery of the School Development Plans project (Hargreaves *et al*, 1989) 'root' and 'branch' innovation had been attended to simultaneously.

Continuity and change had been accommodated. Both the main and subsidiary matters for development were areas where some development work had been done, but where review renewed the curriculum development work in line with current needs, thus building on what had gone before and making progress.

By planning the next year's work in advance some control over the demands on teachers was gained. Particularly effective was the simple technique of counting the meetings available and estimating the time that was realisitically available for development work. The rest of the time was allocated to routine administrative and whole school matters.

Participation had been extended. Previously staff had taken part only in designing materials. Leading the faculty review and development sessions extended and enhanced their participation.

From the point of view of an outsider, these achievements can be seen as part of a wider view of the professional development of teachers. It is clear that the changes to teachers' work affect the conceptualisation of teacher professionality as well as teacher development. It is not possible to say to what extent the professional development of staff which the head of faculty intended had been realised. It is possible however to note that staff had had new experiences, the intention of which was to facilitate their development.

In attending to the professional development of staff in his faculty, Mr. Smithson had been instrumental in his own professional development. This is evident in three respects. First the head of faculty had taken responsibility for negotiating a meaningful nexus between school and staff, between the demands for change and development and between the needs of teachers for professional support and development. Second he had taken seriously the needs of staff as adult learners. As members of the school organisation their motivation and morale needed to be sustained. Third he had given his role as a source of teachers' professional development a higher profile.

A number of points of general interest are illuminated by this case study

Accommodating conflicting priorities

First, it has become increasingly evident that teachers need to learn to give priority to the conflicting demands upon them. There are two consequences which flow from this: establishing what will be first also defines what will not be first; and the impact of such choices on the staff responsible for work of different levels of priority.

School development has been bedevilled by what Handy and Aitken (1986) have called the 'pile of purposes'. In evaluating Guidelines for Review and Internal Development of Schools (GRIDS) Constable *et al* (1988) attributed success to the establishment of agreed priorities. In the design stage of GRIDS what was perhaps considered most important was the agreement to and participation by teachers in the review process. In the implementation stage in schools it was the prioritisation of action by staff which was most significant: what would be worked on first and with most attention and resources and, therefore, what else would be left until some future time.

The establishment of priorities was picked up and elaborated as a strong theme in the School Development Plans Project (Hargreaves *et al*, 1989). The logic of the position is clear in that what is identified as a priority receives attention – including resources such as staff time; what is not identified as a priority will receive no, or less, attention, perhaps being left for prioritisation in the next round of planning, or later.

A rather different consequence of prioritisation is its impact on the staff with responsibility for high and low priority areas. Examine the list of priorities given by the head of faculty and the time he had available to work on these. Consider also the effect of giving low priority to the area of responsibility of a trusted, committed and competent colleague. Imagine a situation in which a whole school policy has been established, for instance concerning equal opportunities, information technology or special educational needs, and imagine further that a teacher is given responsibility for implementing this policy within a department, faculty or even across the school. The effect of putting such work in the 'not a priority' category gives rather clear messages about the importance of the policy and the work of those associated with it. If, for instance, equal opportunities is a policy of the school, then how can it not be a faculty priority? How can a person given responsibility for responding to special educational needs resolve the conflict between the message that this work is important enough for a school policy and for a post with an allowance, but 'not a priority this year in the faculty'?

It is easy to see from this that headteachers and heads of faculties and departments are under pressure to include priorities from the need to keep up staff morale, or at least to avoid demotivating colleagues. Arguably this leads to the identification of more rather than fewer priorities. Mid- and long-term planning needs to be seen in relation to this tendency to include rather than exclude issues and concerns as priorities, with the danger of ending up with the 'pile of purposes'. The skilful use of a change of focus to allow both consolidation and change can help to diffuse the tensions inherent in such situations.

Becoming extended professionals

Second, a government policy which set out to improve standards in schools by emphasising the primacy of classroom practice has in fact had the effect of making teachers take more responsibility for practice beyond their own classroom – a tendency identified some time ago in primary schools in England and Wales (Roger and Richardson, 1985). Devolving budget control to schools, lessening the control of local authorities, reducing the number of advisory teachers, increasing the scope of curriculum and assessment change and accelerating the pace of change have all combined to reinforce this trend. The result has been teachers in schools carrying a huge burden of new and existing demands for the smooth running of the school to which they have had to respond under severe time constraint from within their own resources and expertise. Teachers' work then increasingly involves responsibility for practice beyond their own classroom.

The power structure in schools has reflected a strong element of hierarchy and traditionalism by virtue of the historic position of headteachers. This has been emphasised, exaggerated even, by the managerialist thrust of government reforms. At the same time there has been the appearance of a move towards collegiality. Collegiality works the other way round from managerialism, with transient and changing leadership and changing responsibilities based around the idea of a college of equals. Above all collegiality is voluntary and spontaneous. The idea of each teacher as in some sense the provider of expertise or leadership for others and in turn the recipient of different expertise and leadership in other situations fits in well here. So contemporary teachers have not only to acquire the skills of acting more closely with each other in both collegial and managerial contexts, but also to resolve the different practices of these contrasting imperatives.

Hargreaves (1994) notes the way collegiality has been hijacked by managerialism and the two contrasting approaches added to each other. The sum of the parts (which in this case adds up to less than the whole) he aptly describes as 'contrived collegiality'. It is doubtful whether it is practical to consider operating in these different traditions at the same time. Any teacher surviving thinking about such an idea may wish to skip out of his or her postmodern nightmare and slip into a cool born-again modernity. For the faint hearted a more modernist question which still needs answering would be, 'Where does the time come from to meet all the demands now required of teachers?'

The significance of the contrast between managerialism and collegiality lies in the place of the teacher as a learner. It has, as Fullan and Hargreaves say, been shown 'time and time again that staff or teacher development is closely related to successful change' (Fullan and Hargreaves, 1992, p 3). The managerial school may not be the best place to implement the idea of the teacher as continuously learning adult; it may even be the worst.

Teachers as learners

The need to release the act of teaching from its bonds as a power-bound activity is the third point. It is now necessary, not just good practice, that teachers teach each other or, put another way, help each other systematically to learn. Teachers have of course always learned from each other – picking up pieces of good (and bad) practice and incorporating it into their own. What is newly prominent and not always recognised is the idea of teachers as formal learners.

The rhetoric of teaching and learning suggests teaching may best be seen as a perficient activity, one which causes learning. Teaching is assisting learning to happen. Obviously learning can and does happen without teaching, but teaching is about deliberate plans and activity to make some particular learning happen rather than being left to chance, and happen at some specified time rather than at any time. Learning is something to do with changes in knowledge or skills, and as such teaching and learning carry with them broadly positive connotations: learning is good, teaching helps learning.

However, teachers confront considerable emotional dilemmas in becoming learners, perhaps especially in school and with colleagues. For practising teachers in school, teaching is loaded with acutely felt values. It is embedded in and overlaid by defined power relations. Those who teach are those who control and define the situation; whereas those who learn (the pupils) are controlled. This unidirectional relationship is not a necessary corollary of teaching and learning, as can be seen in many examples, but it is common enough to be recognisable. The conflation of being the learner with being the inferior partner in a human relationship is common in school teaching. The long-standing resentment of many adults for teachers in general may stem from just one or two bad experiences of this kind involving shame, confusion or humiliation. On the other hand, teachers work in conditions which may not be well suited to teaching – one teacher and many pupils, and what is more the pupils are not all enthusiastic learners. The images of war are never far away – rebellion and riot are the dread of beginner teachers; and 'the enemy', and 'over the top' are phrases that have been heard in at least some staff rooms. Failing to learn or to behave as a learner can be greeted with loss of privileges and possibly punishment, including derision. This very partial analysis (in order to make the point) hovers amongst others, colouring working teachers' reactions to and feelings about teaching and learning.

From the dilemmas of control and status comes another shading for teachers which may be difficult to shake off. This concerns mistakes. It is reasonably easy to argue, and indeed to persuade many adults, that getting something 'wrong', making a mistake, things not working out, can and should be seen as the start of a learning cycle, an event to be celebrated and seized upon for the opportunity it offers of new learning rather than a failure to be concealed as best one can. The logic of the matter is unassailable, that if things are not working out there is an opportunity for review and further learning, but teachers have more baggage to carry than that. Not learning, for practising teachers, is associated with pupils' experiences of failure, loss of dignity and possibly status, all of which can be permanently damaging to the esteem in which a person is held. It is not generally associated with exciting opportunities for new learning.

It is not surprising that teachers are not easy to release into a world where teaching and learning are worked out and at, rather than activities laden with values of status and power. By contrast, for managers in pigment factories, computer software installers or bicycle shop owners, the idea of needing to learn, needing to learn continuously and using a professional teacher of some sort to organise that learning may seem straightforward, even obvious and welcome. For teachers in school the baggage that goes with experience can be a significant interference. So although teachers with their skills and understanding of organised teaching might seem in some ways well placed to teach and learn, in other ways they are disabled by their experience.

Releasing the relationship of teacher and learner from the bonds of past experience may be harder for practising teachers than for any other comparable group. And yet it is essential not only for continuous staff development but because the attitudes to learning held by teachers are part of the learning environment for pupils. What is more, attitudes to being a learner are part of the climate for pupils and staff.

Arenas of tension have already been identified in school development planning: the process as both innovation and vehicle for innovation, the contrast between messy reality and schematic models and the exposure of contrasting values. School development planning is at least as problematic in relation to extending teachers professionality.

References

Bowe, R, Ball, S J with Gold, A (1992) *Reforming Education and Changing Schools*, Routledge, London.

Constable, H, Brown, R and Williams, R (1988) 'An evaluation of the implementation of GRIDS in a local education authority,' *Educational Management and Administration*, 16, pp 43–58.

Constable, H (1994) 'Three arenas of tension: teachers' experience of participation in school development planning' in Hargreaves, D H and Hopkins, D (eds) *Development Planning for School Improvement*, Cassell, London.

Eraut, M (1988) 'Management knowledge: its nature and its development' in Calderhead, J (ed) *Teachers' Professional Learning*, Falmer Press, London.

Eraut, M (1994) *Developing Knowledge and Competence*, Falmer Press, London.

Fullan, M and Hargreaves, A (1992) *Teacher Development and Educational Change*, Falmer Press, London.

Handy, C and Aitken, R (1986) *Understanding Schools as Organisations*, Penguin, Harmondsworth.

Hargreaves, A (1994) *Changing Teachers, Changing Times*, Cassell, London.

Hargreaves, D H, Hopkins, D, Leask, M, Connolly, J and Robinson, P (1989) *Planning for School Development: Advice to Governors, Headteachers and Teachers*, Department of Education and Science, London.

Hoyle, E (1972) 'Creativity in the school' paper for Organisation for Economic Cooperation and Development (OECD) Workshop on 'The Creativity of the School', Estoril, Portugal.

Joyce, B and Showers, B (1988) *Student Achievement through Staff Development*, Longman, New York.

Roger, I A and Richardson, J A S (1985) *Self-evaluation for Primary Schools*, Hodder & Stoughton, London.

Schon, D (1983) *The Reflective Practitioner: How Professionals Think in Action*, Basic Books, New York.

Schon, D (1987) *Educating the Reflective Practitioner: Towards a new Design for Teaching and Learning in the Professions*, Jossey-Bass, San Francisco.

Stenhouse, L (1975) *An Introduction to Curriculum Research and Development*, Heinemann Educational Books, London.

Chapter 10

Working with Support Staff in Schools: Relationships between Teachers, Governors and other Staff
Rene Saran and
Hugh Busher

Introduction

There is such a paucity of research into both the management of support staff, (a term we attempt to define later in this chapter) and into relationships between teaching and support staff in schools that it is difficult to discern general trends. Further, most of the literature that is available is based on studies undertaken before the implementation of the local management of schools (LMS) in England and Wales in 1990 under the Education Reform Act (1988). We have tried to supplement this dearth with two case studies. Behind the chapter lies some recent small-scale qualitative research carried out at Loughborough University into the management of support staff in schools.

This chapter focuses on how teaching and support staff and school governors can work together effectively to enact the aims of their schools. Unlike Mortimore and Mortimore with Thomas (1994), we did not set out to explore innovatory uses of support staff, yet what we found was, in part, innovatory because many of the jobs carried out by support staff have changed radically since the implementation of LMS.

A key aspect for the effective working together of teaching and support staff seems to lie in management processes which value the contribution of all staff to the aims and methods of working of a school. This approach fits within a conceptual framework derived from some of the more recent work on school improvement (Hopkins and Hargreaves, 1991; Fullan, 1992; Greenwood and Gaunt, 1995). In this, more successful institutions try to involve all staff in decision-making, value highly the work of staff, whatever role they perform, and value them as people with their variety of talents and needs. Not only is this approach uncommon, apparently, in the management of support staff in schools (Hipkiss, 1992; Busby, 1991), but one which is remarkably successful at making support staff feel valued and, so, committed to the institution in which they work (this chapter; Busher and Saran, 1995).

It is a philosophy towards managing people in institutions which has educational roots as well as commercial ones. Not only does it underpin the *Investors in People Standard* (Employment Department, 1992) but schools have applied it very successfully for many years in the implementation of sytems of pastoral care and discipline. Where pupils have felt involved through the latter with school processes, schools have tended to have pupils who were well motivated and successful in their work and well behaved in their relationships with other people. If this collegial approach to managing staff is as successful as the fragments of data reported here suggest, then it is perhaps time that headteachers and governors began to consider their staff as a whole (as does the headteacher of one of the schools featured in this chapter) rather than continuing to maintain outmoded distinctions between teaching and support staff.

Who are the support staff?

Haigh (1991) points out that a considerable number of people work in every school who are not teachers. Some of them form part of a school's establishment and some of them work for it on a contract basis. Some of them work close to the central processes of a school – the teaching and learning processes – and some work at a remove from this, while still doing essential work maintaining the fabric of the building and providing the clerical and administrative support to facilitate the central processes.

These staff can be subdivided into many categories but Lyons and Stenning (1986) suggested: librarians, technical, secretarial/clerical, caretakers/cleaners, welfare assistants and groundstaff. They have a wide variety of qualifications, ranging from professional through clerical and technical to manual skills. Most of them are employed on the APT and C scales for local authority staff. Most are poorly paid either because they are on part-time contracts or because their jobs are defined by the National Joint Council for Local Authority Staff as relatively unskilled. Most are women, who find the hours of work fit conveniently with their other responsibilities at home (Hipkiss, 1992), but site and groundstaff are usually men.

The number of support staff in school has fluctuated during the last 20 years, though there has been a major increase in numbers since the late 1980s. Riches (1981) observed an increase in the numbers of support staff in schools in the 1970s but this trend did not continue. The School Teachers' Review Body (STRB, 1995) recorded an increase of 31 per cent in education support and clerical staff since 1991, compared with an increase for the year 1994/5 of 0.2 per cent in full-time teaching staff and 2 per cent in pupils. Information on caretakers, groundstaff and kitchen staff are not collected centrally (STRB, 1995). The main reasons for the increase in numbers of support staff seem to have been the introduction of LMS since 1988, with its many administrative demands, and the increased demands of the National Curriculum on teachers, especially in primary schools (HMI, 1992; Bullock and Thomas, 1994).

The Education Reform Act (1988) dramatically affected the locus of responsibility for a school's staffing policies as well as for its financial policies. Prior to the introduction of LMS LEAs allocated support staff to schools, sometimes on the basis of a local formula, to reflect what they considered to be an appropriate ratio between a school's teaching establishment and its other staff. Suddenly county school governors, with headteachers as senior line managers on their behalf, became responsible for supervising the employment of all their teaching and support staff, although the LEA remained legally the employer. This included those posts such as caretakers and senior cooks who, before LMS, had been responsible to an LEA officer rather than to the head of the school in which they worked.

These increased employment responsibilities required school governors to put in place policies for pay, equal opportunities and race relations to comply with the legislation in these fields, as our earlier study *Teachers' Conditions of Employment* (Busher and Saran, 1992) pointed out. Decisions about pay have to be reached either within statutory frameworks laid down nationally and locally or negotiated with the relevant staff unions at site level. When considering the employment of teachers, governors could follow a well-known national statutory framework, set out annually in the *School Teachers' Pay and Conditions Document* (eg Department for Education (DfE), 1994), which allowed limited local flexibility. For support staff there was much less guidance. There was no equivalent annual document issued nationally. Locally, they often lacked comprehensive LEA guidance on how to handle the pay and changing conditions of work of support staff. At the two schools cited in this chapter, governors chose to work within the pay structure negotiated nationally with the support staff unions, mainly UNISON since 1993, and within the job descriptions negotiated locally by their LEA. Such job descriptions were placed at particular points within the pay bands of the national scales. Since the introduction of LMS many job descriptions have been renegotiated to reflect changing duties and responsibilities with a consequent regrading of people's pay scales.

Positively, these new responsibilities allowed school governors the opportunity, within the tight constraints of delegated budgets, to develop staffing structures for support staff which mirrored those for teaching staff. It also allowed governors to reallocate support staff between jobs, especially where responsibilities (such as those of school secretaries and site staff) had changed quite considerably (HMI, 1992). In many cases former caretakers and school secretaries had become site managers and financial managers or administrative officers as they took on a wide range of managerial tasks alongside their former manual or clerical ones.

On the other hand the introduction of compulsory competitive tendering (CCT), under the 1988 Local Government Act, highlighted the conflicts which such responsibilities entail. Under this scheme local authority services which had been provided directly to schools now had to be put out to tender to private companies or to financially autonomous agencies of a local authority, often called direct service organisations (DSOs). In order to balance their delegated budgets, schools had to buy the cheapest services available. Often this meant that existing LEA staff had to be declared redundant, even though they had carried out their work admirably, and replaced with those from the new service providers. Under LMS the redundancy notices had to be issued by a school's governors, not by the LEA as had been the case formerly. School cleaning and meals services fell into this framework.

This meant that governors were frequently faced with a moral dilemma even if their budget left them no latitude of choice: those whom they sacked were often re-employed by the new private provider or DSO to do the same job for less pay under more constrained conditions of service. At the two schools cited in this chapter, governors were most concerned at the impact such enforced redundancies would have on the school and on the individual staff. The cleaners were women living in the local community who had a sense of loyalty to the schools. The implementation of CCT weakened the link between cleaning and kitchen staff and the schools where they worked, making it more difficult for them to be part of the staff team. On the other hand, Hipkiss

(1992) suggested that there was little difference in the degree of allegiance to an institution between part-time and full-time support staff.

Whom do we mean by 'support staff'?

This debate is wider than merely a terminological one since at its heart is the question whether or not the non-teaching staff of a school should be regarded as a homogeneous group for purposes of organisational analysis and management strategy. There is no widely agreed collective noun for the non-teaching or support staff of schools partly perhaps because, by function, they are such a diffuse group. The term 'support staff' is used by the Office for Standards in Education (OFSTED, 1995) and Bullock and Thomas (1994). Mortimore and Mortimore with Thomas (1994) argue that the term 'support staff' does not give any clear view of what the staff are supporting nor of their value to schools. Yet the term 'support staff' describes precisely what such people do in schools, supporting the central processes of teaching and learning. In most organisations cleaning and secretarial services are defined as unskilled or semi-skilled and are relatively poorly paid because it is thought to be quite easy to recruit staff to these posts, but this does not diminish the importance of the work they do. The value of staff to an institution can be demonstrated in other ways apart from their levels of pay, for example by the extent to which they are involved in the decision-making processes of an organisation. The case studies in this chapter give some further illustration of this point.

The term which seems to be used most commonly in schools is 'non-teaching staff' (HMI, 1992; Hipkiss, 1993; Busher and Saran, 1995), although there seems to be a tendency to describe classroom-based non-teaching staff as support staff, ancillary staff or classroom assistants, while reserving the term non-teaching staff for administrative, technical and site staff. Mortimore and Mortimore with Thomas (1994) think the term non-teaching staff is demeaning since it defines people's work by what they are not, a rather negative view of their importance. They prefer their own term, 'associate staff'.

A work characteristic which offers a major distinction between one group of support staff and the others is how closely staff work directly with students, rather than giving support to them at one remove by working with or for teachers. There are some support staff who work mainly directly with students and, for want of a better term, these staff might be described as learning support staff. Like many other members of the support staff they are paid on the APT and C scales for local authority staff. They are sometimes called teaching assistants, welfare assistants or, in the primary school case study in this chapter, primary helpers. Kennedy and Duthie (1975) talk about auxiliary assistants to teachers in the classroom, Mortimore (1989) about para-professionals. Included amongst these people are nursery nurses, education care officers and ethnic minority support staff (Wallace and McMahon, 1993). Bullock and Thomas (1994) use the term non-teaching assistants for these staff but also include librarians and technicians in their ranks. While the former do work directly with students in school libraries, often unsupervised by teachers, technicians usually work at one remove from students in preparatory rooms or workshops, or have only limited contact with students when supplying them with equipment (Busher and Saran, 1995). The term 'ancillary staff' does not seem to be adequate for this group of support staff. Ruthven (1976) used it to cover clerical and technical staff. Howarth (1984) used it as a generic term for all non-teaching staff in a school. Popularly in schools this term is often used to refer to midday or meals supervisors, which is how Loftus (1991) uses it.

The problem of terminology is exacerbated by past political conflicts and the concern of teachers' unions to demarcate clearly between professionally qualified teachers and non-professional classroom helpers. Riches (1981) points out the sensitivity of teachers' unions to the notion of para-professionals or even teacher auxiliaries, a point borne out by one of our case studies. In the early 1990s there was considerable concern expressed by teachers when the then Secretary of State for Education, John Patten, suggested that voluntary parent helpers in classrooms could be relatively easily accredited to provide qualified learning support for large-sized primary classes. But some learning support staff, such as nursery nurses, have semi-professional qualifications. Others have fully professional qualifications, such as librarians and some of the support staff for students with special learning needs. Yet others, such as the primary helpers (classroom assistants) in one of the case studies, have few formal qualifications at all.

Conditions of employment offer another potential framework for classifying non-teaching staff in schools. Riches (1988) draws a distinction between staff who form part of a school's establishment and are based in a single institution (if not always on a single site), staff who visit many schools (such as education welfare officers) and voluntary helpers. Of those who are part of a school's establishment, some are employed full time, such as the site caretaker or senior administrative officer, while others are employed part time, such as midday supervisors and classroom assistants. Some, such as clerical assistants, may be employed full time but only during school terms (Busher and Saran, 1995). In some smaller primary schools there may be no full-time support staff at all, creating an extra administrative burden on senior teaching staff. Since 1990 there have been groups of contract staff in schools, such as cleaners and kitchen staff, who work for private providers or DSOs under the processes of compulsory competitive tendering set up in 1988.

This study prefers the term 'support staff' as the generic term for staff other than teachers in schools, and identifies five major subdivisions by the proximity of their work to the central processes of a school: learning support; technical support; administrative and clerical staff; premises staff (a term used in the Audit Commission (1984) report on non-teaching costs in schools and by OFSTED (1995)); and welfare and catering (see Fig 10.1).

Support Staff in Schools				
Classroom based	Prep room or office based			
Learning support	Technical support	Administration /clerical	Premises and site	Welfare/ catering
School establishment Full-time		Technician – IT, lab, workshop	Senior secretary, administrator, bursar, registrar	Site supervisor, caretaker	
Part-time (includes full-time term only)	Special needs, nursery nurse, librarian, ethnic minority support, language assistants, learning support, ancillary		Clerical assistant, library assistant, receptionist, reprographics	Maintenance	School nurse, meals/midday supervisors
Voluntary	Helpers				
Contract				Cleaners, ground staff	Caterers
Site visitors LEA based	Educational care officer, educational psychologist		Attached part-time bursar		Educational welfare officer
Other	OFSTED Inspector				

Figure 10.1 *Different categories of support staff in schools*

These divisions in no way reflect a scale of relative importance to a school of these different groups of staff. None the less there were detectable differences between the groups, though practice seems to vary between small and large schools. Learning support staff were more likely than other types to be included regularly in teaching staff meetings and to use the teaching staff room for recreation. Other support staff preferred to take a break near to their own work areas (Busher and Saran, 1995). Some laboratory and workshop technicians were included in formal department meetings but many were not. Other support staff, such as the administrative and clerical staff, who provide essential support for the maintenance of the school as an organisation (Torrington and Weightman, 1989), tended to have their own regular staff meetings. This last group were often invited to teaching staff recreational activities. The premises staff, who were responsible for a school's heating, lighting, security and cleanliness, were manual workers who had little contact with teachers and students and were sometimes, apparently, resentful of what little they had (Management in Education, 1991). The catering and welfare staff were usually poorly qualified part-time staff employed only during the school term and who were in school only during lunch breaks. Despite their apparent marginality, senior staff seemed to perceive midday supervisors as key personnel in maintaining order in a school (Busby, 1991; Loftus, 1991). Sometimes some of the welfare staff also carried out other duties, as one of our case studies reports.

This diversity amongst the support staff raised issues for senior teachers and governors about how best to acknowledge the importance of the work of support staff to a school, and how best to involve each of the groups equitably with other teaching and support staff in the decision-making processes of a school. The following case studies begin to address these issues.

Case studies from a governor's perspective

The social–political context

The account which follows is based on governor and chair of governor experiences in two county schools in an inner London borough which was controlled by the Inner London Education Authority (ILEA), until its demise in 1990 as a result of the Education Reform Act of 1988. The schools have been given pseudonyms: Cityland is a primary school and Open Door is a secondary school. Whereas Mortimore and Mortimore with Thomas (1994) studied innovatory uses of support staff in schools, these case studies provide an account of everyday issues that arise in working with such staff.

ILEA policies towards support staff influenced those of the new LEAs which took over from it. For example, ILEA had established a career structure for support staff with good conditions of work. There were reasonable levels of support staff in its schools. The ILEA had acknowledged the importance of support staff to schools by allowing them, along with teachers and parents, to have representation as a group on ILEA school governing bodies. For support staff, this representation ended when school governing bodies were reconstituted by the Education (No 2) Act (1986), depriving them of a direct voice to influence school policies and promote their legitimate interests. Many schools, including the two in these case studies, having benefited from the inclusion of both teaching and support staff on their governing bodies, used their powers of co-option to continue the representation of support staff.

In the schools cited in this study, governors began to think about basic principles concerning pay for the whole staff, not merely for the teaching staff. The pay policies of the two schools contained statements like:

> Under LMS, the governors determine both the teaching and support staff establishments, and judgements have to be made about the appropriate numbers and grades of posts to support the School Development Plan (SDP) priorities.

> A pay policy underpins the whole structure of a school's organisation. It is needed not only to review the pay of existing teaching and support staff but also to assess the appropriate salary each time a new appointment is made.

> The school's curriculum plan and shadow staffing structure [for teaching and support staff], as approved by the governors, will reflect SDP priorities.

> The pay scales of support staff are mostly either APT and C (nationally negotiated) scales or scales negotiated between the LEA and the relevant trade unions. Support staff at school will be paid in accordance with these scales.

At Cityland and Open Door schools relationships between teaching and support staff were good because such policies encouraged people to feel valued as part of a team. However, the processes of arriving at overall staffing structures and of regularly reviewing responsibilities and pay for all staff remained an ever present challenge.

Former ILEA policies influenced how schools worked with support staff in other ways, too. During the late 1970s and the 1980s the ILEA had developed equal opportunities policies to cover the behaviour of its employees in all its institutions on matters of gender, class and race. These were continued after the inner London boroughs became LEAs in 1990 and the schools gained autonomy under LMS. Part of this policy was to reduce discrimination against particular children, their parents and staff in schools. Although raising the awareness of all school staff about this was important, the training of support staff became central to the implementation of these policies. Support staff had a particular part to play in this since it was often they who supervised the playgrounds and classrooms during lunch breaks, especially as many teachers refused to undertake such voluntary supervisory duties after the teachers' industrial action of the mid-1980s. As Saran (1988) points out, they were entitled to do this under the Rossetti School Meals Agreement (1968), so long as they continued to help the headteacher to keep good order in the school. This agreement was the outcome of a working party convened by the Secretary of State and led to an amendment of statutory regulations whereby teachers no longer held the statutory duty to supervise school meals.

Case one: Cityland Primary School

Cityland Primary School was for pupils aged 3–11 years. The nursery and infant pupils numbered over 200 and the juniors around 200. Cityland's total delegated budget in 1995/6 was under £1 million. Leaving aside the kitchen staff who were employed and managed by an LEA DSO, Cityland employed about 20 support staff, many of them part time. Out of the nursery and infant department budget, support staff accounted for 19 per cent and teaching staff for about 67 per cent. Thus the staffing budget absorbed 86 per cent of the total. The equivalent figures for the junior department were: support staff 13 per cent, teaching staff 69 per cent, total 82 per cent. Staffing ratios for early years children are usually higher. National figures for primary schools for 1994/95 were very similar: support staff 14 per cent, teaching staff 69 per cent, total staffing 83 per cent of total delegated budget (Frost, 1995).

The prospectus which Cityland sent to parents covered all aspects of school life, including staffing and the curriculum. Although it did not list staff by name, after its opening sentence: 'Welcome to Cityland School', it informed parents that: 'The teaching and support staff work together to make the school a happy and secure place for children to learn.'

Under a section headed 'School Discipline and Conduct' the team work of staff was further emphasised: 'In our school, teaching and non-teaching staff through their own methods and example encourage and reward good behaviour.'

Even the school meals staff, who were less directly part of the school community for reasons explained earlier in this chapter, were given recognition: 'There is a kitchen on site and meals are prepared by our cook, Caroline Brown, and her team.'

There are countless ways in which the headteacher and governors of a primary school can celebrate the common membership of all staff in the school team. In the entrance lobby to the school, on everyday view in a 'rogues gallery', were photographs of the site manager, primary helpers and the principal administrative officer alongside those of the teachers. In a close-knit community where all staff, children and many parents know each other, social occasions offered further opportunities for this. At Cityland, Christmas was a time for a party for the older children, parents and staff, and for all the staff to get together for a festive drink. Retirement parties were held for all staff and some governors, whether it was the headteacher, the nursery nurse or the primary helper who was joining the ranks of senior citizens. There was also a 'surprise' party for the school secretary's 60th birthday.

Teamwork and sharing helped to make Cityland 'a happy and secure place for children to learn'. At Cityland the staff room was a shared meeting place for all staff throughout the year. Some staff meetings were attended by teaching and support staff when there was an issue of common concern, such as when an antibullying policy was being formulated. As some of the support staff, through their supervision of the playground, would play an important part in implementing this, it seemed sensible for them to be involved in the creation of a workable policy. The unity of staff in implementing school policy was also symbolised by the attendance of *all* staff on the five training days allocated to teachers under the Teachers' Pay and Conditions of Service Act (1987). Support staff also had their own separate regular staff meetings.

The impact of LMS on the support staff at Cityland was evident. By 1995 the job of the school caretaker had been transformed into that of a site manager and the school secretary had become a principal administrative officer in both name and duties. The latter had to acquire a new range of information technology skills to administer and control the school's budget. For this, she received in-service training from the LEA and an increase in salary which took her pay above the level of that for an inexperienced teacher, a reflection, perhaps, of the relative importance to the school of the two posts under LMS. She was not unusual amongst the support staff in receiving in-service training from the LEA.

LMS brought about shifts in previously stable expectations about what certain jobs entailed, although changes in duties were not always, at least immediately, accompanied by changes in pay. An interesting example of this were changes in the roles of the primary helpers at Cityland School. By 1995 these staff, who had previously mainly undertaken unskilled supervisory work in the playground and for school meals, had become involved in supporting teachers in the classroom. In particular they helped with statemented special needs pupils, taking over these duties from the part-time support teachers who, at one time, had come into the school and worked individually with such pupils. Their involvement in classroom duties raised issues for relationships between teaching and support staff. It also caused concern to the teacher unions. The local NUT, for example, called a meeting for all its members in the LEA at Cityland and other schools, and for involved support staff, to discuss the issue.

An elected teacher governor raised the matter at a school governors' meeting on the grounds that primary helpers were not being given proper recognition for the new tasks which they were undertaking. This governor, together with a co-opted governor, a primary helper, then was asked to collect evidence about the pay and responsibilities of primary helpers. Their report revealed that primary helpers were paid at an hourly rate of £4.50; that some of the same people also acted as midday supervisors, for which they were paid at a higher rate, £6 per hour; and that the senior meals supervisor received £8.50 an hour. Not only had the nature of the work of primary helpers changed, but their pay did not reflect this. The report was referred to the governors' personnel and staffing subcommittee for action.

In June 1995, as part of the school's preparation for an OFSTED inspection, the headteacher negotiated new job descriptions with the primary helpers to reflect their actual responsibilities, although their rates of pay were not changed immediately. At the same time the governors brought the problem to the attention of the LEA in the hope that it would lead to a regrading of the primary helpers' jobs and a more adequate valuing across the LEA of the contribution which support staff made to the work of schools.

A combined staffing and pay policy for teaching and support staff
By 1995 at Cityland School the headteacher and governors were in the process of facing a whole new challenge: trying to devise a staffing structure for all staff to meet the framework of the SDP which was within the school's budget. This meant reviewing not just the jobs of the support staff but also those of the teachers, including those of the deputy head and the headteacher. The latter were reviewed in the light of the common spine pay points and the different duties and responsibilities which staff carried out.

This review came at a time of heightened awareness of the extent to which LMS had increased the pressures on school administration. In 1994 the STRB recommended that the professional duties of deputy headteachers be rewritten to give them a clearer managerial role (STRB, 1994, para 137), a view accepted by the Secretary of State for Education in the *School Teachers' Pay and Conditions Document* of that year (DfE, 1994, Part X, para 34). At the same time research by Mortimore and Mortimore with Thomas (1994) had revealed the types of innovatory posts for support staff which some primary and secondary schools had created to try to enhance school effectiveness.

It was in this climate that the governors asked the headteacher to examine the SDP and raise with the personnel and staffing subcommittee any staffing implications from it. The governors expected that the 'staffing issues to be considered should include the role of primary helpers and other support staff. Such an exercise will help governors and staff to know where the school is going and the opportunities for staff development and career advancement.'

At two subsequent meetings of the subcommittee the headteacher presented the SDP, stressing the need for the school to move forward through consultation and consensus. The discussion, especially with regard to the staffing implications, proved difficult. In large part this was because, in an established school, history and accretion shape the existing staffing structure. The SDP reflects the expertise of current staff and their collective wisdom, alongside the view of the headteacher, about what needs to be undertaken to meet the internal needs of a school and to face the external pressures upon a school from the local community, the LEA and central government. Formulating a new SDP and the consequent staff restructuring which that might entail is a different and more painful process from what it would be in a newly established school.

The headteacher argued that the provision of the National Curriculum to all children had to be at the core of the SDP. This left relatively little time and few resources for other activities. Members of the subcommittee then raised questions about how best a staffing structure for support staff could be devised which adequately mirrored that for teaching staff. To lay the foundation for a new shadow staffing structure the headteacher and vice-chair of governors, an experienced manager of staff, set out to generate a short factual statement about how pupil numbers were related to the allocation of all staff, teaching and support, in the school.

Open Door Secondary School

Open Door Secondary School served pupils aged 11–18 years. It was an inner London multicultural comprehensive school with over 1000 students and a large sixth form providing academic and vocational courses. The school budget for 1995/6 was about £3.7 million. Apart from the kitchen staff who were employed under a CCT contract, the school managed 24 support staff who accounted for 9 per cent of the budget. Teaching staff absorbed 70 per cent, making staffing 79 per cent of the total budget. National figures for secondary schools for 1994/5 were: support staff 7 per cent, teaching staff 73 per cent, all staffing 80 per cent of total budget (Frost, 1995).

Several years ago the governors organised a large welcome party for their newly appointed headteacher. All staff were invited, a move fully supported by the new head. Support staff, including cleaners, were heard to comment, 'this never happened before', suggesting that they were unused to feeling included and recognised as part of the staff team.

The new headteacher was convinced that crucial to the successful management of staff, regardless of what job they did, was the attitude of senior staff. Relationships must demonstrate that everyone is valued and treated equitably. The decision of the school to apply for the Investors in People award in 1995 was perceived as evidence of this. It became accepted practice that all staff were listed in alphabetical order in the school's list of staff. The staff room was available for all to use and technicians as well as administrative staff were to be seen there during morning breaks. The weekly staff briefing meeting was for all staff, although some were prevented from attending regularly because of the nature of their duties. Most support staff participated in an annual appraisal of their work on the same basis as the teachers. In-service training was accessible to support and teaching staff. In matters of punctuality, health and safety at work, and co-operative working in pursuit of school aims, the headteacher applied the same code of conduct to all staff.

Widening the use of support staff to meet the challenges of LMS
LMS has led to an increase in support staff jobs in schools, not to the reverse as was at first feared. This has been a necessary increase to cope with the changes brought about by LMS, not a wanton indulgence in extra clerical support to make life easier for teachers. When the school office at Open Door School changed over to a co-ordinated information technology (IT) system to cope with the demands of LMS there were fears of redundancies among clerical staff. By 1995 the opposite had occurred, with the school office handling more work than ever before, releasing teachers from a variety of clerical work to undertake professional duties. The use and development of IT and technology across the curriculum also resulted in new jobs for support staff to service and maintain equipment. The delegation of funding under LMS

to departmental level generated new jobs for support staff. One department, for example, decided not to appoint a temporary replacement teacher but used the money to buy a clerical assistant to help with curriculum development instead.

Not only was there some shift in the school's resources towards the employment of more support staff but more sophisticated use was made of the skills of support staff. For example, the headteacher's personal assistant also served as clerk to the governors and was involved in supporting the head's national activities which indirectly benefited the school. The governors' finance subcommittee included two senior members of the support staff: the principal administrative officer, a co-opted governor who was widely recognised in the school and in the LEA for her efficient management of the school budget; and the site manager, who was invited by virtue of his office. His work, too, had been widely commended as during his stewardship he had saved the school thousands of pounds by running the school services more efficiently and had also improved the cleanliness and security of the school environment.

The impact of the school pay policy on support staff
Drafting the school's pay policy, which began in 1992, was a seminal experience for the governors and the school. By 1995 two annual reviews had produced no major hiccups, though it tended to be teachers' rather than support staff pay which was reviewed. However, it was becoming apparent that the pay of the principal administrative officer and the site manager no longer reflected their level of work, so greatly had the nature of their jobs changed to embrace a wide range of managerial tasks.

As the personnel and staffing subcommittee reviewed the pay of teachers and the governors had a policy of equitable treatment for all staff, it seemed reasonable to review the pay of two of the most senior support staff. Apart from then raising a further issue about the need for the subcommittee to review the jobs and pay of all support staff, the review process uncovered several difficulties. It was discovered, for example, that whereas class teachers, deputies and headteachers had statutory job descriptions, the support staff did not. The principal administrative officer therefore collected details of the job descriptions of the support staff, finding that some long-established staff had none and, in a few cases, nor could the LEA supply any. Furthermore, there were no general guidelines for reviewing the jobs of support staff in the LEA, although such staff did qualify for cost-of-living annual pay rises and annual incremental increases within the pay band of their job under the APT and C scales for local government staff. The sub-committee then realised that the only way to raise an individual employee's rate of pay within the national negotiated scales was to give the person a new job description and regrade their job. Alternatively schools could carry out their own site-based negotiations with the support staff unions for restructuring jobs and pay.

As the governors of Open Door School wanted to remain within the LEA network, which they valued, and to keep broadly in line with the other schools in the LEA, they decided in future to review the job descriptions of all the support staff regularly, although this was a massive undertaking. They began by asking the site manager and the principal administrative officer, in consultation with the deputy head who was their line manager, to draft new job descriptions which reflected the work which they actually did. In due course this led to a regrading of their posts and an increase in pay, after consultation between the governors' finance subcommittee and the personnel and staffing subcommittee. At the same time the subcommittee asked the headteacher to have drawn up valid job descriptions for all support staff, although this raised further questions about what should constitute the generic component of such job descriptions and what should be specific to individual responsibilities. Teachers, too, have job descriptions which include generic and specific components.

Conclusion

The Education Reform Act (1988) made all staffing the responsibility of school governors in England and Wales, including those postholders, such as school caretakers, who were formerly the responsibility of LEA officers rather than of headteachers. To ensure that support staff in schools are used effectively, inspections of schools by people working for OFSTED under the Education (Schools) Act 1992 consider the way in which support staff are deployed. The OFSTED *Handbook* (1993) points out that:

> staffing is not necessarily a fixed cost. In some schools more effective use has been made of resources by altering the balance between teaching, administrative and curriculum support staff... In cost-effective staffing, non-teaching staff are used effectively to relieve more expensive teaching staff of non-educational tasks.
>
> (OFSTED, 1993, Part 5, Technical Papers, paras 19–20, pp 52–3)

Attempts to alter the balance by developing new staffing structures, redefining job specifications and regrading support staff posts may strain relationships between support and teaching staff unless senior staff and governors bring about change through processes of consultation and collaboration. Multiunion involvement in such restructuring processes may pose a considerable challenge to headteachers, LEA officers and other managers in schools. Teacher unions as much as support staff unions, such as UNISON, are concerned to protect the jobs of their members and ensure that pupils receive the best education possible. Changes in staffing are likely to be eased where these can be adequately funded and where senior staff involved in the negotiations utilise high-quality and open negotiating skills.

In Cityland and Open Door Schools leadership from headteachers, senior staff and governors had created an ethos where all staff were valued for their contributions to their schools' aims and to the creation and maintenance of a good learning environment. Although LMS had resulted in flexibilities in the use of resources, restructuring expenditure between teaching and support staff to recognise this was no easy matter as staffing costs absorbed so much of the budget. This made it more difficult for headteachers and governors to shape a staffing structure for support staff to mirror that of teaching staff.

In both schools the development of a pay policy for all staff and its application during individual staff pay reviews raised the level of awareness among governors about issues of equal treatment for support and teaching staff. This threw up challenges to school management about appropriate job descriptions for posts, regrading posts and thinking about the school's present and future staffing structures in relation to the aims and targets in the schools' development plans.

This suggests that the management of support staff is an integral part of the management of all school staff and relationships between teaching and support staff are a key element in the culture of a school. Support staff need to be valued as much as teaching staff, to experience relationships of mutual respect with teaching staff, to know about and accept a school's aims and to be involved in the creation and committed to the implementation of a school's development plan.

References

Audit Commission (1984) *Obtaining Better Value in Education: Non-Teaching Costs*, HMSO, London.

Bullock, A and Thomas, H (1994) *The 'LMS' Impact Project: Final Report*, National Association of Headteachers, London.

Busby, S (1991) 'The management of children in the dining room at lunchtime' in Lomax, P (ed) *Managing Better Schools and Colleges: The Action Research Way*, *BERA Dialogues 4*, Multilingual Matters, Clevedon.

Busher, H and Saran, R (1992) *Teachers' Conditions of Employment*, Bedford Way Papers, Kogan Page, London.

Busher, H and Saran, R (1995) 'Discovering school support staff: an under-researched organisational underclass' paper given at the European Conference for Education Research (ECER) '95 Conference, 15–17 Sept, University of Bath.

Department for Education (1994) *School Teachers' Pay and Conditions Document*, HMSO, London.

Education (No 2) Act (1986), HMSO, London.

Education Reform Act (1988), HMSO, London.

Education (Schools) Act (1992), HMSO, London.

Employment Department (1992) *Investing in People*, HMSO, London.

Frost, R (1995) 'Overview of the impact on quality and standards: the evidence from OFSTED' paper given at the Education/SIMS Seminar, London, 3 February.

Fullan, M (1992) *The New Meaning of Educational Change*, Cassell, London.

Greenwood, M and Gaunt, H (1995) *Total Quality Management for Schools*, Cassell, London.

Haigh, G (1991) 'In the wings', *Times Educational Supplement* 26 April 1991, p xiii.

Hipkiss, J (1992) 'Non-teaching staff in a secondary school', unpublished MA dissertation, Loughborough University.

Hipkiss, J (1993) 'Non-teaching staff in a secondary school: a case study' unpublished mimeo, Department of Education, Loughborough University.

HMI (1992) *Assessment, Recording and Reporting*, A report by HMI on the Second Year of the National Curriculum 1990-91, HMSO, London.

Hopkins, D and Hargreaves, D (1991) *The Empowered School*, Cassell, London.

Howarth, S (1984) *The Head's Legal Guide*, Cromer Publications, London.

Kennedy, K and Duthie, J (1975) *Auxiliaries in the Classroom*, HMSO, Edinburgh.

Loftus, J (1991) 'Bringing about a more effective working relationship between teaching and ancillary staff in an infant school' in Lomax, P (ed) *Managing Better Schools and Colleges: The Action Research Way, BERA Dialogues 4*, Multilingual Matters, Clevedon.

Lyons, G and Stenning, R (1986) *Managing Staff in Schools*, Hutchinson, London.

Management in Education (1991) 'A head's month: course thoughts by a junior school headteacher', *Management in Education* 5, 1, pp 2–3.

Mortimore, B (1989) 'Life with the para-professionals', *Times Educational Supplement* 13 October, p 35.

Mortimore, P and Mortimore, J with Thomas, H (1994) *Managing Associate Staff in Schools*, Paul Chapman, London.

Office for Standards in Education (OFSTED) (1993) *Handbook for Inspection*, HMSO, London.

OFSTED (1995) *Handbook for Inspection*, HMSO, London.

Riches, C (1981) 'Non-teaching staff in primary and secondary schools', *Block 6 Course E323*, Open University, Milton Keynes.

Riches, C (1988) 'Managing Staff in schools', *Block 4 Course E325*, Open University Press, Milton Keynes.

Ruthven, B.T (1976) *Ancillary Staff in Secondary Schools: A Report for the Scottish Education Department*, HMSO, Edinburgh.

Saran, R (1988) 'School teachers' pay and conditions of employment in England and Wales' in Saran, R and Sheldrake, J (eds) *Public Sector Bargaining in the 1980s*, Gower, Aldershot.

School Teachers' Review Body (STRB) (1994) *Third Report* Cm 2466, HMSO, London.

STRB (1995) *Fourth Report* Cm 2765, HMSO, London

Torrington, D and Weightman, J (1989) *The Reality of School Management*, Blackwell, Oxford.

Wallace, M and McMahon, A (1993) 'Ethnic minority staff in primary schools: a deprofessionalised semi-profession?' *School Organisation* 13, 3, pp 303–17.

Chapter 11

Managing Staff Professionally
Hugh Busher and
Rene Saran

Introduction

In the 1970s and 1980s a considerable amount of research (eg Rutter *et al*, 1979; Mortimore *et al*, 1988; Reynolds and Cuttance, 1992) was undertaken into the internal characteristics of effective schools. Harber (1992) suggests that, on the face of it, these appear to be largely common sense, and lists what he considers to be the main findings. These may be summarised as emphasising the importance of:

- the leadership of the headteacher and senior staff;
- schools being well-managed and orderly communities;
- the quality of the culture of a school so that
  a) staff are happy and operate with agreed policies;
  b) teachers always adhere to a strong professional code of practice;
  c) students believe that high achievement is important;
  d) students identify with a school through influencing its running and organisation;
- there being high quality teaching;
- the curriculum being appropriately differentiated for students of all abilities;
- students being kept informed of how well they are performing so that they can improve.

In addition to these factors Harber points out that the socio-political environment at both macro- and local levels has a vital influence on schools, shaping the way their staff are able to operate. Unfortunately, as Ball (1987) argued, how such contextual factors affect the internal decision-making of a school is little researched, although Busher (1992) makes reference to how parents' attitudes affect the actions and decisions of teachers. He also discusses through what mechanisms some policies implemented by an LEA influence the way in which a school uses some of its resources. Harber (1992) cites three case studies on this topic to show that the environment affects the culture of a school. Becoming involved in marketing may be one means through which schools can become more responsive to their local communities as well as to the views of their students, who may be said to be part of a school's internal environment or market (Devlin and Knight, 1990). Rudduck *et al* (1995) document how well students understand what makes schools effective.

Leadership and management are two different but interrelated facets of helping people in school organisations to work together effectively. These people may be school-aged students, clerical and technical staff or professionally qualified teachers. Brighouse and Tomlinson (1991) support this view, identifying leadership, and management and organisation, as two of seven characteristics to be found in successful schools. The others are collective review, creating the environment, staff development, teaching and learning, and parental involvement. The last bears witness to Harber's view that school effectiveness research may have overlooked this, so far, as an important factor contributing to the success of a school.

Leadership is intimately bound up with the development and maintenance of values and beliefs by senior people in an organisation or part of an organisation. Headteachers are important creators and maintainers of educational and social values in their schools. Cohen and March (1983) point out that school leaders face ambiguities in four key areas of running schools as organisations, either because the preferred outcomes are not clear or because there are several possible outcomes but not all of them can be achieved. The four areas of choice lie in deciding:

- the purposes of a school to meet the differing needs of the students and parents;
- how to use the power which they are given as leaders;
- what they can learn from their experiences as leaders to inform their future practice;
- how success in institutional and personal terms can be defined.

The styles of leadership which, for example, a headteacher or a head of department embraces to cope with these ambiguities will affect the way in which other staff treat each other (Busher, 1992). A headteacher who works in an autocratic manner is likely to provoke staff to act in a similar manner towards their colleagues, their students and the students' parents. Within departments in a school senior postholders will exercise a similar influence. These styles will depend on the educational and social values which leaders hold and will reflect how they perceive the processes of teaching and learning; their views of appropriate relationships between teachers and students; and their perceptions of and interactions with the people, both teaching and support staff and governors, with whom they work. We try to summarise the range of possibilities this implies in Figure 11.1.

Leadership and the management of professional teachers

Possible relationships between leadership style and school culture

1. Autocracy		Co-operation			Autonomy
2. Tells	Sells	Persuades	Listens	Delegates	Abdicates
		Corporate Managerialism		Collegial Empowerment	
3.		Contrived Collegiality		Genuine Collegiality	
4.		Consultation		Negotiation	
		(Participation)			
5.		Process Participation		Content Participation	
6. Dependent Teachers		Quasi-Interdependent Teachers		Interdependent Teachers	Independent Teachers

Figure 11.1 *Leadership and management of professional teachers.*
Sources: line 1 Campbell (1985), SED (1988), Southworth (1988); line 2 Tannenbaum and Schmidt (1973); line 3 Hargreaves, A (1991); line 4 Packwood (1981); line 5 Busher and Saran (1992); line 6 Ribbins (1992). From Busher and Saran (1994a).

Leaders may be effective or ineffective. Gibb (1947) described those people who held office ineffectually in an organisation as merely having headship. To be an effective leader, ideas and values have to be translated into a vision for the future and communicated to those people whose opinions and work need to be co-ordinated and affirmed so that that vision may be enacted. The distinction which Brighouse (1991) draws between leadership and management activity is a useful one. He suggests that if the former is concerned with vision and having an idea of how to achieve it, the latter involves working with people in creating a particular climate or environment in a school, helping staff to develop their skills, organising and co-ordinating the work of a school and keeping the school process under review. Effective leaders, then, have to engage in managerial processes, whether bureaucratic, interpersonal or micro-political. Blase and Blase (1995) point to the importance of all three.

This chapter considers how leaders at any level in a school organisation might manage with staff to implement, professionally and effectively, the teaching and learning processes which are at the core of schooling.

Who are the teachers?

Several authors in this book have commented on the nature of teacher professionality, of the autonomy that is implicit in it and of necessity part of it. Although teachers in schools may be interdependent, at least when schools are managed collaboratively (Ribbins, 1992), they usually work separately from their colleagues. On the other hand they also usually work with large groups of students, helping the students as a group and individually to learn and to manage their own learning. Greenwood and Gaunt (1994) likened the teacher of a class to a chief executive, needing both to understand the 'business' thoroughly and the socio-political environment in which it operates, and to be able to help people (the students) to carry out their work effectively. Teachers have to work with students not only collectively, perhaps when explaining a task or delivering some information, but also individually, making judgements about how best to help each student on the basis of their subject knowledge and their knowledge of a student's needs. Mortimore (1993) suggested that teachers need five different types of knowledge – curriculum, pedagogical, psychological, sociological and organisational and a wide range of skills 'so that the dynamics of individual learners can be effectively co-ordinated and... so that teaching itself can be continually improved' (pp 61–2).

An important part of professionality is the ethical code which teachers bring to their work, their sense of how it is appropriate to carry out their jobs. Many teachers subscribe to what might be described as a vocational ethic, that is they put the interests of their clients, the students, before their own particular interests. The term client is used most carefully here to suggest somebody with whom a service provider (teacher) is contracted to work to create an effective service (teaching and learning) tailored to the needs of that person. Teachers are indirectly contracted to the students who choose their school through the schools which employ them to teach a particular curriculum. This process of collaborative working between client and provider creates a very different relationship from that between consumer-purchasers and providers (Gray, 1991). In the latter case customers tend to know little about the providers of an object or service, and have little personal contact with them, however much they may know about the product. Morgan (1992) points out that businesses listen to the views of their clients in order to tailor the processes of service provision to meet client needs. He suggests that schools should accord the same respect to the views of their students and parents as it would provide teachers with insights into how well their courses were adapted to student needs and parent concerns. Along with other performance indicators such as student test results, records of achievement and National Curriculum Standard Assessment Tests (SATs), these would help teachers to judge the quality of their work. Harber (1992) explained that such attentiveness is already a characteristic of effective schools. Some schools have used this approach successfully to tackle behaviour problems, such as bullying or undervaluing the work of midday supervisors (Busby, 1991).

Teachers at work

Apart from the research evidence of people such as Nias (1984) on why teachers teach and the myriad anecdotes of teachers who profess to put the interests of their students before their own, there seem few other explanations able to account for the working hours teachers apparently willingly undertake to fulfil their duties, particularly as their pay is not linked in any way to the hours they work. The School Teachers' Review Body (STRB) noted that full-time classroom teachers in primary schools in 1994 worked on average 48.8 hours a week, of which some 39 were spent on teaching or student-related activities while a further four or so were spent on school management and administration or curriculum matters. The use of time amongst secondary school teachers was substantially the same, although heads of departments spent two or three hours longer on management and administration (STRB, 1995, para 146, Chart 4).

These figures have to be set in two contexts in order to gain an appreciation of their impact on teachers' lives: the number of hours outside the working day in which teachers are regularly engaged and the number of people with whom they work. The STRB claimed that teachers, on average, worked each weekend for 4½ hours and after 6 pm on weekday evenings for 1½ hours per night (STRB, 1995, tables 33, 34 and 37). Many teachers claim they spend many hours during school holidays on curriculum development and preparation. Like professional staff in many other jobs, teachers have to prepare, during their own time, papers and other materials to support their work and undertake professional development and renewal. None the less teachers would seem to work substantially harder than the national average working week of 37 hours, even allowing for their notionally long holidays. Further, their rates of pay compare unfavourably with those of police constables and junior officers in the armed services with whom such comparisons, conventionally, have been made, and bear no comparison at all with other professional workers such as doctors, solicitors or managers in industry, particularly when the non-financial rewards of the latter are taken into account.

If this were not sufficient to suggest the dedication with which teachers undertake their work, it is enlightening to consider briefly the span of control involved in supervising students in classrooms and to compare this with industrial and commercial practices. Most professionals, such as solicitors or doctors, and semi-professionals, such as nurses or bank staff, usually work with clients on an individual basis, one at a time. They might well argue that it is impossible to do otherwise as they have to make complex judgements about the individual needs of their clients, as teachers have to with their students. Apart from these judgements, teachers in most maintained schools in England and Wales, often working with between 25 and 30 students at once, additionally have to make judgements about the likely and actual interactions between students when they are presented with particular materials and learning opportunities at particular times in the day or week. During lessons, teachers usually have to give guidance and support to students individually as well as to the class as a whole. Most of the work which students do involves a variety of conceptual and, in some lessons, physical manipulations and transformations. In industry it is usually suggested that when work is semi-skilled, involving the possibility of some conceptual or technical problems, managers can, at most, supervise effectively only between eight and ten people. With routine manual work this recommended span of effective control is usually stretched to 15 people, but no more. In no way could the process of teaching and learning be classified as routine manual work, yet many teachers normally supervise double that number of people.

The changing meaning and context of supervision

The cultural transposition of practices and language is a difficult matter, whether between business and education or between different countries and education systems. Terms used in an industrial context, such as supervisor, may not have the same meaning in education (Burlingame, 1979). Transferring terms carelessly also risks importing, along with the language, values which may be appropriate in one sphere but are inappropriate or destructive in another. Davies (1994) in *Beyond Authoritarian School Management* points out how the use of language such as 'school leaders' has brought with it the application of military metaphors to some of the rituals and ceremonies of schools, such as assemblies. In turn, such language has brought with it notions of conflict and hierarchy that fit uncomfortably with the practice of teachers working alongside students, and might heighten tension in a school where there are already strained relationships between teachers and students.

For example, as Smyth (1991) points out, supervision in education is different from that in commerce or industry. In education it involves processes of dialogue between teacher and student that can on occasions outweigh relationships of hierarchy and control based on expert knowledge. Although Smyth is talking about the supervision of trainee teachers, the point can be more generally applied to relationships between teachers and students of all ages. Part of that dialogue contains a process of empowerment by teachers allowing and acknowledging that students may learn and practise effectively in ways other than those which the teacher has recommended. In industry, supervisors usually ultimately remain in control of deciding how jobs should be done, if only through being the hierarchically appointed arbiters of the differing opinions, including their own, put forward for the solving of problems in a particular sphere of activity.

Following Smyth's argument it is as reasonable to consider teachers engaged in the process of empowering students through helping them to learn how to learn, as it is them providing students with a service of supervision. Teachers work with and alongside students as well as guiding and assessing their performances. An important aspect of this perspective is that teachers, and perhaps other staff in schools, too, are themselves engaged in learning as well as taking a leading part in maintaining a community of learners. Constable, in Chapter 9, points to the tensions this can cause teachers. Such interactive or emancipatory views of teaching and learning imply the need for more interdependent relationships between people in school organisations than is portrayed in conventional hierarchic–bureaucratic descriptions of them. Such relationships might more aptly be conceptualised by the notions of genuine collegiality put forward by Hargreaves (1991; 1994) or of leaders wielding power through or with people (Blase and Blase, 1995) than by leaders and senior managers having power over staff and students.

Trust: the key to collaborative forms of management

Being empowered as a teacher means being part of a school which works as a community or a series of teams but which also delegates autonomy to its members' decision-making, at least within limited spheres, such as the classroom or the department or a particular task like developing records of achievement. In turn this implies that staff are encouraged to take initiatives which will improve the quality of the service provided, such as the learning undertaken. Hopkins and Hargreaves (1991), amongst many others, argue that this will lead to staff being committed to their work and highly motivated. Greenwood and Gaunt (1994), again amongst many others writing about total quality management, describe this as removing the sense of fear which many staff have in organisations that however they act or whatever initiatives they undertake their work will always be criticised. This atmosphere of judgement is the converse of an atmosphere of trust in an organisation. Sadly for those managers and theorists oriented to rational models of management, the provision of detailed job specifications and tabulated descriptions of staff competences, intended to promote efficient and effective organisations, is likely to foster fear – because each member of staff will anxiously compare their every step with what is laid down in their contract. The implicit messages of such prescriptions is a lack of trust in colleagues – why else try to control so tightly how people act? – and a discouragement of autonomy and initiative. Everybody may know their place, but nobody dare step out of line for fear of criticism from senior management or from their colleagues, whose role definitions they might breach when taking an initiative.

The culture or atmosphere of a school has important repercussions on the way people work, whether teachers or support staff, students or governors. The culture of an organisation is the summation of the values, attitudes and beliefs which are widely shared amongst most of the people who work in it. It provides what some might describe as the natural way of doing things in a school, against which the actions of staff and students are judged. When visiting different schools it is obvious that each has its own 'atmosphere' or 'climate', though how this is so starkly revealed is not so easy to define. Headteachers and senior staff are amongst the most important definers of school culture, not only through their public actions and speech but also through their personal relationships. The culture of a school is not permanently fixed but changes, usually slowly, in response to changes in members' views and needs and in the external environment. Sparkes (1991) points out that although an organisation's culture contains many elements of tradition it is in a constant state of being renegotiated by the members of the organisation.

Harrison (1995) suggests that in order to construct a culture which promotes effective collaborative learning, which school effectiveness research suggests is positively linked with effective schools, staff in schools need to construct effective collaborative management. The lead in establishing this has to come from those in positions of greatest formal power, the senior staff and school governors. This, he perceives, is not an abdication of a leader's authority but its relocation through delegation (p. 8). Hopkins *et al* (1994) take a similar view when emphasising the importance of team work through collaborative planning and the use of effective strategies for co-ordinating activities.

In a more emancipatory paradigm of school governance or management the key aspect is the maintenance of trust between followers and leaders: students, teachers and support staff, on the one hand, and headteachers and governors on the other (Locke, 1992; Blase and Blase, 1995; Esp and Saran, 1995). Drucker (1990) argues that organisations have to be based on trust because they can only operate effectively if there is mutual understanding between people. Not only do attempts to prescribe behaviour tightly (perhaps through competence statements or detailed job descriptions) appear to indicate a lack of trust by senior staff in their colleagues, but they almost invariably lead to subversion as individuals try to preserve some autonomy of action and sense of self. Ganderton (1991) points out that subversion plays an important part in school organisations, allowing the perspectives of individuals to be sustained in dialogue with the perspective of the collectivity, which is often dominated by formally powerful senior staff.

Although trust requires all parties to act in an open and honest manner it does not exclude the micro-political processes which riddle institutions and through which participants try to influence decisions. It is more a matter of how these processes are carried out, in public arenas rather than in cabals behind closed doors, than whether or not they exist. Micro-politics emerge for various reasons. One is that it is impossible to prescribe through rules how members of an organisation should behave on every occasion. A second is that different people in organisations have legitimately differing professional and personal interests. In schools many teachers' expressed professional interests are likely to be predicated on deeply held personal educational and social beliefs about the purposes and processes of schooling. Some are to do with how a school is managed and resources allocated, others focus on the processes of teaching and learning. Some of these may be congruent with the aims and purposes of a school and some may not (Busher, 1992). In order to pursue their interests staff will tend to form into factions and coalitions, some through the formal structures of a school such as departments and some through informal channels. Although Hoyle (1986) perceived micro-political negotiations as being confined to an organisational underworld, other authors (Ganderton, 1991; Busher and Saran, 1994b; Blase and Blase, 1995) perceive them as part of everyday life in schools, facilitating the leadership activities of people within a school's organisational structures.

Trust is seen by Locke (1992) as a means by which formally powerful people, be they headteachers or school governors, empower other staff to take part openly in decision-making. In doing so they assume colleagues will behave in predictable and acceptable ways. Acceptable, here, means behaviour that enacts values and policies agreed between people. For example when appointing a new teacher, using a variety of techniques and interviews, the headteacher and school governors provide a school community with reasonable grounds on which to expect that the new colleague will behave acceptably. An important aspect of trust is that people will exercise it in the interests of the collectivity or organisation rather than in pursuit only of their self-interest (Locke, 1992). Such altruism seems rather suitable grounds for empowering vocationally oriented staff, such as teachers, to take part in decision-making at school and classroom level and to exercise autonomy of action in those activities where they are agreed to behave professionally. As trust is so highly valued in institutions and legal systems such bodies usually impose stiff penalties on people who betray it.

Such an approach to managing school organisations requires participants of whatever status to acknowledge that the school is a community of interdependent members (Sergiovanni, 1994) – staff, students, parents and governors – with shared responsibility for the success and successful management of the school (Harrison, 1995) and with continued commitment to staff development and learning. It requires individual staff to take responsibility for the success of the whole school, not just for the students in their classes or the efficiency of their clerical work – becoming extended professionals, to use Hoyle's term (1981). It requires headteachers and governors to empower staff to do so by facilitating collaborative forms of management.

Facilitating collaborative management

To manage schools in a collaborative way requires a shift in the style of leadership in schools from a traditionally bureaucratic–authoritarian one which focuses on control (Harber, 1992) to a more emancipatory one which encourages members to participate in decision-making at school-wide as well as classroom level. Everard (1988) described this as a facilitative style of leadership which supports and empowers staff while sustaining and renegotiating core institutional values. Hopkins *et al* (1994) prefer the term 'transformational leadership' but appear to mean much the same thing. Such views put forward for schools those same flat management processes advocated by Deming and others for industry and commerce under the framework of total quality management (Greenwood and Gaunt, 1994).

Blase and Blase (1995) prefer to envisage more 'democratic' forms of school governance. This is a significant shift in language away from the organisational overtones of managerialism; corporate mission statements, which may generate a new conformity rather than a new empowerment of workers (Ozga, in Chapter 2); and hierarchy, however flat. It moves emphasis in understanding the workings of organisations away from the bureaucratic and the structural towards the micro-politics of negotiated decision-making. This latter perspective does not deny the existence of bureaucracies and structures, but does emphasise the interactive processes of people in them and through them.

More collaborative styles of school governance require the involvement of staff in the systematic collection and review of school-based data to focus efforts towards school improvement; the involvement of staff in planning continuity and change at school-wide, department and classroom level; the greater responsiveness of a school to the identified needs of its clients and their proxies, whether students, parents or the wider community; and the adequate provision of relevant in-service education for teaching and support staff to allow them to meet the changing requirements of their jobs. Within this paradigm the process of school development planning, discussed by Constable in Chapter 9, is a powerful tool if carried out in a consultative manner.

Trust is fostered through collaborative or collegial decision-making at school-wide and department level as well as at classroom level, although decision-making is constrained by the external social and political pressures surrounding schools and the internal social dynamics of each institution. In maintained schools in England and Wales these will tend to be focused round the effects of schools' delegated budgets.

Formally trust can be promoted through the use of regular staff meetings, though who has membership of these and when they are held may raise important questions for who feels empowered and who feels excluded. Meetings which always fall at such a time that particular staff have difficulty attending are likely to leave those staff believing that their opinions are not given equal weight with those people who can attend, although informal processes of consultation may reduce this impression to some extent. From some recent small-scale qualitative research (Busher and Saran, 1995) it would seem unusual for support staff to be included with teaching staff in department meetings in secondary schools. Where staff of a certain level of seniority only are invited to attend particular meetings, without these meetings and agenda being notified to other staff, it is likely to leave those not included, and usually of a lesser status, feeling marginalised. This in turn can lead to disaffection or lack of enthusiasm amongst such staff. How staff meetings are conducted also affects the extent to which people feel empowered by them.

Monitoring and reviewing performance can be the key to school improvement as it helps teachers adapt to a changing environment and meet the needs of students and the community. Yet the Office for Standards in Education (OFSTED, 1994) identified these processes as a major weakness in schools. Teachers as a matter of course monitor students' performances to guage how well they are progressing. The performances of students in the upper secondary school have been assessed through public examinations for many decades. Since the early 1990s in the UK these have been supplemented by SATs at the various Key Stages of the National Curriculum. Greenwood and Gaunt (1994) recommend the development of statistical assessments of the value added to students' performances by attendance at a series of lessons in a subject.

The evaluation of staff, school and student performance can be carried out collaboratively or hierarchically, for internal audiences in an organisation or for external ones (Thomas, 1985). In a rational model of evaluation, emphasising hierarchical control and internal audiences, the review process might use checklists and target setting which purports to allow senior staff to make judgements on the performance of colleagues and students. Such approaches often rely on the expertise and authority of external supervisors, whether OFSTED or providers of psychometric tests. They tend to disempower the practitioners by preventing them using their own professional expertise to control the processes or purposes of evaluation, requiring them only to act as clerical staff administering the processes of evaluation. Such approaches are likely to reduce the sense of shared responsibility held by staff for a school because they appear to indicate a lack of trust by school management in their staff and reduce the autonomy of decision-making which staff have in their own particular spheres of activity. Such approaches are the antithesis of collaborative management and are likely to produce staff who have adequate levels of commitment to an institution to maintain it but insufficient to make it dynamically responsive to the needs of its students.

School review includes not only the performances of students but also, for example, the effectiveness of clerical procedures, teaching methods and, perhaps, management processes. For example, central government requires the appraisal of teaching staff under the Education (No 2) Act (1986) and *Circular 12/91* (DES, 1991), though the appraisal of support staff does not yet seem to have become firmly established. Although the processes of teacher appraisal are essentially hierarchical, albeit with a focus on staff development needs, not on judgement and without connecting the outcomes to teachers' pay or security of job, teachers are able to shape the focuses of classroom observation in many schools.

Alternative collaborative processes of critical review, which Brighouse and Tomlinson (1991) call collective review, tends to create effective schools which perform like the communities of learners recommended by Harrison (1995) or Hopkins *et al* (1994) and which Blase and Blase (1995) show to exist. Here staff are encouraged to work together by and with senior colleagues and school governors to review their practices in a structured way to meet pressures in the external institutional environment and students' needs, adapting teaching, learning and management processes to do so. They encourage their students to do likewise. Smyth (1991) perceives this as a process of collaborative learning among teachers which may, as Constable suggests in Chapter 9, cause some uncomfortable cultural confusion for some teachers. There are various techniques for carrying out such emancipatory review processes, such as the processes of action research or action enquiry of which Lomax (1990) gives several examples. To be effective, staff need to make rigorous use of data to address questions of practical concern which arise out of their own working practices, whether at classroom or school-wide level. After reviewing practice the next step is to implement and monitor change, whether following an action research cycle or a school development planning cycle.

The structural organisational support needed both for the process of review and for the implementation of outcomes is in three forms. One is the investment of school resources, though how much can be provided will be limited by budgetary constraints. This can take the form of time, for a team of teachers to define the focus of the review, collect the data, evaluate them, and not be available for doing other things; materials with which to collect the data; and money, either directly to buy resources, such as substitute teachers to cover the classes of those doing the review, or imputedly. Failure to provide resources by senior staff or to take note of the findings of a review, ie not lending authority to its outcomes, is likely to lead to demoralistion by the staff involved in undertaking it and a loss of a sense of empowerment.

Second, it requires the support and approval of senior staff and governors. Not only can they empower staff by providing the financial, material and time resources but they can also lend authority to other teachers' work. Praising the work which staff are doing or taking an enthusiastic interest in it may be as important as material support, particluarly if this incorporates expert advice on how to surmount problems. Helping to create a supportive or non-threatening culture for change and innovation in a school is also important. Staff need the support of their colleagues, either as part of the team carrying out a review or as people providing information to that team, or as professional colleagues being sympathetic to what such work involves.

Third and possibly most important it needs the provision of staff development. The importance of staff as a key resource in schools and other service industries is widely recorded. Since 1987 teachers in the UK have been given five days training each school year and central government part-funds teacher in-service training on short courses where school and LEA priorities accord with its own as set out annually in the grants for educational support and training funding scheme.

Staff development

Staff development takes many forms, but may be said to have three stages: induction, for staff entering a school at any level; widening expertise; and preparation for the next career phase, including retirement and long-term leave of absence for any reason. All staff need induction to become familiar with the culture of a school, its values, beliefs, rules and regulations. They also need to become aware of the different responsibilities of their colleagues and to know practically where resources are stored and how they are accessed. Many of these aspects may be incorporated in a school handbook or prospectus. It forms part of the information which maintained schools have been required by the UK central government to make available to parents and the local community since the early 1980s. Informally, new staff in a school are likely to want to know who are influential people in a school, as well as who are the formally powerful.

An important, if specialist aspect of induction is the initiation of trainee teachers into the profession. In addition to the types of support already discussed, such staff will need specialised support and guidance. Reid *et al* (1994) consider at some length the range of issues involved in inducting trainee or student teachers. Initial teacher education is part of staff development, not only for the trainees but also as a professional development opportunity for established staff. It allows established teachers to reflect on their practice when having to give guidance to novitiates on how to prepare themselves for lessons and evaluate their performances both in the classroom and as members of the staff of a school.

Established teachers need to develop a deeper understanding of their classroom activities and how these are influenced by a wide range of organisational and external pressures. They may also want to become familiar with the wide range of tasks involved in managing a school. Busher (1988) explored the range of jobs which teachers in one humanities faculty undertook outside their classrooms to further the work of the department. He argued that the involvement of as many staff as possible in these jobs not only reduced the strain on the head of department but also contributed to the professional development of the other staff. Undertaking these jobs could be organised on a rotating schedule so that all staff eventually knew about every aspect of the work of a department. Some staff might be resistant to this because it increased their workloads, ie there may be some staff in a department or school who find the practice of extended professionality threatening and the responsibilities of empowerment unwelcome.

As well as farming out jobs within schools and departments, enabling people to take part in decision-making as full participants will help to develop their professional expertise as well as their understanding of organisational processes. As long ago as 1982 Rudduck suggested the involvement of teachers with education colleagues, both internal and external to a school, in observing and researching what goes on in classrooms. Another approach to staff enrichment she recorded was of teachers visiting other schools to see them at work. Both processes are now partly contained within teachers' conditions of service. Teacher appraisal uses some minimal levels of classroom observation to help teachers consider aspects of performance which they want to improve. Public examinations, including the National Curriculum SATs, encourage teachers to moderate their evaluations of students' work with colleagues from other schools. Busher and Hodgkinson (1995) comment on the widespread development of inter-school networks by teachers in one area of England to foster curriculum development, amongst other things.

In drawing to a close this discussion on appropriate forms of school management for professional staff, some reference must be made to how effective schools manage their external environments, since this, too, can be a means of facilitating collaborative management. Traditionally schools have been reluctant to encourage communities to share their facilities and see their classrooms at work. Traditionally, too, teachers have tended to claim professional expertise as a reason for paying little heed to community and student views on school and classroom processes. On the other hand some schools have had close and successful involvement with their local communities for many years and claim to be adept at tailoring their management and curriculum processes, within the regulations for their type of educational institution, to meet their needs.

The market-oriented approach of local management of schools (LMS) has forced all maintained schools since 1988 in England and Wales to be more responsive to the needs of their clients and potential clients or risk not attracting sufficient students to generate enough income to sustain the school budget. However such a quasi-commercial relationship is not the same as that engendered by a school working in partnership with its local community to create the range of educational opportunities which will best serve the needs of a community's students. In the latter partnership paradigm, ironically perhaps, teachers are once again trusted professionals who are believed by the community to know how to construct a high-quality school experience with and for the students. But in this case it is because there is an open and honest dialogue between teachers and the community about how education is undertaken – not, as formerly, because of teachers' claims to a great and mysterious expertise. Promoting such a dialogue may involve schools and teachers using a range of marketing techniques, not as glib sales devices, but to research how best a school can begin to meet the educational wants and needs which its students and potential students and their parents have.

References

Ball, S (1987) *The Micro-politics of the school*, Methuen, London

Blase, J and Blase, J (1995) 'The micropolitical orientation of facilitative school principals and its effects on teachers' sense of empowerment', paper given at the American Educational Research Association (AERA) Conference, San Francisco, April.

Brighouse, T (1991) *What Makes a Good School?*, Network Educational Press, Stafford.

Brighouse, T and Tomlinson, J (1991) *Successful Schools,* Institute for Public Policy Research, London.

Burlingame, M (1979) 'Some neglected dimensions in the study of educational administration' *Educational Administration Quarterly* 15, 1, pp 1–18.

Busby, S (1991) 'The management of children in the dining room at lunchtime' in Lomax, P (Ed) *Managing Better Schools and Colleges: The Action Research Way BERA Dialogues 4,* Multilingual Matters, Clevedon.

Busher, H (1988) 'Reducing role overload for a head of department: a rationale for fostering staff development', *School Organisation* 8, 1, pp 99–103.

Busher, H (1992) 'The politics of working in secondary schools: some eachers' perspectives on their schools as organisations' unpublished PhD thesis, School of Education, University of Leeds.

Busher, H and Hodgkinson, K (1995) 'Managing interschool networks: across the primary/secondary divide', *School Organisation* 15, 3.

Busher, H and Saran, R (1992) 'Changing Professional roles of teachers in the UK' paper given at the BEMAS Annual Conference 12–13 September University of Bristol, Bristol.

Busher, H and Saran, R (1994a) 'The politics of school management' in Public Finance Foundation (1994) *How to Manage a School: Conference Proceedings,* Chartered Institute of Public Finance and Accountancy, London.

Busher, H and Saran, R (1994b) 'Towards a model of school leadership', *Educational Management and Administration* 22, 1, pp 5–13.

Busher, H and Saran, R (1995) 'Discovering school support staff: an under-researched organisational underclass', paper given at the ECER 95 Conference, University of Bath, 15–17 September.

Campbell, R (1985) *Developing the Primary School Curriculum,* Holt, Rinehart & Winston, New York.

Cohen, M and March, J (1983) 'Leadership in an organised anarchy' in Aldridge, J and Deal, T (eds) *The Dynamics of Organisational Change in Education,* McCutchan, New York.

Davies, L (1994) *Beyond Authoritarian School Management,* Education Now Books, Ticknall.

Department of Education and Science (1991) *Circular 12/91,* HMSO, London.

Devlin, T and Knight, B (1990) *Public Relations and Marketing for Schools,* Longman, Harlow.

Drucker, P (1990) *Managing the Non-Profit Organisation,* Butterworth Heinemann, London.

Esp, D and Saran, R (1995) *Effective Governors for Effective Schools,* Pitman Publishing, London.

Everard, K B (1988) 'Learning to manage' paper given at the BEMAS Annual Conference, September 1988, Oxford Polytechnic, Oxford.

Ganderton, P S (1991) 'Subversion and the organisation: some theoretical considerations' *Educational Management and Administration* 19, 1, pp 30–6.

Gibb, C A (1947) 'The principles and traits of leadership' in Gibb, C A (ed) (1969) *Leadership*, Penguin, Harmondsworth.

Gray, L (1991) *Marketing Education*, Open University Press, Milton Keynes.

Greenwood, M S and Gaunt, H J (1994) *Total Quality Management for Schools*, Cassell, London.

Harber, C (1992) 'Effective and ineffective schools: an international perspective on the role of research', *Education Management and Administration* 20, 3, pp 161–9.

Hargreaves, A (1991) 'Contrived collegiality: the micropolitics of teacher collaboration' in Blase, J (ed) (1991) *The Politics of Life in Schools: Power, Conflict and Co-operation*, Sage, London.

Hargreaves, A (1994) *Changing Teachers, Changing Times*, Cassell, London.

Harrison, B T (1995) 'Regenerating leadership, authority and service in education: empowerment through teamwork', inaugural lecture, Division of Education, University of Sheffield, 14 June.

Hopkins, D, Ainscow, M and West, M (1994) *School Improvement in an Era of Change*, Cassell, London.

Hopkins, D and Hargreaves, D (1991) *The Empowered School*, Cassell, London.

Hoyle, E (1981) 'The process of management' in *Management and the School E323 Block 3* Open University, Milton Keynes.

Hoyle, E (1986) *The Politics of School Management*, Hodder & Stoughton, London.

Locke, M (1992) 'The application of "Trust" in the management of institutions', paper given at the British Educational Management and Administration Society Annual Conference, University of Bristol, 12–13 September.

Lomax, P (ed) (1990) *Managing Staff Development in Schools: An Action Research Approach, BERA Dialogues 3*, Multilingual Matters, Clevedon.

Morgan, G (1992) 'Children are clients: what have primary pupils got to say about equal opportunities?' *Education Management and Administration* 20, 3, pp 193–7.

Mortimore, P, Sammons, P, Stoll, L, Lewis, D and Ecob, R (1988) *School Matters: The Junior Years*, Open Books, Wells.

Mortimore, P (1993) 'Managing teaching and learning: two sides of the same coin: The search for a match' in Busher, H and Smith, M (eds) *Managing Educational Institutions: Reviewing Development and Learning*, Sheffield Papers in Education Management, Centre for Education Management and Administration, Sheffield Hallam University, Sheffield.

Nias, J (1984) 'Definition and maintenance of self in primary teaching', *British Journal of the Sociology of Education* 5, pp 267–80.

Office for Standards in Education (OFSTED) (1994) *Improving Schools*, HMSO, London.

Packwood, T (1981) 'Policy-making in Schools' *Management and Administration in Education Course E323* Open University Press, Milton Keynes.

Reid, I, Constable, H and Griffiths, R (eds) (1994) *Teacher Education Reform: Current Research*, Paul Chapman, London.

Reynolds, D and Cuttance, P (eds) (1992) *School Effectiveness Research, Policy and Practice*, Cassell, London.

Ribbins, P (1992) 'What professionalism means to teachers' paper given at the British Educational Management and Administration Society Fourth Research Conference, University of Nottingham, 6–8 April.

Rudduck, J (1982) 'Teachers in partnership', *Inspection and Advice* 16, pp 3–6.

Rudduck, J, Chaplain, R and Wallace, G (1995) *School Improvement: What Can Pupils Tell Us?* David Fulton, London.

Rutter, M, Maughan, B, Mortimore, P and Ouston, J (1979) *Fifteen Thousand Hours*, Open Books, Shepton Mallet.

School Teachers' Review Body (1995) *Fourth Report Cm 2765*, HMSO, London.

Scottish Education Department (SED) (1988) *Effective Secondary Schools: A Report by HMI*, HMSO, London.

Sergiovanni, T (1994) 'Changing our theory of schooling', *Management in Education* 8, 1, pp 9–11.

Smyth, J (1991) *Teachers as Collaborative Learners*, Open niversity Press, Milton Keynes.

Southworth, G (1988) 'Primary headship and collegiality' in Glatter, R *et al* (eds) *Understanding School Management*, Open University Press, Milton Keynes.

Sparkes, A C (1991) 'The culture of teaching, critical reflection and change: possibilities and problems', *Educational Management and Administration* 19, 1, pp 4–19.

Tannenbaum, R and Schmidt, W (1973) 'How to choose a leadership pattern', *Harvard Business Review* 51, 3, pp 162–80.

Thomas, H (1985) 'Perspectives in evaluation' in Hughes, M, Ribbins, P and Thomas, H (eds) *Managing Education: The System and the Institution*, Holt, Rinehart & Winston, London.

Index

7577